Storytelling, Special Needs and Disa

Now in a fully revised and updated second edition, this innovative and wide-ranging book shows how storytelling can open new worlds for individuals with special educational needs and disabilities.

Providing a highly accessible combination of theory and practice, the contributors to this book define their own approaches to inclusive storytelling, describing the principles and theory that underpin their practice, whilst never losing sight of the joy at the heart of their work. Topics include therapeutic storytelling; language and communication; interactive and multi-sensory storytelling; and technology. Each chapter includes top tips, and signposts further training for practitioners who want to start using stories in their own work, making this book a crucial and comprehensive guide to storytelling practice with diverse learners.

This new edition:

- has been fully updated to reflect the way in which this field of storytelling has grown and developed
- uses a broad range of chapters, structured in a way that guides the reader through the conceptualisation of a storytelling approach towards its practical application
- includes an additional chapter, sharing the lived experiences of storytellers who identify as having a disability.

Full of inspiring ideas to be used with people of all ages and with a range of needs, this book will be an invaluable tool for education professionals, as well as therapists, youth workers, counsellors and theatre practitioners working in special education.

Nicola Grove has a background in English teaching, speech and language therapy and university lecturing. She founded the charity Openstorytellers, and the Storysharing® approach, and is currently an independent consultant and researcher. She has published widely on augmentative and alternative communication, literature and storytelling for people with intellectual/learning disabilities, and has worked internationally with storytellers, educators and therapists. In 2020 she set up a website to collect the pandemic stories of people with learning disabilities. She is an Honorary Fellow of the Royal College of Speech and Language Therapists and a member of the Open University Social History of Learning Disabilities Research Group.

Storytelling, Special Needs and Disabilities

Practical Approaches for Children and Adults

Second edition

Edited by
Nicola Grove

Routledge
Taylor & Francis Group

LONDON AND NEW YORK

Cover image: © Robin Meader

Second edition published 2022
by Routledge
2 Park Square, Milton Park, Abingdon, Oxon OX14 4RN

and by Routledge
605 Third Avenue, New York, NY 10158

Routledge is an imprint of the Taylor & Francis Group, an informa business

First edition published by Routledge 2012

British Library Cataloguing-in-Publication Data
A catalogue record for this book is available from the British Library

Library of Congress Cataloging-in-Publication Data
Names: Grove, Nicola, 1948- editor.
Title: Storytelling, special needs and disabilities : practical approaches for children and adults / Edited by Nicola Grove.
Other titles: Using storytelling to support children and adults with special needs.
Description: Second edition. | Abingdon, Oxon ; New York, NY : Routledge, 2022. | "First edition published by Routledge 2012" -- Title page verso. | Includes bibliographical references and index.
Identifiers: LCCN 2021030895 (print) | LCCN 2021030896 (ebook) | ISBN 9780367746872 (hardback) | ISBN 9780367746858 (paperback) | ISBN 9781003159087 (ebook)
Subjects: LCSH: Storytelling in education. | Special education.
Classification: LCC LB1042 .U85 2022 (print) | LCC LB1042 (ebook) | DDC 372.67/7--dc23
LC record available at https://lccn.loc.gov/2021030895
LC ebook record available at https://lccn.loc.gov/2021030896

ISBN: 978-0-367-74687-2 (hbk)
ISBN: 978-0-367-74685-8 (pbk)
ISBN: 978-1-003-15908-7 (ebk)

DOI: 10.4324/9781003159087

Typeset in Galliard
by Taylor & Francis Books

Contents

Illustrations

Figures

Tables

Foreword

In the ten years since the first edition of this book came out, interest has continued to grow in the power of stories and storytelling to transform the lives of people who face marginalisation and discrimination, and thus change our communities for the better. The invitation to produce a second edition has provided an opportunity to include many new contributors, and I am extremely grateful to the publishers for their generous endorsement of the way the book has expanded along the way. Inevitably though, there will be story innovators who are missing from these pages – to whom I apologise.

The new edition was put together during the tumultuous and chaotic time of the Covid 19 pandemic. Thanks are due to the authors, who responded magnificently to a series of demands and deadlines, including original contributors who took the time to update their chapters – in a few cases this has not been possible, and the original is retained from 2012. Thanks also to Sue Cope for her diligence as a copy editor and Jashnie Jabson as the Production Editor.

Leah Burton has been my guiding support throughout the process; her deep understanding of the purpose of the book making her a superb editor and sounding board.

Finally, I would like to dedicate this book to James Hogg and Loretto Lambe, whose shared passion for storytelling and the rights of people with learning disabilities has left an enduring legacy.

Nicola Grove
May 2021

Contributors

Mary Atkinson worked for many years as a complementary therapist in a hospice. She is co-founder of the Story Massage Programme, and has authored many books on the topic. She has an MA in Transpersonal Arts and Practice. In 2020, she was awarded Complementary Therapist of the Year by the Federation of Holistic Therapists (FHT) for her work in lockdown running live sessions for schools and families.

Rolf Black has a background in mechanical and bio engineering and has worked with children with complex disabilities since 1993. He lectures in Educational Assistive Technology at the University of Dundee and is a member of the augmentative and alternative communication (AAC) research team, co-initiating many projects to support narrative skills.

Louise Coigley is a speech and language therapist, trained storyteller and curative educator (Camphill). Her work has taken her to four continents, to work with children and teenagers, parents, teams of speech and language therapists/pathologists (SLTs/Ps) and teachers. She runs bespoke training, mentors therapists and parents internationally and is founder of the UK Clinical Excellence Network for Storytelling in SLT.

Valerie Critten was an information technology (IT) teacher and coordinator at a special school for children with physical and learning disabilities. She holds an EdD from the Open University. She has published research into children and young people with physical disabilities, with learning and communication disabilities and people living with dementia. Her latest projects have included researching into programming and coding with preschool children.

Justine de Mierre is a Cambridge psychology graduate and Clore Cultural Leadership Fellow. Her multi-faceted storytelling practice *So ... what's the story?* began in 2008 and has taken her as both performer and trainer to festivals, events, schools, pubs, libraries and prisons across the country including the Cambridge Folk Festival, Bath Literary Festival, Edinburgh Literary Festival, Hay Festival and the National Centre for the Folk Arts.

Jem Dick is a creative therapist and performance storyteller who holds a diploma in person centred counselling. He has worked with people with learning disabilities for over 40 years. He was one of the original trainers and developers of the Openstorytellers company.

Janet Dowling is a traditional oral storyteller with a background in mental health and creative writing. She has worked in hospitals and schools helping children facing trauma, bereavement and loss. She has published two books of folktales. She has been a volunteer with Cruse Bereavement Care for 15 years, and was awarded a Churchill Memorial Trust Fellowship in 2006 for *Storytelling in the Care of the Dying and the Bereaved*.

Barbara Fornefeld recently retired as Professor of Education for People with Mental Disabilities at the University of Cologne, Germany. Previously she was a special education teacher and university professor in Ludwigsburg/Reutlingen and Heidelburg. Her field of research was the education and development of people with profound disabilities in national and international contexts.

Chris Fuller taught in mainstream and special schools. She founded and led Bag Books, employing skilled craft artists to produce story-packs. Multi-sensory storytelling and training tours throughout the UK followed. Bag Books has now provided training in Europe, produced and distributed over 18,000 story-packs and won charity awards. Now retired, Chris remains a consultant on new titles for the charity.

Joanna Grace is a sensory engagement and inclusion specialist, author, trainer, TEDx speaker and founder of *The Sensory Projects*, working to contribute to a future where people are understood in spite of their differences. This runs on the principle that with the right knowledge and a little bit of creativity inexpensive items can be used as effective sensory tools for inclusion.

Carol Gray is President of the Gray Centre for Social Learning and Understanding, a non-profit organisation serving people with autism spectrum disorders and those who support them. She has many years' experience as a teacher and consultant, an international reputation and is the recipient of several awards for her contributions to the field.

Nicola Grove has been an English teacher, speech and language therapist and university lecturer, with a PhD from London University. She founded the charity Openstorytellers, and in 2020 set up a website to collect pandemic stories of people with learning disabilities. She is an Honorary Fellow of the Royal College of Speech and Language Therapists and a member of the Open University Social History of Learning Disability Research Group.

Jane Harwood is a musician and project manager who uses music, story and personal narrative to develop communication, creativity and self-confidence for individuals and groups. A founder member of Openstorytellers, Jane has led on Storysharing projects for the charity, working in adult social care settings and schools, and delivering staff training programmes.

Sue Jennings is the pioneer of Neuro-Dramatic-Play, Embodiment-Projection-Role and Theatre-of-Resilience; the European Federation of Dramatherapists awarded her the honorary title of Professor of Play. She is Director of Training (www.ndpltd.org) and supervisor across many cultures. She is co-editor of the award-winning *International Handbook of Dramatherapy* and *Handbook of Play, Therapeutic Play and Play Therapy*.

Victoria Joffe is Professor of Speech and Language Therapy and Dean of the School of Health and Social Care at the University of Essex. She is co-editor of *Child Language Teaching and Therapy*, and is currently working on three National Institute Health Research (NIHR)-funded projects on new innovative interventions for children with social communication disorders, children who stammer and children with Down Syndrome.

Steve Killick is a clinical psychologist, storyteller and trainer. He now works in independent practice, is a Visiting Fellow of the George Ewart Evans Centre for Storytelling, University of South Wales and a trustee of the Beyond the Border International Storytelling Festival. He has published widely on the theme of emotional literacy and storytelling.

Sayaka Kobayashi is a storyteller from Toyota city in Aichi Prefecture Japan. In 2019 she was awarded the Toyota Culture New Face Award from the City Cultural Promotion Foundation.

Mascha Legel is a visual anthropologist, filmmaker and researcher in the field of augmentative and alternative communication (AAC), based at Radboud University, Nijmegen, the Netherlands. She is the director of the charity Com in Beeld, which runs a film production house, where a mix of young people with and without disabilities work together.

Loretto Lambe founded Promoting A More Inclusive Society (PAMIS), University of Dundee, developing support services for families caring for people with profound disabilities across Scotland. Amongst her many creative initiatives were Changing Places toilets, so that families could go out for the day; healthy lifestyles and leisure and support in bereavement and dying. Loretto passed away in 2015 but her legacy keeps her memory very much alive.

Beth McCaffrey has a PhD from the University of Exeter. She is a teacher with wide experience in learning disabilities and complex needs, with a particular interest in the development of empathy through story.

David Messer is a developmental psychologist, Emeritus Professor at the Open University and Visiting Professor at City University, London. His current research concerns communication, language, literacy and technology in young people with disabilities. He was an academic advisor to the BBC series 'Child of Our Time'.

Jenny Miller is an occupational therapist by profession and CEO of PAMIS. She is involved in national and international networks, amplifying the voice of people with PMLDs and their family carers. She is a member of the Scottish Government leadership group for policy for people with ID; the Kings Fund and GSK Impact award winners' leadership network; co-chair of the Changing Places toilet consortium and an RSA fellow.

Anne Nafstad is a psychologist specialising in dialogical approaches to communication and congenital deafblindness (CDB) working at Statped, Oslo, a national service for special needs education. She has worked extensively in higher education, lecturing at the University of Groningen, and is currently a guest lecturer in the study of atypical communication at the University of South East Norway.

Christopher Norrie holds a PhD from the University of Dundee and is an inclusive design technologist specialising in human computer interaction. His background is as a web author and multimedia developer, contributing to the development of the e-learning object metadata standards. His doctoral research focused on the application of socio-cultural research approaches in special education.

Openstorytellers (OST) is a community arts organisation providing progressive opportunities for people with a learning disability. The award winning storytelling company research, create and perform stories that challenge, inspire and promote inclusion.

Keith Park worked as a specialist teacher in visual impairment in many settings in the UK and Australia. He is a writer and performer, running inclusive workshops using Interactive Storytelling in community and heritage settings.

Maureen Phillip has worked with PAMIS for over 20 years in a research, development and family support capacity. She has an MA (hons) in English Literature and a MSc in Information Science and Research Methods. She has designed creative and innovative programmes supporting inclusive story-telling practices to ensure increased opportunities to access and participation in the arts.

Tuula Pulli is a retired specialist in AAC and multiple disabilities, community rehabilitation, drama and transdisciplinary teamwork. She has a doctorate from the University of Jyväskylä, Finland.

Bec Shanks is a senior specialist speech and language therapist within a multi-disciplinary neurodevelopmental team in North Wales. She has spent her career forging positive working relationships with education to integrate therapy in schools. The Speaking and Listening Through Narrative approach arose in Stockport in 2001 as one of these collaborative projects. She continues to develop and extend a range of resources with Black Sheep Press.

The Arts End of Somewhere (TAEOS) is a creative and performing arts collective formed in 2019 in Dumfries, Scotland with PAMIS. The group are dedicated to working closely with, and learning from, people with profound learning and multiple disabilities in creating new stories and performances to increase access to local culture and heritage sites.

Gunnar Vege worked for 30 years as a special pedagogue and as an adviser at the Signo Deafblind Centre, School and Resource Centre in Norway. He has just retired from his post in the Psychological-Pedagogical Services in Sandefjold and Vestfold og Telemark. He has an MSc from the University of Groningen, and his research and practice is focused on language development and co-created narratives for deafblind individuals. He has lectured widely on this topic to international audiences.

Annalu Waller is Professor of Human Communication Technologies at the University of Dundee. A chartered rehabilitation engineer, she manages several interdisciplinary research projects within the field of AAC. Her recent research has used natural language generation and technology to automatically generate jokes and narratives for nonspeaking children. She was awarded an OBE in 2016, and is an Honorary Fellow of the Royal College of Speech and Language Therapists.

Robin Meader is an artist who runs his own business as an illustrator and graphic facilitator. He has worked on many projects, including commissions for the NHS, BILD, *Community Living* magazine and Openstorytellers, to name but a few. His artwork ranges from historical images to illustrations of everyday life. His work has been used for information resources, books, publications and animation. Robin is a keen storyteller with a passion for myths and legends. He loves to see his images tell a story and help people to understand the world. His own learning disability has helped him to see how his work can support and empower the voices of others. Contact: robinmeader-artist@gmail.com; https://www.facebook.com/pages/category/Artist/Robin-Meader-Artist-109351024154084.

Introduction

Nicola Grove

Telling stories is one of the simplest, most enjoyable and most transformative activities on earth. With this book we hope to inspire everyone with an interest in the lives of children and adults with special needs and disabilities – in homes, classrooms, arts and heritage facilities, social and health provision – to feel confident to tell stories in ways that are fun, creative and empowering.

We know that many children enter school with limited language skills, and leave with poor levels of literacy and oracy, which affects their life chances. Recent years have seen no diminution of the challenges faced by individuals with disabilities and those who support them. Around 10 per cent of the global population live with a disability; in the USA, the figure is put at 14 per cent of school age children.[1] In the UK approximately 20 per cent of the school population at any one time are said to have special educational needs and disabilities (SENDs). Between the ages of 5 and 7 years around half of these needs are identified as speech and language difficulties. These problems have a knock-on effect; as pupils get older, the main difficulties reported relate to literacy, and in adolescence behavioural difficulties seem to predominate (ICAN/RCSLT, 2018). The same report and its update[2] demonstrate that children with SENDs continue to severely underachieve, and are disadvantaged when leaving school and making choices of further study or a career. The advent of the global pandemic has increased health inequalities and levels of stress in the population, particularly affecting people with disabilities, children with special needs and their families[3] (APPG, 2021). At the same time, we have all been made aware of the importance of sharing our stories to help us survive these difficult times (see also Vanaken et al., 2021).

How can storytelling help?

This ancient creative art form has been used in all societies to entertain, record events and instruct. Through stories we find out about new experiences and ideas, develop empathy and imagination and learn how to face challenges and solve problems. Storytelling is a powerful practical tool that we can use to understand the perspectives of others and release our imaginations; a proven method of engaging learners (Haven, 2007). It is also a crucial entry skill to social participation, which predicts levels of socialisation, advanced language skills, literacy and educational achievement over time (Spencer & Petersen, 2020; Lenhart et al., 2018). This is not surprising. Telling stories is a demanding task that requires co-ordination of many different abilities: memory, sequencing, manipulation of complex linguistic structures and a wide vocabulary, understanding and expression of causal and temporal relationships, whilst simultaneously paying attention to the listener and managing

DOI: 10.4324/9781003159087-101

expectations and shared knowledge (Melzi & Caspe, 2008; Reese, Suggate et al., 2010). Increasingly, professionals use narrative tasks as a way of identifying children's difficulties in learning and socialising (Auza, Towle Harmon & Murata, 2018; Spencer & Petersen, 2020).

No surprise, then, that research demonstrates consistently that children with a range of learning and developmental disabilities have problems in both understanding and telling stories. Profiles differ somewhat according to the nature of the disability. To summarise some of the main findings, autistic children (without intellectual disability) may be able to retell a sequence, but find inferencing and overall coherence difficult, with underlying problems in working memory and theory of mind (Kuijper et al., 2017; Norbury & Bishop, 2002). Children with developmental language difficulties, as you would expect, struggle with linguistic aspects, cohesion and story structure (Boudreau, 2007; Fichmana & Altman, 2019). Intellectual disabilities are associated with poor memory, coherence, structure, length and detail (Brown et al., 2018; Hessling & Brimo, 2019).

Although Favot, Carter and Stephenson (2020) caution that many studies are flawed, oral storytelling has been shown to yield many benefits: increased language comprehension, emotional well-being, empathy, a sense of identity, imagination, creativity, literacy skills and recovery from trauma (see, *inter alia*, Brinton & Fujiki, 2017; Curenton, Jones Craig & Flanagan, 2008; Griffin et al., 2004; Haven, 2007; Hibbin, 2016; Lenhart et al., 2020; Reese, Suggate et al., 2010; Reese, Yan et al., 2010; Schauer, Neuner & Elbert, 2017; Snow Burns & Griffin, 1998; Van Puyenbroeck & Maes, 2008).

Defining storytelling

Because storytelling is such a diverse practice, there are many different perceptions of what it involves. All oral tellers are used to wearily correcting misunderstandings: 'No, we don't read stories aloud, we tell them', 'No, it's not just for children', 'No, we aren't creative writers as such' (though oracy and literacy clearly interact). Oral tales are handed down 'from mouth to ear',[4] sometimes mediated by written forms. If you are deaf, the stories will have been (literally) handed down manually between hand and eye through sign language. Deaf people are amazing storytellers (Sutton-Spence & Kaneko, 2016), as anyone who has been privileged to sit amongst a gathering of signing friends will testify. The main focus of this book is the live interactive construction of stories, rather than the creation of stories as output (written or digitised), although this may indeed be an important goal or tool in the process. As the Story Museum in Oxford[5] puts it, storytelling involves direct, immediate, face-to-face interactions that engage attention and require active listening and interpretation.

However, in educational settings, oral components of story are often minimised. In the UK speaking and listening has been subordinated to literacy for the last 20 years. In 2021, alarm was raised by an All Party Parliamentary Inquiry about the downgrading of oracy, and a clear decline in young people's abilities to express themselves effectively (APPG, 2021). Storytelling has an important role to play in addressing this problem – as long as its oral nature is valued. In the current curriculum (England and Wales), virtually everything relating to story and narrative is subsumed within literacy, with some use of it in drama. This may explain why teachers tend to emphasise reading and writing. Some years ago I contributed a section on oral narrative tasks for young people with SENDs to a manual for newly qualified teachers, and subsequently led some face-to-face training. Some months later

I was asked to support teachers who were finding the training difficult to implement. One young woman told me, 'I tried doing what you suggested but it just didn't work'. I enquired further: 'Who were her students?' They turned out to be teenage boys with emotional and behavioural difficulties. 'What was the problem?' 'Well,' she said, 'they are just really scared of reading and writing.' Maybe I had not been clear enough originally, but the chapter she was working from specifically stated that this was an oral approach. More recently, I told a story to an entire primary school during UK National Storytelling Week, and when I sat down, a teacher turned to me and commented, 'It's all about Talk for Writing,[6] isn't it?' At which point I had to prevent myself shouting '*No!* it's about Talk for Talking!'.

About this book

The field of special needs has seen an upsurge in storytelling approaches that have transformed the learning experience of individuals with a wide range of difficulties. However, as McCabe (2020) pointed out, there is no one approach that will suit everyone. The many options on offer are exciting, but also challenging. What kind of storytelling do you want? How do you know what will best suit your students? How does a particular approach fit with your working priorities – and indeed your own interests and skills?

This book grew from a short survey I conducted in 2009 with colleagues using storytelling in different ways in different settings. I heard from those who had been working for many years, but I also discovered innovative new projects which would inevitably take some time to write up and publish. However, in my many visits to schools and centres, I found that professionals were often only aware of one or two ways of telling stories. This overview of both tried and tested formats, and new developments, aims to introduce the range and variety of styles on offer.

Many years ago, when I was beginning to explore the potential of stories and storytelling, a colleague suggested Michael Bamberg's book *Narrative Development: Six Approaches* (1977).[7] Taking its title from Wallace Steven's famous poem, 'Thirteen Ways of Looking at a Blackbird', which itself drew on William Empson's essay, *Seven Types of Ambiguity* (1930), this is a collection which facilitates the study of complex perspectives on narrative by addressing the same set of questions in each chapter. It suggests that no one approach is superior to any other, but that it is critical to understand the varied frameworks and their founding principles, in order to ask the right questions and interpret what you observe in your own practice. In real life, ways of telling may merge – for example, using call and response techniques alongside multi-sensory resources, or Bag Book formats with literature as well as tales specifically composed to fit the schema. However, it is important to be aware of what elements you are combining, and why.

I want readers to understand what different approaches involve, and the history, theory and principles that guided their development. Next, to illustrate how the approach works in practice, to know what the outcomes are likely to be and to have access to relevant evidence. As not all approaches will necessarily work for everyone, there are issues and potential limitations to consider. Cultural factors are important in all interventions, and storytelling is no exception. Finally, readers should feel inspired to go and try things out for themselves, to be given really practical tips and to know where to go for training.

The following issues are discussed in each chapter, bearing in mind that authors have addressed them at different levels of detail and in different ways, appropriate to their philosophy and practices. The final chapters diverge from this framework, sharing the lived experience of storytellers who identify as having a disability.

- **Background**

    - A description of the particular approach and a definition of the terms 'story' and 'narrative'
    - Relevant *history*, sometimes very personal
    - Theories and principles that underpin the practice

- **Work in practice**

    - A description of a typical session
    - The use of different kinds of stories – fictional, personal, traditional or a combination
    - How the work is evaluated – *outcomes*, relevant *assessments*, *evidence* that a participant is learning, progressing or simply enjoying and engaging
    - *The story of* …. An illustration or two of how an individual or group responded to the approach. *All the names used here are pseudonyms unless otherwise indicated.*

- **Contexts of learning** relevant to this approach
- **Issues to consider**

    - Any limitations or problems that may arise, with suggestions for tackling them
    - Any groups who need special consideration
    - *Cultural factors* that affect the involvement of diverse communities

- **Try it yourself**

    - *Top tips* for practitioners who want to start using stories in their work
    - *Where to go* – further information and resources

The contributors to this book are all highly creative practitioners in the art of story, whether myths and legends, written literature, personal stories, life stories and biography or stories created by participants themselves. The purposes and methods are diverse. Therapeutic, educational, cultural and leisure aims can be identified; usually we are looking at a happy mixture of all four. Different models and frameworks are used in the design and to assess, progress and evaluate outcomes. Some authors have been in a position to undertake rigorous research – reported here. The evidence from others is based more on their long experience, observations and reports from colleagues and the many children, adults, families and professionals who have benefited from their work.

The first chapters (1–3) come from a specifically therapeutic perspective. Janet Dowling, a counsellor, Steve Killick, a psychologist who works with foster carers, and Sue Jennings, a play and drama therapist, describe the ways they have worked with children facing emotional crises caused by illness and injury, and by neglect and abuse. This sets the tone – the provision of a healing, regenerative space is one of the most important gifts we can offer through story, even if we are not specifically trained in therapeutic methods, as Beth McCaffrey (Chapter 4) demonstrates in her account of a successful and creative storytelling project in a special needs classroom. McCaffrey's work involves a complex mixture of literacy, oracy and drama. Working in a range of settings, Louise Coigley (Chapter 5) shares with Keith Park (Chapter 6) an emphasis on drama, ritual and repetition (as does Tuula Pulli's work, Chapter 16). Park's storytelling provides access to culture not only through the stories that are told, but via historic settings, a theme shared with Grove and Phillip and performance storytellers (Chapters 11 and 25).

The next four chapters (7–11) all focus on explicit teaching of narrative skills. Bec Shanks –and her colleague Judith Carey – have long been influential in the nursery and primary sector, and have recently extended their programme to an upper age of 14 years. Both Shanks and Victoria Joffe (Chapter 8), whose programme targets secondary-aged pupils and young adults, focus on strategies for helping learners master the structural elements of storytelling, using visual prompts and carefully prepared questions. The two following chapters address the learning styles and needs of young people who communicate non-verbally. Digital apps are now ubiquitous, and David Messer and Valerie Critten (Chapter 9) describe a story creation tool that can be used with speaking and non-speaking children and adults alike. Rachel Sutton-Spence, working with deaf children in Brazil, uses folklore stories to develop language skills in sign (Chapter 10).

Access to culture is an important theme for Sutton-Spence, and provides a link to the work of Nicola Grove, Maureen Phillip and Barbara Fornefeld (Chapters 11 and 12), who explore strategies for sharing literature and folktales with individuals with a wide range of communication difficulties. Multi-sensory techniques are central to their approaches, and have proved to be essential in the now well-established traditions of storytelling with children and adults with profound disabilities and sensory impairments.

Multi-sensory storytelling is to the fore in chapters by Chris Fuller (who was the pioneer in this field), Mary Atkinson, Joanna Grace, Tuula Pulli and Loretto Lambe, Jenny Miller and Maureen Phillip (Chapters 13–17). Grace works with a range of stories, and here provides a novel dimension by considering non-fiction – telling stories from science. Pulli, drawing on work by Grove, provides a framework for evaluating response to literature and folktale. Another perspective is provided by Mary Atkinson's massage storytelling (Chapter 14).

At PAMIS, the charity founded by Lambe, storytelling is multi-faceted, but their chapter (17) on 'sensitive stories' describes ways of enabling young people with profound disabilities to explore difficult emotional situations, such as sexuality, health and bereavement, grounded in personal experiences. Likewise, Carol Gray (Chapter 18) has pioneered an approach for those with autism or similar social cognition problems to understand and adapt to the many confusing situations they encounter in daily life. Gray's 'social stories' can be considered scripts for accessing routine, predictable events – what usually happens in the day. By contrast, Nicola Grove and Jane Harwood (Chapter 19) describe a framework for sharing experiences that are 'tellable' because somewhat unexpected. Storysharing® is a technique based on collaborative anecdotal telling which is also applicable to fictional, traditional stories, and to factual accounts. The theoretical basis of their work is shared with Gunner Vege and Anne Nafstad, whose chapter (20) follows.

Memory for a personal experience can be conceptualised as a sequence of sensorimotor impressions. This is the basis for Vege and Nafstad's revelatory work on developing personal experience narratives with deaf blind individuals. Arguably, this is the population presenting the greatest challenge to storytellers wanting to support access to stories for identity and cultural access. Vege and Nafstad's description of planned choreography and the creation of bodily emotional traces (BETs) has application for other groups with sensory and intellectual impairments.

Continuing the theme of personal narrative, Annalu Waller and Rolf Black and Mascha Legel and Chris Norrie work with young people with complex needs using using augmentative and alternative communication (AAC). Waller and Black (Chapter 21) created a programme to support the recoding and sharing of personal stories. Legel and Norrie (Chapter 22) have pioneered film training so that youngsters can incorporate filmed footage into their retellings of personal stories. In so doing, they become producers of cultural artefacts. Common to all personal storytelling is the necessity for careful preparation and adaptation to individuals so that each story is uniquely owned and told.

The final three chapters feature storytellers with lived experience of disability. Nicola Grove and Jem Dick (Chapter 23) lay some of the groundwork by describing the course that was developed over three years to build the company Openstorytellers. We then hand over to the storytellers themselves. Justine de Mierre (Chapter 24) is a seasoned professional who was recently diagnosed as on the autism spectrum. Her chapter is a wake-up call to all of us to accept and learn from neuro-diverse communities. Finally, there is testimony (Chapter 25) about what it means both personally and publicly, to work as storytellers with learning disabilities – from Sayaka Kobayashi in Japan, The Arts End of Somewhere in Scotland and Openstorytellers in England.

Terminology

Special educational needs and disabilities

As defined within the UK education sector, these are needs that affect a child's ability to learn and function in school and daily life: *cognitive and learning; language and communication; social and emotional; sensory* (e.g. visual and hearing impairments) and *physical.* Some are temporary; for example, a pupil may have specific emotional needs in response to a crisis, or physical difficulties resulting from an illness, which subsequently are resolved. Other needs will be pervasive and result in people identifying themselves, or being identified by others, as having disabilities in adult life.

The individuals described here have a wide range of difficulties and disabilities. Some of the approaches are designed for a particular group, others are inclusive. Many contributors work with adults as well as with children.

Storytelling

Storytelling is proving so popular that we practitioners are struggling to define approaches in ways that are precise and indicative. Most authors here identify a multi-sensory dimension to their work: what we might call generic (small 'm') multi-sensory. Lambe, Miller and Phillip and colleagues in Europe use the term Multi-sensory Storytelling — MSST ('big M') as their trade name. Similarly, all oral storytelling is interactive (small 'i') but Park coined the term Interactive Storytelling (big 'I') for his call and response approach, because this is the element that he felt was most distinctive in his work. In this volume we have tried to recognise the commonalities between approaches as well as respecting professional boundaries.

Narrative and story

Each author was invited to provide a definition of the broad category of narrative and the narrower category of story – and many have done so. In all cases, narrative is defined as the conveying of a sequence of events that are linked in time (*temporality*) and by consequence (*causality*). One event, as we say, leads to another. Story, however, is another matter, and the way that authors chose to define this was governed by their own perspectives. These definitions offer options to the reader; if you want to emphasise a particular aspect of story then look for a definition that meets this criterion. For example, Shanks places the focus on cognitive and language skills, whereas Park focuses on the poetic, and Pulli focuses on social and aesthetic elements. Vege and Nafstad are concerned above all with the co-construction of meaning to enable people who are deaf blind to build memory and identity. Gray sees her social stories as more like narratives, as the entertainment aspect is not prominent. However, what Social Stories[TM] demonstrate very clearly is the ancient educational role of storytelling in illustrating how we should conduct ourselves in our relationships with others and in different situations. Of course, you do not have to be restricted by any one definition: McCaffrey used a multidimensional framework for her research.

Types of story

Most authors work with many different genres: traditional (myths, legends, wonder tales and fables), authored fictional, factual, personal experiences and stories that the teller, or the child, invents to suit the occasion. Some authors use predominantly one type, others mix and match. One issue is that genre does influence the ease with which children master narrative structure. Everyday accounts (such as those involved in Social Stories[TM]) and personal narratives seem to pose less of a challenge than retold fictional stories or composed stories, both for typically developing children (Allen et al., 1994; Hudson & Shapiro, 1991) and those with language impairments (McCabe et al., 2008; Westerveldt & Gillon, 2010), particularly if they have been directly involved in the experience (research reported by Brown et al., 2018). However, as Waller and Black suggest, in some circumstances it may be that fictions are easier than personal narratives — when they are known and predictable, and offer structured opportunities for participation; or where receptive skills are particularly poor (Spencer & Petersen, 2020). In children's development, it is clear that there is an interaction between types of narrative; as children become more exposed to literate fictional stories, there is feedback into their own narrative constructions (Fox, 1993). We need to nurture all types of stories and storytelling, and it is clear from these chapters that individuals thrive when the storyteller is able to tailor the selection of the stories to their particular circumstances and interests.

It follows therefore that choice of story type is critical when determining an individual's level of narrative competence. There are several published assessments available, but as Duinmeijer et al. (2012) point out, you need to be specific, choosing tools that are appropriate to the underlying questions, purposes and functions of the approach you are using.

Styles of telling

Because of the long association between books and stories, the term 'storytelling' ubiquitously refers to *reading* as well as oral *telling*. There is also a close relationship between *telling*, as narration, and *performing*, as dramatisation. At the extremes there are clear distinctions (e.g. in drama, characters engage in dialogue in real time, whereas in narrative, speech is reported). But one of the joys of using story is that it is possible to move between different modes. Thus McCaffrey starts by reading, moves into drama and then towards telling and writing. Fuller, Fornefeld, Lambe and her colleagues locate their work firmly within the tradition of reading stories out loud, but include opportunities for interaction. They use pre-written scripts in order to ensure consistency of delivery and opportunities for repeated learning, as do Atkinson, Grace and Gray. Legel and Norris, Messer and Critten and Waller and Black are of necessity composing scripted stories because of the constraints and affordances of technology. Vege and Nafstad emphasise the importance of planned choreography for narrating with deaf blind individuals. Other authors (Dowling, Jennings, Grove, Coigley, Pulli, Dick, Harwood, Killick and de Mierre) operate more spontaneously, in accordance with a fundamental principle of oral storytelling that each story is told anew because the teller is responsive to the particular audience. However, the anecdotes developed by Grove and Harwood do eventually become scripted through repeated telling and sharing. And Park, whose call and response approach is highly oral, keeps to a script every bit as strictly as those who read out stories, because of the importance of the metrical beat. Grove and Phillip, working with literary texts, ensure that the original words of authors are used (selectively), as well as paraphrased to move the plot along. As for storytellers with disabilities, Kobayashi needs a consistent script that she can memorise, whereas de Mierre excels at extemporising to incorporate the challenges of her audience.

Participation and response

Most of the chapters cover strategies for telling *to* children and adults with disabilities but they all insist on active response *by* individuals in the process, and consider engagement as fundamental. Some have a more explicit focus on the development of narrative skills, moving towards independent narration (telling *by*) and for others telling *with* is a critical outcome. In all cases, the concern is to develop the potential of the individuals involved in the storytelling. The main dimensions of learning and development are *emotional and social* (what might be termed therapeutic or relational); *cognitive and linguistic* (educational/psychological); *creative* (arts practice); *community participation; leisure/enjoyment* and, finally, *empowerment*. In some approaches there is one particular focus; in others the purposes are intertwined and inseparable. We can all agree with Alida Gersie (Gersie & King, 1990) that it is most important for eyes to light up and to build confidence and resilience.

Cultural factors

In the world of oral storytelling, cultural styles and cultural ownership are hotly disputed topics. How we can authentically tell stories from other traditions than our own poses real ethical problems. Many of the tales that are circulating readily in published books were taken down by (largely white, Western) anthropologists, tidied up and divorced from their original sacred or ritual contexts.

> Within our culture there's a number of categories of stories: public stories, sacred stories, sacred secret stories, men's and women's stories. A woman cannot tell a man's story to a group of men and men cannot tell women's stories – I don't know the men's stories — I only know the female, the public, the women's and sacred stories – stories just for women.
>
> (Pauline McLeod, Aboriginal storyteller, interviewed in 1998 by Helen McKay for *Telling Tales*[8])

Eric Maddern, an experienced storyteller and traveller, puts the challenge head on:

> By what right do storytellers tell stories from Africa, Native America, Aboriginal Australia and other similar cultures? Isn't appropriating and telling these peoples' stories an extension of colonialism? We stole their lands and livelihoods; we decimated their cultures; we virtually drove them to extinction. Now we want to tell their stories. Isn't this just the latest stage of colonial theft? It's not surprising that some survivors from such cultures think so.[9]

So we need to be culturally sensitive in choosing the stories we tell. We also need to be aware of cultural variation as we seek to develop oral skills of telling, which can differ considerably between ethnic traditions and language backgrounds, and within different genres of story. In particular there are marked cultural influences on styles of narrating personal experiences.

Westby (2020) characterised some fundamental differences between cultures that map broadly onto Eastern and Western traditions. *Collective* cultures privilege interdependence, shared responsibility and relationships, with group goals prioritised over individual goals. Expression of emotions at a high level of arousal is discouraged, and 'low arousal' feelings such as calmness, serenity and peacefulness are valued. Narratives focus more on others, on context, social engagement and moral correctness, description of an event is often generalised. Children from cultures which value low arousal may resist expressing feelings directly. *Individualistic* cultures focus more on the self, autonomy, personal evaluations and detailed description. High arousal feelings are valued, such as drama, suspense, excitement and adventure.

Comparative research from the USA demonstrates the serious consequences of mismatches between the expectations of teachers and the experiences of pupils (Dickinson, 1991; Heath, 1982; Michaels, 1981; McCabe & Bliss, 2003). For example, Vernon Feagans and co-researchers (2002) showed that despite having superior skills in vocabulary and narrative, the storytelling abilities of African American boys from low-income families were *negatively* associated with literacy and educational outcomes, probably because their elaborated, sophisticated retellings did not conform to the simple and straightforward paraphrases that their teachers required. McCabe (2020) characterised different styles of telling:

- *European American*: telling single events in sequence, at medium length, emphasising adherence to facts, goals and resolutions.
- *Japanese and Chinese*: succinctness, told in brief turns, inclusion of two or more similar experiences in same narrative. She reports that Chinese children's stories often ended without resolution – which certainly in a Western school context would lead them to be judged incomplete.
- *African American* children may include several experiences within one story; narratives are embellished and performed.
- *Latinate* stories focus on the importance of social networks and tend to be embedded in conversation rather than narrated as linear monologues.
- *Haitian* narratives are highly descriptive, showing an emphasis on poetic, repetitive, parallel structures rather than overly concerned with plots or internal goals.

Many contributors have worked successfully with children and adults from a wide range of cultural backgrounds, but there still remains a great deal to research and learn about indigenous traditions and what they can teach us.[10] Spencer and Petersen (2020) stress the importance of equipping young people with the skills that are required to succeed in the society where they are growing up, not replacing their own traditions, but through code-switching; however, the evidence shows how easy it is to suppress rather than celebrate cultural diversity in this context.

What else?

The focus of this book is the process of live, dynamic, face-to-face storytelling. There are other important ways of telling stories that are not covered here. Life-history work (Atkinson et al., 2010; Salman, 2020) is a distinct discipline within disability studies which is assuming increasing importance as people start to take control of their own lives and their own biographies. Books written for people with learning disabilities, to explain situations is a speciality of the charity Books Beyond Words.[11] Next Chapter Book clubs enable people with severe communication disabilities to enjoy many different book genres.[12] In these fields, the emphasis tends to be on reading – on testimonies as transcribed texts, and on the books as ways of transmitting information, rather than on the process of oral telling. One has to draw boundaries somewhere – this book could have become a never-ending story, such is the reach of narrative into our lives.

And we all lived ...

There is a Seneca legend about how stories came into the world.[13] A magic story rock tells tales to a whole community who come to listen, but then commands the people to go out and tell for themselves. In the words of Brian Marshall, a founder member of Open-storytellers, 'We all have stories, don't we?' But many people lack a voice to tell, so let's enable everyone to be heard and everyone to enjoy the power of story.

In conclusion, we all hope that this book will prove a resource for readers to develop their own creative practice. There are as many stories as there are stars in the sky – and as many ways of telling.

> The creation myth is the story that enacts the creative power of stories, the many narratives that are going on in us all the time, and in which we live. Scheherazade, herself a story, tells tales to you non-stop to keep you awake, and thereby saves your life as well as her own.
>
> (Cupitt, 1991: 55)

Notes

1 https://www.disabled-world.com/disability/statistics/; https://nces.ed.gov/programs/coe/indicator_cgg.asp (Accessed 27.4.2021).
2 www.bercow10yearson.com/wp-content/uploads/2018/03/337644-ICAN-Bercow-Report-WEB.pdf (Accessed 27.4.21).
3 https://reliefweb.int/report/world/covid-19-and-its-impact-persons-disabilities (Accessed 15.5.21).
4 www.sfs.org.uk (Accessed 1.5.21).
5 https://www.storymuseum.org.uk (Accessed 1.5.21).
6 See https://www.talk4writing.com (Accessed 27.4.21).
7 Thanks to Professor John Clibbens, University of Essex, for this recommendation.

8 https://australianstorytelling.org.au/interviews/pauline-mcleod-nsw-aboriginal-perspective (Accessed 1.5.21).
9 https://mechanicaldolphin.com/tag/eric-maddern (Accessed 1.5.21).
10 www.marilynkinsella.org (Accessed 1.5.21). Advice on telling stories from different cultures.
11 https://booksbeyondwords.co.uk (Accessed 27.4.21).
12 https://www.nextchapterbookclub.org (Accessed 1.5.21).
13 www.firstpeople.us/FP-Html-Legends/The-Origin-Of-Stories-Seneca.html (Accessed 27.4.21).

References

Allen, M., Kertoy, M., Sherblom, J. & Pettit, J. (1994). Children's narrative productions: A comparison of personal event and fictional stories. *Applied Psycholinguistics*, 15, 149–176.

APPG: All Party Parliamentary Group for Special Needs & Disabilities (2021a). Forgotten, left behind, overlooked. The experiences of young people and their educational transitions during the COVID19 pandemic in 2020. Available at: https://www.naht.org.uk/about-us/organisations-we-support/all-party-parliamentary-group-on-send (Accessed 6.5.21).

APPG: Oracy All Party Parliamentary Group (2021b). Speak for change: Executive summary. Available at: https://oracy.inparliament.uk/sites/oracy.inparliament.uk/files/2021-04/Executive%20Summary-Oracy%20APPG%20final%20report.pdf (Accessed 4.5.21).

Atkinson, D., Holland, C., Humber, L., Ingham, N., Ledger, S. & Tilley, E. (2010). *Developing a 'living archive' of learning disability life stories: Project report*. Milton Keynes: Open University Press.

Auza, A., Towle Harmon, B. & Murata, C. (2018). Retelling stories: Grammatical and lexical measures for identifying monolingual Spanish speaking children with specific language impairment (SLI). *Journal of Communication Disorders*, 71, 52–60.

Bamberg, M. (1997). *Narrative development: Six approaches*. Mahwah, NJ: LEA.

Boudreau, D. M. (2007). Narrative abilities in children with language impairments. In R. Paul (Ed.), *Language disorders from a developmental perspective* (pp. 331–356). Mahwah, NJ: LEA.

Brinton, B. & Fujiki, M. (2017). The power of stories: Facilitating social communication in children with limited language abilities. *School Psychology International*, 38, 523–540.

Brown, D. Brown, E., Lewis, C. & Lamb, M. (2018). Narrative skill and testimonial accuracy in typically developing children and those with intellectual disabilities. *Applied Cognitive Psychology*, 32, 550–560.

Cupitt, D. (1991). *What is a story?* Norwich: SCM Press.

Curenton, S., Jones Craig, M. & Flanagan, N. (2008). Use of decontextualized talk across story contexts: How oral storytelling and emergent reading can scaffold children's development. *Early Education & Development*, 19, 161–187.

Dickinson, C. (1991). Teaching agenda and setting: Constraints on conversation in preschools. In A. McCabe & C. Petersen (Eds), *Developing narrative structure* (pp. 255–303). Hillsdale, NJ: Lawrence Erlbaum Associates.

Dodwell, K. & Bavin, E. (2008). Children with specific language impairment: An investigation of their narratives and memory. *International Journal of Language & Communication Disorders*, 43, 201–218.

Duinmeijer, J., De Jong, J.Scheper, A. (2012). Narrative abilities, memory and attention in children with a specific language impairment. *International Journal of Language & Communication Disorders*, 47, 542–555.

Empson, W. (1930) *Seven types of ambiguity: A study of its effects on English verse*. London: Chatto & Windus.

Favot, K., Carter, M. & Stephenson, J. (2020). The effects of oral narrative intervention on the narratives of children with language disorder: A systematic literature review. *Journal of Developmental and Physical Disabilities*. doi:10.1007/s10882–10020–09763–09769 (Accessed 27.4.21).

Fichmana, S. & Altman, C. (2019). Referential cohesion in the narratives of bilingual and monolingual children with typically developing language and with specific language impairment. *Journal of Speech, Language & Hearing Research*, 62, 123–142.

Fox, C. (1993). *At the very edge of the forest: The influence of literature on storytelling by children.* London: Cassell.

Gersie, A. & King, N. (1990). *Storymaking in education and therapy.* London: JKP.

Griffin, T., Hemphill, L., Camp, L. & Wolf, D. (2004) Oral discourse in the preschool years and later literacy skills. *First Language*, 24, 123–147.

Haven, K. (2007). *Story proof: The science behind the startling power of story.* Westport, CT: Greenwood Publishing.

Heath, S. B. (1982). What no bedtime story means: Narrative skills at home and school. *Language in Society*, 11, 49–76.

Hessling, A. & Brimo, D. (2019). Spoken fictional narrative and literacy skills of children with Down syndrome. *Journal of Communication Disorders*, 79, 76–89.

Hibbin, R. (2016) The psychosocial benefits of oral storytelling in school: Developing identity and empathy through narrative. *Pastoral Care in Education*, 34, 218–231.

Hudson, J. & Shapiro, L. (1991). From knowing to telling: The development of children's scripts, stories and personal narratives. In A. McCabe & C. Petersen (Eds), *Developing narrative structure* (pp. 89–136). Hillsdale, NJ: Lawrence Erlbaum Associates.

ICAN/RCSLT. (2018). *Bercow: Ten years on.* Available at: www.bercow10yearson.com/wp-content/uploads/2018/03/337644-ICAN-Bercow-Report-WEB.pdf.

Kuijper, S., Hartman, C., Bogaerds-Hazenberg, S. & Hendriks, P. (2017). Narrative production in children with autism spectrum disorder (ASD) and children with attention-deficit/hyperactivity disorder (ADHD): Similarities and differences. *Journal of Abnormal Psychology*, 126(1), 63–75.

Lenhart, J., Lenhard, W., Vaahtoranta, E. & Suggate, S. (2020). More than words: Narrator engagement during storytelling increases children's word learning, story comprehension, and on-task behavior. *Early Childhood Research Quarterly*, 51, 338–351.

McCabe, A. (2020). Working with the grain: Appreciating rich narrative traditions from diverse cultures. Paper presented at *ASHA Webinar Series, Personal Narratives across Diverse Cultures*, Rockville, MD, 3–7 August .

McCabe, A. & Bliss, L. (2003). *Patterns of narrative discourse: A multicultural lifespan approach.* Boston, MA: Pearson Education.

McCabe, A., Bliss, L., Barra, G. & Bennett, M. (2008). Comparison of personal versus fictional narratives of children with language impairment. *American Journal of Speech-Language Pathology*, 17, 194–206.

Melzi, G., & Caspe, M. (2008). Research approaches to narrative, literacy, and education. In N. Hornberger (Ed.), *Encyclopedia of language and education* (2nd ed., Vol. 10, pp. 151–164). New York: Springer.

Michaels, S. (1981). 'Sharing time': Children's narrative styles and differential access to literacy. *Language in Society*, 10, 423–442.

Norbury, C. F. & Bishop, D. V. M. (2002). Inferential processing and story recall in children with communication problems: A comparison of specific language impairment, pragmatic language impairment and high-functioning autism. *International Journal of Language & Communication Disorders*, 37, 227–251.

Reese, E., Suggate, S., Long, J. & Schaughency, E. (2010). Children's oral narrative and reading skills in the first 3 years of reading instruction. *Reading and Writing*, 23, 627–644.

Reese, E., Yan, C., Jack, F. & Hayne, H. (2010). Emerging identities: Narrative and self from early childhood to early adolescence. In K. McLean & M. Pasupathi (Eds), *Narrative development in adolescence: Creating the storied self* (pp. 23–43). New York: Springer.

Salman, S. (2020). *Made possible: Stories of success by people with learning disabilities in their own words.* London: Unbound.

Schank, R. C. & Abelson, R. (1977). *Scripts, plans, goals, and understanding.* Hillsdale, NJ: Lawrence Erlbaum Associates.

Schauer, M., Neuner, F. & Elbert, T. (2017). Narrative exposure therapy for children and adolescents (KIDNET). In M. A. Landolt, M. Cloitre & U. Schnyder (Eds), *Evidence-based treatments for trauma related disorders in children and adolescents* (pp. 227–249). Paranaque City, Metro Manila: Springer International.

Snow, C., Burns, S. & Griffin, P. (1998). *Preventing reading difficulties in young children.* Washington, DC: National Academy Press.

Spencer, T. & Petersen, D. (2020). Narrative intervention: Principles to practice. *Language, Speech, and Hearing Services in Schools,* 51, 1081–1096.

Sutton-Spence, R. & Kaneko, M. (2016). *Introducing sign language literature: Creativity and folklore.* Basingstoke: Palgrave Press.

Vanaken, L., Bijttebier, P., Fivush, R. & Hermans, D. (2021) Narrative coherence predicts emotional well-being during the COVID-19 pandemic: A two-year longitudinal study. *Cognition and Emotion.* doi:10.1080/02699931.2021.1902283 (Accessed 27.4.21).

Van Puyenbroeck, J. & Maes, B. (2008). A review of critical, person-centred and clinical approaches to reminiscence work for people with intellectual disabilities. *International Journal of Disability, Development and Education,* 55, 43–60.

Vernon Feagans, L., Scheffner Hammer, C., Miccio, A. & Manlove, E. (2002). Early language and literacy skills in low income African American and Hispanic children. In S. Neumann & D. Dickinson (Eds), *Handbook of early literacy research* (pp. 192–210). New York: Guilford Press.

Westerveld, M. F. & Gillon, G. T. (2010). Oral narrative context effects on poor readers' spoken language performance: Story retelling, story generation, and personal narratives. *International Journal of Speech-Language Pathology,* 12(2), 132–141.

Westby, C. (2020). *Telling our stories: Developing cultural identity.* Paper presented at ASHA Webinar Series, Personal Narratives across Diverse Cultures, Rockville, MD, 3–7 August.

Chapter 1

Therapeutic storytelling with children in need

Janet Dowling

Background

I use 'therapeutic storytelling' as a term to describe telling a range of stories that are used to help listeners explore metaphors that enable them to experience a change in perception about themselves and their situation. These metaphors are a way of describing something as if it is something else. So, for example, if someone were very shy, a metaphor for shyness could be a hedgehog that has lost its mirror and is looking for it. The story of looking for it, finding help along the way and eventually finding it would be a metaphor for dealing with and overcoming shyness. The telling is purposeful, targeted and intended to support and develop the listener regardless of their level of cognitive functioning. The content is important, but so too are the ways in which the story is told and the multisensory elements that are brought into the story-telling. All have an impact on the listener at a conscious and unconscious level. A narrative is a retelling of a sequence of events as a statement and history of those events. A story explores the emotional and sensory components and relationships of those events.

Theories and principles

Storytelling as a therapeutic process is well documented (Dent-Brown & Wang, 2006; Gersie & King, 1989; Gersie, 1992; Lawley & Tompkins, 2000). Lahad (1992) suggested that using metaphor and storytelling with people with post-traumatic stress, for example, enables them to address the emotional content of their experience without having to relive the actual traumatic moment.

Attachment theory is an important foundation of the process. This emphasises the need in early childhood for relationships that provide security and comfort on the one hand and the scope for excitement and exploration on the other (Bowlby, 2011). Telling and listening to stories is one way that listeners can be in comfortable and secure settings whilst exploring and experiencing excitement through their imaginations in short, time-limited, self-contained settings. Stories allow the exploration of frightening things – to experience the fear and elation, the tension and the release, the joy and the sadness (Bettelheim, 1976). Stories also allow the learning of social norms and the development of emotional literacy (Killick & Thomas, 2007; Killick 2018, Killick & Okwedy 2020), and bring the promise of hope – that this too shall pass, something will happen to put right the bad things that have happened, but also that if at first you don't succeed, try, try, try again.

Other research that has contributed to the development of therapeutic storytelling comes from neuroscience. Sunderland (2001, 2003) discusses how 'fear kills play and can block the

DOI: 10.4324/9781003159087-1

ability to learn and the wish to explore the world' and relates this to the brain's emotional memory system. If a fearful incident has happened in the past, a similar occurrence in the present can trigger the same intensity of emotional response. Emotional memories can be laid down by sensory events that occur even before the child can create a memory they can consciously recall.

The brain works through metaphor, storing information and memory as stories describing the relationship between things. From that relationship the brain can develop and build tension, release and calm that can become building blocks of learning experience and feeling safe. The easiest way to access the memory is through emotion, and stories (when well told) create an emotional response. By listening to and exploring the emotional content of stories the listener is accessing their own experiences, even when those emotional issues are too difficult to consciously express. As the character in the story grows, explores options and matures, the listener unconsciously learns about their own emotions, experiences and feelings to help them make sense of what has happened to them, and decide how they want things to be in the future.

Structuring the story

There are various traditional story formats. I use a basic version of the mythic structure loosely derived from Campbell (2008) and which I find fits most (but not all) situations.

Stories begin with the *initial situation*, in which we are introduced to the main characters and the setting. Then something happens – the *problem* or *change* – which calls the hero to respond: typically, something dark to overcome or a partner to be wooed and won. The hero will then *prepare for the quest* – be given advice, meet helpers, find magical objects, learn skills – or do nothing at all. Then arise the *challenges, obstacles* or *hazards* that have to be overcome to achieve *transformation*, where the challenge is resolved. This leads to a *celebration* of success. The cycle then begins again.

The challenges generally occur in threes and allow recognition of the pattern of events – the try, try, try again, relating to how the brain deals with information. Most folk tales have it – *Goldilocks and the Three Bears* and *The Three Little Pigs*. The first time an event happens, it is registered: 'Aha! something happened'. The next time it occurs it is recognised: 'Oh, that happened before'. And the third time it is remembered: 'Oh yes, I have been here before'. And as it is remembered the listener starts to anticipate the next part of the story: 'I know what's happening next'. With anticipation comes learning and thus the possibility of change (Dowling, 2009, 2010).

Work in practice

The focus of this chapter is on the work at the Children's Trust in Tadworth, Surrey between 2004 and 2007 with children who have acquired brain injury from traumatic events such as road traffic accidents, near drowning or strokes. However, it has application to all children (and indeed adults) who are in need of support to deal with the challenges they face in life and I have applied the same principles in my bereavement work with children and adults for the past 15 years.

Before the session, information was gathered about the child – such as hearing, vision, preferred position, preferred movement. I started (and finished) a session with a short song. This 'punctuated' the time and using the song voice differentiated from the talking/telling voice. Then I offered my hand and introduced myself, before moving into the storytelling.

I used fictional, traditional and personal stories, plus helped the children to make up a story about themselves. This was particularly relevant for children recovering from traumatic brain injury, where part of the process was enabling them to create a vocabulary and emotional literacy to describe what had happened to them and how they felt about it. Just being able to name the feelings was very important and to recognise that they were not the only ones experiencing them. The trauma of injury may well leave children in a mental and emotional state where they have no words to describe or convey how they are feeling. Listening to and taking part in a made-up story about familiar characters allows them to name and explore the emotions and then relate them to themselves.

I used the *visual, aural* and *kinaesthetic* modalities at as many points as appropriate – providing more opportunities for the child to participate and process information. Using tone of voice and sensory objects with different textures (e.g. rough scouring pads, smooth and silky material, knotted string, red stretchy material) I provided metaphors for the emotions that they might be feeling, and then introduced the words to describe these feelings.

Parents and carers were asked about favourite stories from the past. Sometimes it was fairy tales (*Little Red Riding Hood* seemed to be popular). Sometimes it was a book (*Harry Potter*), or sometimes a TV show (e.g. *SpongeBob SquarePants* or *Tracy Beaker*). By basing the work on familiar stories we don't have to establish an emotional connection with a character, as that is already in place. The focus is then on putting the characters into new situations where they might feel as the child feels. This enables the child to access their current new experiences and develop their emotional vocabulary. The experiences and memories of the past are used to help them find a place in the present. Sometimes I made up a story that was a metaphor for the child's experience, incorporating elements of their family story; but not quite their family. There has to be enough distance from reality for a story to be a metaphor rather than a retelling of personal history. Most important is for the intention to be clear in telling a particular story. For example, was I telling *Jack and the Beanstalk* as a story to address bereavement, self-esteem, anxiety, displacement or transition? My intention affected how I told the story, what words I used and, in turn, what the child experienced. However, everyone is different, and my intention for the story might not always match the child's response. The child would experience the story at a level they could deal with at the time, and that would determine the course of the post-story work.

Harry Potter has much potential for exploring traumatic injury. He falls from his broom in the Quidditch match and lies in the sick wing. His bones grow back but very slowly – there is no sudden magic response. *Harry Potter and the Prisoner of Azkaban* was particularly relevant as the background story for enacting and telling new stories that addressed metaphors for physical and mental trauma. The dementors suck all the good experiences out, leaving the person with just the negatives emotions – depression. It is also in this book that through his relationship with the Weasleys, Harry finally understands what a good, functional, loving family has to offer, and really starts to grieve for the loving family he never had. In particular, the Patronus spell that Harry has to learn to use for his own protection could be seen as basic cognitive behavioural therapy. A key part of the work involved enabling the child to find their own positive metaphor – their 'Patronus'– to hold back their own demons and deal with depression and bereavement.

Outcomes and evidence: what I look for

Outcomes are related to the child's behaviour and responses, and feedback from the therapy team and other staff familiar with the child.

For verbal children, I look to see whether they are actively involved in the session, and their recall from previous sessions. Sometimes a child will refer to a story that had been told some weeks earlier, wanting it to be retold, or to share a retelling of it, perhaps incorporating changes in it. This indicates that they have internalised the story and indirectly related it to their own situation.

For children unable to communicate directly, and with varying levels of cognitive functioning, their participation is a positive outcome, as is the way they physically present themselves. For example, actively reaching for objects, responding to different physical textures of materials, and vocalising. I watch for eye movements; changes in breathing; small gestures with the head, hand or arm, or even a startle response; and changes in muscle tone from tense to relaxed. For some children the outcome is a change in behaviour – a child who is restless outside the sessions may be more settled, whereas a child who is normally passive outside may become more active inside the sessions. Feedback from staff was used to discover any differences observed as a result of the sessions; for example, being more settled and less distressed, and in their sessions with other therapists, such as being able to talk about their feelings and referring to the stories we had used.

The story of Georgina

Georgina was 15 years old. A short illness had left her with a muscle wasting condition, unable to speak above a whisper, and using a voice amplifier to help communication. She was in a wheelchair and effectively paraplegic, although she had no specific diagnosis. She was bright and intelligent but found the classroom fatiguing. I was asked to see her for an initial exploratory session. We eventually met for 10 sessions of about 45 minutes, which was longer than staff had anticipated.

I used a combination of encouraging her to make up stories and my telling (or making up) traditional tales focusing on female protagonists who initially seemed weak and powerless but, through their own devices and with the support of others, prevailed and became stronger women, such as *Cinderella, Cap O' Rushes*[1] and the *Silent Princess*.[2] They would all experience the same pattern of loss, developing personal resources and overcoming three challenges before experiencing transformation. Along the way there would be an exploration of feelings of depression which the heroines might have experienced. At various points in the story I would stop and 'wonder' what the characters might be feeling and invite Georgina's point of view. Even though it was a struggle for her, she tried to respond most of the time. On days when she was too tired she would just listen, and I would still 'wonder' and leave space to enable her to be thinking, even if she could not respond actively. This space was very important. To be able to explore some of the emotional and physical choices of the characters, she had to draw on her own experience, meaning that she was processing and maturing her own experiences through the character's development. Sometimes this could only be done in her head, with no verbal input either from me or herself.

Georgina loved horses, and her own stories often featured a heroine riding on a horse – in sharp contrast to her own situation. Sometimes she was too tired to tell herself, but would tell me who she wanted in the story, and what the problem was. I would follow my version of the mythic structure in making up the story, and at appropriate points I would ask her what happened next, or give her a choice of two possibilities that she could signal with her eyes if necessary. We generally finished the sessions with a recap of the main points of the story, highlighting her comments and contributions.

The staff regularly commented that she looked forward to our sessions and was disappointed if I could not attend. They felt the sessions were supporting her and that she was more relaxed after them. Indeed, she actively chose to come to our session rather than attend the Christmas show.

Georgina eventually returned home after various treatments that enabled her to build up her strength and manage on a day-to-day basis. I believe the storytelling also enabled her to build her inner strengths, and I recommended a book of tales of strong women that her family could continue to read to her. As I had used a regular pattern of questioning and facilitating her to consider the emotions of the characters, it is my hope that she is able to continue to do that for herself as she listens to other stories

Contexts of learning

If the child is able to speak then we can talk about the different characters in the story and how each of them might feel, finding a physical gesture, drawing a picture or making a sound, then finding the words to express that feeling.

If a child is unable to speak, but does have some way of communicating, then the story is simply told, with objects and choices. Some children have gestures or sounds that they use repetitively. I took a gesture or sound that the child produced, replicated it and then incorporated it. One boy would fling his arms around with his fingers pointing out. I put a butterfly finger-puppet on his finger, and all of a sudden he was part of the story and being rewarded for it; eventually in our sessions he followed me on the arm flinging, in tune with the story, rather than the random movements made previously.

When there is no obvious physical movement or cognitive functioning, the storytelling is more sensory based, focusing on repeating sequences: the same three stories every week for six weeks, then another three stories. This allowed the development of a pattern of sensory experiences using voice, body, words and multisensory objects. That pattern of sensory experiences became their emotional literature.

A voice output communication aid such as a Big Mack[3] was used to record short elements of a story, such as a refrain (e.g. the bloodcurdling 'Fee Fi Foh Fum'), that the child could use during the story, increasing their sense of participation as they began to register, recognise, remember and then anticipate – reaching out for the communication device.

Issues to consider

The work described in this chapter is appropriate for individuals working with a therapist who has had training and supervision. However, the principles that I have outlined can be used in classrooms and with groups of children where stories are told for enjoyment and participation without any attempt to interpret or to force the storyteller's point of view. At all times it is the child's view of the story that is central, and not what the storyteller intends to be the point of the story. The storyteller's role is to listen to and observe the child's responses and to maximise those responses, either through exploring the language or by a physical representation. Whilst it is important to be clear about your own intention for telling the story, the impact on the listener might be quite different and it's important that you follow the consequences, rather than steer them towards your intent.

If you are working therapeutically, a basic training in counselling skills is important to learn listening and responding skills as well as boundaries and confidentiality. Access to supervision is important for the storyteller to reflect on the effect their work is having on themselves as well as the clients. This should be provided within the agency through which the activity is done. Where this is unavailable or inappropriate, 'creative supervision' is available to support arts practitioners working in health and social care settings, and professionals who use storytelling in their work (see 'Where to go').

Cultural factors

Working with children from different cultures, I was open to using traditional tales from their own cultures and would often ask to meet the parents to establish this. However, most of the parents would refer to traditional European tales such as *Goldilocks and the Three Bears* and *Little Red Hen*, as well as mainstream TV programmes like *Tracy Beaker, SpongeBob SquarePants* and films or books like *Harry Potter*. For example, the mother of a small Arabic boy with very little English said *Little Red Riding Hood* was most definitely his favourite story. Fortunately I used a half-sized puppet with a red hoodie top in my stories, to which he positively responded even though he didn't have the language; he was able to follow the story through the tone, pace and pitch of my voice and by interacting with the puppet.

Try it yourself

Top tips

- Assume that the child is cognitively functioning, can understand a story and use stories with simple concepts appropriate to their age and ability.
- Have a sound story structure (beginning, middle and end) because that affects the pacing of the story, know what your intention is for the child to be telling that story and be prepared for the impact may be different from what you had anticipated.
- XXTell stories that maximise the child's sensory stimulation, always looking for new opportunities to stretch and stimulate ('push' and 'pull') and, where appropriate, their previous experience.

Where to go

There are basic storytelling courses where you can learn and develop skills as a storyteller, such as the International School of Storytelling at Emerson College: http://www.emerson.org.uk/. Other courses can be found through the Society for Storytelling: www.sfs.org.uk.

I run therapeutic storytelling workshops: www.JanetTellsStories.co.uk, as does Sue Jennings (see Chapter 2).

Healing stories can be found at: https://storynet.org/groups/hsa/healing-story-alliance-hsa.

Resources

- Big Mack (www.inclusive.co.uk/ablenet-bigmack-p2039)
- Puppets
- Box of materials of different textures
- Large pieces of nylon material in different colours for sea, sand, earth, rainbow

Notes

1 www.longlongtimeago.com/llta_fairytales_caporushes.html.
2 www.sacred-texts.com/asia/ftft/ftft08.htm.
3 A simple voice output device: a verbal person records a message of up to 90 seconds, which can then be activated by a person with communication difficulties. See www.ablenetinc.com.

References

Bettelheim, B. (1976). *The uses of enchantment: The meaning and importance of fairy tales.* New York: Knopf.

Bowlby, R. (2011). Presentation by Richard Bowlby on the work of John Bowlby at Glastonbury, April 2011. Refers to Bowlby, J. *Attachment and loss* trilogy, first published 1969.

Campbell, J. (2008). *The hero with a thousand faces* (3rd ed., first published 1949). Novato, CA: New World Library.

Dent-Brown, K. & Wang, M. (2006). The mechanism of storymaking: A grounded theory study of the 6-part story method. *The Arts in Psychotherapy*, 33(4), 316–330.

Dowling, J. (2009). The alchemy of number in storytelling. *IBBYLink*, 26, 2–3.

Dowling, J. (2010). The power of three: Storytelling and bereavement. *Bereavement Care*, Spring, 29–32.

Gersie, A. (1992). *Storymaking in bereavement: Dragons fight in the meadow.* London: Jessica Kingsley Publishers.

Gersie, A. & King, N. (1989). *Storymaking in education and therapy.* London: Jessica Kingsley Publishers.

Killick, S. (2018). 'Building relationships through storytelling' for the Fostering Network. Available at: https://stevenkillick.files.wordpress.com/2018/04/building-relationships-through-storytelling.pdf.

Killick, S. & Okwedy, P. (2020) *Feelings are funny things: A storyteller's toolkit.* Cardiff and Central South Joint Education Service (CSCJES)Â. Available at: https://tinyurl.com/y923ntmw.

Killick, S. & Thomas, T. (2007). *Telling tales: Storytelling as emotional literacy.* Blackburn: Educational Printing Services.

Lahad, M. (1992). Storymaking in an assessment method for coping with stress: Six-part storymaking and BASIC Ph. In S. Jennings (Ed.), *Dramatherapy: Theory and practice* (Vol. 2, pp. 150–163). London and New York: Routledge.

Lawley, J. & Tompkins, P. (2000). *Metaphors in mind: Transformation through symbolic modeling.* London: Developing Company Press.

Sunderland, M. (2001). *Using storytelling as a therapeutic tool with children.* Oxford: Speechmark.

Sunderland, M. (2003). *Helping children with fear.* Oxford: Speechmark.

Chapter 2

Feelings are funny things

Using storytelling with Children Looked After and their carers

Steve Killick

Background

This chapter describes how storytelling can help children and adults become more aware of aspects of emotional literacy through a process that can contribute to building relationships, personal confidence and engagement in learning. This approach is particularly important to those children facing issues related to attachment and developmental trauma and has been most specifically aimed at Children Looked After (CLA) or those that have experienced a number of Adverse Childhood Experiences (ACEs). It can be delivered in home settings by parents and foster carers and in schools by staff taking a relational approach.

Why use stories?

'Narrative' and 'story' are terms that may be easy to recognise but are harder to define. For the purposes of this chapter, I see narrative as the bringing into words of experiences and ideas, with story as a particular form of narrative. A story is a structured narrative and characteristically involves dealing with a problem or difficulty of some sort. Haven (2007) defined a story specifically as 'a detailed character based narration of a character's struggle to overcome obstacles and reach an important goal'. This definition focuses on the very human elements of a story. Stories such as fables featuring animals, myths of gods, wonder tales with magical elements, indeed all kinds of stories illustrate and illuminate what it is to be human; stories evoke emotions, offer understanding of characters' intentions, relationships and dilemmas. They enable us to see the consequences of actions and to deepen our understanding of our values and what is right and wrong.

Stories are essential to our social and emotional development. Sunderland (2000) said 'Everyday language is not the natural language of feeling for children. Their natural language is that of image and metaphor, as in stories and dreams'. Many children will experience their first stories from their parents and carers where telling strengthens bonds through the 'intersubjective' experience. That experience is characterised by affective attunement and the shared enjoyment of the story. Stories also broaden children's social and physical experience of the world (Frude & Killick, 2011). Reading fiction has been demonstrated to increase empathy in real life (Oatley, 2016). An assumption of this work is that the telling of stories (as opposed to reading aloud or to oneself) amplifies these effects, especially with children who may have less exposure to the world of reading either through an impoverished environment or lagging cognitive or literacy skills.

DOI: 10.4324/9781003159087-2

Stories and storytelling then are excellent vehicles for helping to develop an emotional understanding of oneself and others, especially for children with developmental trauma, who are looked after or have experienced adversity or abuse.

Theory and principles

This project grew from the author's experience of oral storytelling traditions in community and performance settings, and applying this to help foster carers build relationships with the children in their care. CLA have often experienced developmental trauma with subsequent negative impact on socio-emotional, cognitive development and, at times, increased vulnerability to mental health problems. This manifests in difficulties in forming attachments, emotional regulation or disturbed behaviour. Storytelling was combined with ideas and techniques from Dynamic Developmental Psychotherapy (Hughes, Golding & Hudson, 2015) based on attachment theory. Here, parents, carers and facilitators take a stance of Playfulness, Acceptance, Curiosity and Empathy (PACE) in helping children, rather than focusing on using 'reason' or overly strict discipline. The PACE approach allows for relational growth and repair. As such, the relational space between people is seen to be critical to emotional health.

The work with foster carers was then applied to working directly with vulnerable learners (identified as having additional learning needs due to developmental trauma) in schools, incorporating ideas from philosophy in education (e.g. Worley, 2014), Circle Time and third-wave cognitive behavioural therapies such as Acceptance and Commitment Therapy (Greco & Hayes, 2008).

The approach focused on three aspects of storytelling; the *content* of the stories and the *process* of telling person to person, which places an emphasis on nonverbal communication (NVC) aspects such as eye contact, tone of voice, facial expression and posture. NVC often conveys the emotional aspects of communication, so telling stories gives additional emotional information. The final aspect is that of the conversation that can take place around the stories – stories can emerge from this conversation, conversation may be incorporated into the story, or may be used to reflect on the story afterwards. This is the *Talen* model based on the triad of tale, telling and talking and named from the old Anglo-Saxon word that is the root of these three words.

Traditional tales were chosen because they are well crafted stories shaped by many tongues and tested by time as well as reflecting different cultures and values. Also, the image based language and repetitive patterns and phrases make them easier to learn to tell. Personal stories and fictional texts are also incorporated.

An important aspect of the work is to establish a group or dyad that is both safe and playful. This is essential for children to feel they can offer ideas and opinions without fear of being negatively judged for getting things right or wrong. This approach can be used in groups as small as two, for instance a carer and child, through to a whole class in a school or other setting. The optimal size to allow for discussion is between 8 and 12.

Work in practice

Working in schools

A typical 'session' is best run by two facilitators working together (although it can be run by one person) for a period of at least six weeks. It is beneficial for at least one facilitator to have an expertise in emotional health and wellbeing.

The warm-up

A session would normally begin by arranging the group into a circle with sufficient space for the exercises. The sessions are usually introduced as an exploration into feelings, providing a place where we will talk safely about emotions and try and make sense of them, as they can be strange and mysterious; pleasant and unpleasant. The exercises are designed to be active, encourage interaction and develop over each lesson. They involve emotion regulation, encouraging awareness of bodily states, and both raising and lowering energy and arousal levels.

Typical games are interactional, sensory, non-competitive and participative. For instance, sending a 'clap' around the circle where one participant makes eye contact with someone on one side of them and then claps. This second student then turns to the partner on their other side, makes eye contact and claps. So it continues around the circle until it returns to the originator. This game can be developed over the weeks as it becomes more familiar, for instance, working together to clap synchronically. Another game might invite participants, again going round the circle, to say whether they are feeling more like a cat or a dog today. Over time the range of animals can be extended or they can express themselves through movement and gesture. Riddles or expressing an emotion through facial expression or posture are used. One exercise, the 'Rain-dance' involves working through a series of movements from rubbing hands together, lightly patting them, clapping, slapping thighs, stamping on the floor then reversing the sequence to return to rubbing hands together. It works through an emotion regulation sequence of calm to high intensity action in a structured way. The function of these warm-up exercises is to establish an atmosphere where is it safe to participate. The challenge for the facilitator is create the right tone whilst also establishing a degree of focused work. It can be useful to establish the 'boundaries' of the group such as listening to each other and – as feelings can be sometimes also be painful – taking care not to hurt others' feelings. As the group develops, the reasons for these boundaries can be explored farther. Popular exercises are often repeated as these help provide a sense of familiarity through repetition and ritual. New exercises or development of old ones maintains curiosity and engagement. A key aim is to produce an atmosphere of focused calm in the group which is both playful and thoughtful.

The main action

This will usually involve either a 'Story Inquiry' or a 'Storytelling Skills' exercise.

A Story Inquiry will involve telling a short story usually a folk-tale or fable. Typical stories might be *Stone Soup*, the *Fearsome Giant, The Boy Who Lost His Luck* or *Tonguemeat*.[1] The story may fluctuate in its emotional intensity, perhaps using a 'call-and-response' to energise or using tone of voice to lower the mood. Either at the end or at structured points along the story, students are asked what feelings or emotions they notice in the characters, the story or themselves as listeners. Their contributions are written down on a flipchart or whiteboard. If an emotion such as 'happy' or 'sad' is given, participants are encouraged to give more information, for example, 'Could you say more? What kind of happy? Pleased? Excited?' and so on. As the group develops a vocabulary of emotion words, various exercises are used to explore more about the specific emotions or related themes. For instance, the topic of friendship may emerge which can be explored in a 'community of inquiry' style with questions such as 'What makes a good friend?' 'How does having a friend help when you are feeling sad or low?' or 'What kind of friend would you like to be?' It might lead to an exercise or discussion on listening skills. Other exercises might involve placing feeling words, written on cards, into the primary emotion groups: happy, sad, anxious or angry. The triggers and functions of emotions can be explored as ways of coping with those feelings or actions characters might take. Socratic and reflective questions, which are open-ended, encourage deeper exploration. Internal process such as thoughts, beliefs and the choices which can lead to further actions can be explored. Here it is important to use the PACE approach to ensure the questions come from a place of curiosity, are accepting of the viewpoints of the learners and empathic to their emotional responses and the mood is light-hearted when appropriate.

Storytelling Skills sessions involve teaching students stories that they themselves can tell to others and begin when a group has established itself. This gives the opportunity to teach the various cognitive and communication skills necessary to 'relate' a story. Storytelling involves such skills as memory of key information and imagination, it requires the both verbal and non-verbal skills of listening, eye-contact, gesture and tone of voice. The very act of storytelling enables practice of these skills in a way that is both playful and spontaneous. In the sessions, learners are encouraged to tell stories in pairs rather than 'perform' to a whole group. As confidence increases they are encouraged to work with partners or small groups to tell stories, and to tell stories to friends or family outside the session. In some cases this has led to performances in assemblies and younger year groups or to groups in other schools. It is important not to let the pressures of creating good enough 'content' to perform from overshadowing the 'process' of engagement and enjoyment. It does, however, allow the possibility of exploring and mastering the anxieties of performing.

The wind-down

Like the warm-up, the wind-down involves emotional regulation activities although there may be an emphasis on exercises encouraging reflection and relaxation. Such exercises may include 'Checking-in & Checking-Out', a round where each person says what they enjoyed about the session, anything that could be better and what they might take away, or breathing exercises such as 'finger-breathing' where you run the tip of your finger up and down the side of the fingers on your other hand synchronically as you breathe in and out. These and other exercises help to make learners aware of their breathing and lay the foundation for learning mindfulness skills.

A story may be told as part of the wind-down, particularly if there has been less emphasis on listening and discussing the story in the main action. Here there is no intention to discuss the story but to enter into a deeper and more imaginative state of listening. Wonder tales, with moments of awe and wonder, are ideal for this purpose and longer stories can be broken into 10-minute chunks and the story told over several sessions.

Sessions with foster carers

Training sessions for foster carers typically take place over a day and, like the school sessions, focus both on listening to and discussing stories and storytelling skills. Emotion regulation techniques focus on exercises that can be done with 2–3 people reflecting family size. Additional content includes looking at the role stories have in family settings and recalling childhood experiences of stories. It has been possible to integrate story-making and encouraging social storytelling and communication techniques through integrating techniques such as 'Storysharing' (Grove, 2014; see Chapter 19) for young people with more severe communication difficulties. Ways of introducing and creating 'spaces' and ways into storytelling are also introduced, such as telling tales on a walk, with a meal or having a storytelling time (Killick, 2022).

Outcomes and evidence: what to look for

Assessment is built into the process as the participants' emotional vocabulary becomes evident in the exercises. The principle is to work where the group is and to gently extend the members' emotional vocabulary, recognition and comprehension skills through modelling and scaffolding. Stories are adapted to give learners the information they need through both verbal and non-verbal cues. Participants are not corrected or instructed directly if they get it wrong, but alternative and multiple ways of seeing things are encouraged. More difficult emotional content such as loss or anger can be introduced as the group becomes more cohesive and skilled. One useful assessment framework is based on the five dimensions of emotional intelligence as adapted to UK schools (Goleman, 1995; Killick, 2006). This involves observations on both individual students and the group-as-a-whole's level of functioning in the areas of:

- Awareness – ability to name and express different emotions appropriate to age.
- Emotion regulation – ability to engage with activities appropriate to the exercise.
- Motivation – in this case for different activities in the group.
- Empathy – ability to recognise others' emotions and perspectives.
- Social skills – such as listening, friendship or conflict resolution skills.

The 'Feelings are Funny Things' programme was recognised as good practice by the Welsh Government for CLA in 2021. It has run in 15 different primary schools and similar groups have also run in other schools, a pupil referral unit and an adolescent mental health unit. The programme has been delivered with either whole classes of Year 5 or 6 learners with a high proportion of CLA or where small groups of vulnerable learners were brought together from different schools as part of a transition to a secondary school project. Evaluation data collected included teacher ratings of engagement in learning and confidence before and immediately after the intervention. Of the 61 children identified as having emotional, behavioural or additional learning needs who were rated by their teachers, 69 per cent had improved ratings in engagement and 80 per cent had improved ratings of perceived confidence. Follow-up data suggested that these levels of engagement and confidence had declined slightly three months after the intervention was finished but were still higher than prior to the intervention. Evaluations of learners found they much enjoyed story listening and telling as well as learning about emotions. These results, on small numbers and lacking control comparisons, do suggest that the intervention has impact and acceptability to schools and would benefit from a more thorough evaluation.

The stories of 'David' and 'Kara'...

School staff reported that many children showed marked improvements in their ability to talk to them about their feelings and to talk more confidently in classroom settings. 'David', an 11-year-old who had a history of behavioural problems and non-engagement discovered a role for himself as a storyteller for younger children in the school. There were significant improvements in his behaviour and how he perceived himself. 'Kara', a 10-year-old girl who was very unmotivated about school work and often distracted in class, became extremely engaged in discussing and talking about the stories with subsequent improvement in participation in school work and a greater ability to talk about her own thoughts and feelings.

Contexts of learning

These sessions have been delivered in different formats: weekly sessions, one-day sessions over a series of weeks and as three-day intensives. They can be delivered by school staff, outside facilitators or a mix of the two. Our target group is children with a high number of ACEs, are CLA or are struggling academically and/or socially. A principle is always to work at learner's ability level and gently extend this. Some degree of verbal ability is necessary even if learners may be lower than average. The approach has been specifically aimed at pupils aged from 7 to 14 years (Key stages 2 and 3) but is applicable to all ages although using it with adolescents demands a higher degree of confidence and skill in storytelling by facilitators. More complex stories such as myth and epic (e.g., *The Odyssey*) or dilemma stories can be effective for this group.

Issues to consider

The approach is geared to vulnerable learners and to those who have additional learning needs. Although it can work with whole classes smaller groups of 8–12 are more desirable allowing for more reflective discussions. Having an appropriate environment – quiet, free from distractions, either indoors or outside, is essential.

This structure of the group allows for the development of the content of the work with the group to include doing more therapeutic, psycho-educational or other creative activities. For instance, it might be appropriate to move into therapeutic story making (e.g. Golding, 2014, Jennings Chapter 3 this volume) or visual art activities.

For foster carers, training sessions have often been provided through statutory and third-sector foster care organisations. Sessions could be organised through schools and include parents as well as carers and may provide a useful bridge between home and school.

Cultural factors

The work has so far taken place in South Wales in urban and rural areas, some very deprived, with predominantly White British children, a proportion of Black, Asian and Minority Ethnic (BAME) and some refugee and asylum-seekers with a wide range of ability. As stories can reflect many different cultures they can, if used with sensitivity, be a powerful tool for inclusion. It is essential to be aware of the cultural backgrounds of learners and of the schools and of cultural issues in stories, to see cultural differences as an opportunity for learning and as an issue demanding reflection and supervision.

Try it yourself

It can be daunting for practitioners to tell, rather than read, stories to groups of children although, strangely, they may do this frequently in social or family settings. However, it is through practice that sufficient confidence and skill to tell stories to engage children in discussion develops. Even a little training and/or experience can quickly develop the expertise necessary.

Top tips

- Practise storytelling wherever you can to gain confidence and see how people react. Do it with just one other person and do it for the pleasure of sharing a story rather than to trigger an outcome. Try going to any local story circle, watch storytellers live or on YouTube or get some training in storytelling.
- When running groups select a comfortable, quiet and attractive environment. If you can transform it with cushions, rugs or throws in some way so much the better.
- Let go of your ideas of what the story means or why characters make certain actions – be open to the discoveries made by learners – they are frequently surprising and insightful and deepen your own understanding of the story. Choose stories you enjoy telling. Tell a story and watch what happens.

Where to go: training and resources

Feelings are Funny Things: A Storytellers Toolkit contains activities and stories that can be used and is available for free download in English or Welsh from the Cardiff and Central South Joint Education Service website, https://tinyurl.com/y923ntmw, and www.stevenkillick.co.uk which includes information about online training.

A manual for supporting foster carers, *Building Relationships through Storytelling – A Foster Carer's Guide to Attachment and Stories* can be downloaded from the Fostering Network website, https://tinyurl.com/hpufpcv.

The Society of Storytelling website has many resources and information about storytelling, especially events and where to learn about storytelling – www.sfs.org.uk.

Acknowledgements

To Phil Okwedy who co-developed many of the structures described in this chapter, Siriol Burford of the Cardiff and Central South Joint Education Service (CSCJES) and The Resilience Project, NHS Cardiff & Vale University Health Board, for their support of this project.

Note

1 Stories available in *Feelings are Funny Things: A Storytelling Toolkit*. A downloadable manual. See 'Where to go: training and resources'.

References

Frude, N. & Killick, S. (2011). Family storytelling and the attachment relationship. *Psychodynamic Practice*, 17(4), 441–455.

Golding, K. (2014). *Using stories to build bridges with traumatized children*. London: Jessica Kingsley Publishing.

Goleman, D. (1995). *Emotional intelligence*. London and New York: Bantam Books.

Greco, L. A. & Hayes, S. (2008). *Acceptance and mindfulness treatments for children and adolescents: A practitioner's guide*. Oakland, CA: New Harbinger.

Grove, N. (2014). *The big book of storysharing*. London: Routledge.

Haven, K. (2007). *Story proof: The science behind the startling power of story*. Westport, CT: Libraries Unlimited.

Hughes, D., Golding, K. & Hudson, J. (2015). Dyadic Developmental Psychotherapy (DDP): The development of the theory, practice and research base. *Adoption & Fostering*, 39(4), 356–365.

Killick, S. (2006). *Emotional literacy at the heart of the school ethos*. London: Sage.

Killick, S. (2022). Fostering storytellers: Helping foster carers to build attachments and enhance emotional literacy through stories and storytelling. In C. Holmwood, S. Jennings & S. Jackstics (Eds), *The international handbook of therapeutic stories and storytelling*. London: Routledge.

Oatley, K. (2016). Fiction: Simulation of social worlds. *Trends in Cognitive Sciences*, 20(8), 618–628.

Sunderland, M. (2000). *Using storytelling as a therapeutic tool with children*. Bicester: Speechmark.

Worley, P. (2014). *Once upon an if: The storythinking handbook*. London: Bloomsbury.

Chapter 3

Healing stories with children at risk

The StoryBuildingTM approach

Sue Jennings

Background

This is an interactive chapter where you are invited to respond to different examples of stories and events in your own journal, so please choose a writing book with a stiff cover to record your reactions. You may wish to respond visually with pictures or patterns, think of crayons or paints as well as a book.

The telling of stories in times of trouble is not a new concept; however, it is a practice that needs to be rediscovered in our highly technical age. It is both built on received wisdom from ancient civilisations and informed by contemporary therapeutic practice. Since the publication of the first edition of this book, we have had to deal with a major global crisis that many countries have not faced before. Loss, permanent disability and stress and anxiety are major outcomes from the recent pandemic of Covid 19. Storytelling is needed more than ever.

A healing story may be an old traditional tale, or it could be adapted to address the particular needs of an individual or a group. Some people create their own stories for children; others prefer to use existing tales. We need to be aware of what the story is that a child, or group of children, needs to hear. We focus on the story the child needs to tell, as well as the story the child needs to hear.

Write in your journal a story about any time in your life that you felt invisible or not noticed by others. Children who are overlooked can suffer loss of self-esteem and belief in themselves.

The StoryBuilding approach consists of a formula or structure known as the '5 Ws + H'; that is, 'Where? Who? What? Why? When? + How?' The structure is applied in an order and follows gradual steps of learning, whereby each step builds on the foundation of the previous step and moves both the experience and the story forward. Although rooted in every individual's creative capacities, the approach follows a developmental sequence in clear stages in order to build the story (Jennings, 2010).

The StoryBuilding approach is used for children and young people to express therapeutic needs in story form, creating stories to suit the needs of a particular child or children in particular situations. However, it can also be used to explore existing stories in order to deepen understanding and therapeutic experience, explore emotions and life challenges (Grove & Park, 1996). In my own work I do not differentiate between story and narrative, and as Polkinghorne (1988) suggests, they can be used as synonyms. I find it more helpful

DOI: 10.4324/9781003159087-3

to have a big umbrella under which there are many different types of stories: epic stories, myths, legends, fairy tales and so on.

Many of the therapeutic stories that develop through this approach move into other artistic activities, especially drama (Crimmens, 2006). Stories can be danced, painted, explored with puppets and dramatised. And dramatisation can involve costumes, props and masks.

Theories and principles

Although I have always developed the use of stories in therapeutic work in education (Jennings, 1973), there have been certain moments when other people's work and writing have given me sudden bursts of illumination and clarity. The StoryBuilding approach was profoundly influenced by the work and writing of Viola Spolin and her seminal book *Improvisation for the Theater* (1963), in which she discusses a system for helping performers bring truth to their roles and characters, now elaborated in *Theater Games for the Classroom* (1986). Dorothy Heathcote's work on drama in education (Heathcote, Johnson & O'Neill, 1991) pioneered a story form of drama that combines a structured approach with scope for improvisation. The 'zone of proximal development' from the writings of Vygotsky (1973) illustrates the space between the pupil's known and safe area and the next step they can move towards with appropriate help and support. The extensive writing of Alida Gersie, in particular *Earthtales: Storytelling in Times of Change* (1992), has shown me many ways into story forms, especially through her techniques of 'storymaking' (Gersie & King, 1990; Gersie, 1991).

Sensory foundation of storytelling

Creative play, stories, the arts and their therapeutic emergence and, indeed, our social and cultural world grow from our basic sensory experiences.

Sensory proto-play is necessary for the development of healthy attachments and the expansion of the child's place in the social world. Mothers and carers use stories to reinforce this early sensory experience in touch and singing games. However, the senses themselves need to continue to develop as they did in our primitive past. For example, we need our sense of alertness, our sense of intuition, our sense of fear to as yet invisible danger. Only then can we make sense of these experiences by telling stories about them. I am certain that we need to pay more attention to the most basic sensory development in babies and young children, and not to neglect it in adulthood (see Cozolino, 2002). We need to be alert to infant and child disorders that can emerge not only through lack of sensory stimulation but also through 'sensory overdose' and undifferentiated sound (Emmons & Anderson, 2005; Jennings, 2011).

> *Write a story about your own sensory experiences: are there particular smells or tastes or sounds that you like or don't like? How many of these belong to your early childhood experience? Were any of them copied from the adults around you?*

Work in practice

What is StoryBuilding?

The StoryBuilding approach is my focus in schools for creating narratives with individuals and groups, as is exploring folk and fairy tales as a means of deepening understanding and facilitating therapeutic expression. It is a way of 'unpacking' a story that can be personal or newly created or that already exists in some form.

The approach is usually carefully developed in the stages of 'Where? Who? What? Why? When? + How?': *Where* is the story taking place? *Who* are the characters? *What* is going on? *Why* is it happening? *When* is it happening? *How* will it all end?

The first three are interchangeable in terms of starting a story – we can start with: Where is it happening? or Who is in the story? or What is happening? – and progress to the other two. However, the second three – Why is it happening? When is it happening? How does it end? – are more complex concepts and may prove difficult for some children with learning needs. As facilitators we need to be flexible in order to apply the StoryBuilding sequence in relationship to the educational capacities of the participants. The Why?, the When? and the How? need to be introduced slowly and safely.

Who is involved in StoryBuilding?

It is ideally a model for teachers working with children with special needs or children at risk, but it can also be developed within the curriculum with mainstream students. StoryBuilding can be used with all subjects in schools to facilitate learning and the development of communication skills. Creative arts therapists and speech and language therapists also use StoryBuilding for building communication and narrative skills.

Children with special needs may be children with learning difficulties or physical challenges, children who have been neglected or abused, and not forgetting the child who is never seen: 'She was so well behaved I never noticed her', said one teacher; 'No trouble at all, looks after himself, doesn't bother me, what a help!', said a mother of one boy who was so 'invisible' that he had forgotten how to talk. Below is a built story about a child who 'disappeared' that I create with individuals and groups who feel that they are 'invisible'.

Why use StoryBuilding?

The built story enables a sense of achievement and can increase self-esteem and confidence. It also has the added advantage of improving sequencing skills and making sense of a 'through line' of narrative. The through line (Stanislavski, 1950) helps the individual experience how one thing leads to another before coming to a resolution. This is especially important for children with special needs, since life can often be a series of events or happenings, without coherence or a sense of cause and effect. As Alida Gersie (1992) states, one of the reasons that we create stories is that we require and acquire 'an awareness of sequentiality, causality, the accidental, the unexpected and the anticipated, the predictable and the unpredictable' (p. 19).

When is StoryBuilding used?

It is helpful if there can be a regular session every week or, for some groups, every day. Bearing in mind that the StoryBuilding process underpins other forms of learning; regular input can reinforce the retention of information as well as the means of learning and thinking. StoryBuilding can be used as a crisis intervention when there have been sudden or shocking events in the life of the school, or in the life of the individual. The built story can help to 'ground' the experience, and the metaphor of rebuilding the wall is a useful metaphor for the lives of children that have crumbled or collapsed.

How is StoryBuilding applied?

It is important that attention is paid to the sequencing of the built story. The idea of stories is introduced and pupils are able to reflect on possible themes during the massage and sensory development which often precedes the main storytelling.

The following example shows how some stories need to begin with simple sensory experience, and have a simple through line of sequence. It can be used to develop trust and give reassurance and as a warm-up for further StoryBuilding.

A massage story

Create the massage story on the child's back in a one-to-one setting, 'shoulder to waist' (Jennings, 2004/2017, Jennings 2018 see also Chapter 14) or with a group or class. A child goes through an adapted sequence with their hand and fingers on their other arm. Encourage them to make the weather noises of the rain and thunder.

> It is raining very gently (using tips of fingers), then more rain and more rain … Then you can hear thunder (using hands), and then there is more rain, more thunder; then there is lightening (using sides of the hands); slowly the thunder gets less (gentle use of hands), a little more rain and then it stops … The sun comes out (use both hands making a big circle), and then there is a rainbow (using one hand making an arc).

The massage warm-up encourages the focusing of the senses and a feeling of alertness for the following story, which is built on the stages described above: by starting with bodily experience we can engage children in sensory communication that can help build the story through the stages of 5 Ws + H.

The children are invited to listen to the story and to create sound effects when it is appropriate. The task is for the children to find their own healing in a built story that addresses their issues. The children record their own responses through pictures they have drawn and receive feedback at the end. However, it is important that the children do not feel pressured to respond – the story is usually working on their 'inner life' through the symbols and images.

> *Experiment yourself with this exercise using one hand and fingers on your arm, and see what you recall about rainbows. Can you recall a seeing a rainbow as a small child? Draw a rainbow in your journal and write a story about your early rainbow experience.*

The child who disappeared

When telling this story, encourage the children to make any sound effects so that the story becomes truly interactive.

> It is a very stormy night and there is a lot of noise and movement in the forest: branches creak, leaves swirl and rain lashes against the windows of the house of the forest family.

They are surprised by a knock on the door. Their cousin is there, and she tells Mum that she has bought a child with her that no one can see because her aunt was so critical of her that she disappeared. Now she wears a bell round her neck so people know where she is.

Mum sends her own children to bed. She tells the child to follow her upstairs and is very relieved when she hears the tinkle of a bell following her. She puts on the night-light in a little bedroom that has a warm, thick bedcover, and says she will fetch a warm drink. Mum realises she does not know the child's name. She suggests that the child should ring the bell if she says the name that is right for her. Mum tries several names until, at the name Mary-Jane, the bell rings several times. 'Right Mary-Jane, we have a name for you.' When Mum comes back with the warm drink of milk and honey, she can see the bump under the bedcover so she knows the child is in bed. She puts the drink by the bed, says good night and leaves the door open and the landing light on.

Downstairs, she looks in Grandmother's recipe book for all the ways to make invisible children visible. She sits up and sews a little red dress and scarf for Mary-Jane and puts them at the end of the bed. The next morning the family can see a pair of legs and feet coming down the stairs wearing a red dress, but no face.

The story continues, showing how small acts of love and inclusion allow Mary-Jane to reclaim her identity.

Class discussion can follow using the StoryBuilding sequences: 'Where does the story happen? Who is in the story? What happens? Why do you think that Mary-Jane became invisible? When did it happen? [time of day, season] How can Mum help her to become completely visible? Can Dad and the other children help too?'

The story can be told again, integrating any new information that the children have suggested. The story can then be made active, with children moving and dancing all the scenes, or by choosing puppets to tell it again and create an ending. The whole group could draw a picture on one piece of paper that tells the story as a whole. Greater learning is retained through the activation of the story, and the children's creativity is enhanced. The session ends with children drawing their own favourite moment in the story.

> *Write in your journal the ending you would choose for the story of the* Child who Disappeared *and note any similarities to your own experience or those of children you know.*

Outcomes and evidence: what to look for

The story of six boys

I chose the story of *Mihai the Shepherd Boy* as a story for a group of six boys aged 7–8 years who had been selected by teachers because of their combination of mild learning difficulties and behavioural challenges. The aim was to enhance their social learning so they could see that all our actions have consequences. The class could also see that it is possible to find solutions through the imagination and that life does not always have to be predictable. The story is based on a Romanian folk tale in which a young shepherd boy wants to hide in the forest to watch St Peter when he tells all the wolves what they are allowed to eat. All the wolves – young, old, families and lone wolves – gather in the clearing and Peter tells each one what they may eat and they appreciate the gifts and walk away. An old lame wolf arrives very late and Peter is at a loss to suggest some food. Then he says, 'There is a young shepherd boy hiding up that tree'.[1]

I chose this story as it flags up the opportunity for social learning as well as providing a strong image of the wolf, and wolves (like ourselves) are also organised in family structures. The fact that the story does not have a definite ending allows the pupils to explore the outcome of actions and to see the consequences.

We explored where the story was taking place and who was involved. We did some drama games using wolf calls and growls – being able to tiptoe out of the house without disturbing anyone, being able to walk through snow without slipping and so on. In two groups of three the boys discussed the ending. One group decided that Mihai promised the wolf that he would look after him, and took him safely home. The other group said that Mihai would trick the wolf by throwing down his sheepskin jacket and then running home quickly. We then explored what might be said to Mihai when he got home, either with the wolf or without his jacket!

The group were intently involved in this story and all had concerns for Mihai's safety. Later we made wolf masks and everyone enjoyed playing different kinds of wolves. The children all responded, were engaged with the story and created their own imaginative solutions.

There is no doubt that this approach works; hundreds of children in diverse cultures have been engaged with StoryBuilding and have helped to create stories that mattered to them. They have found positive outcomes for their characters instead of their customary 'negative cycle'. There has been an increase in feelings of optimism, both for pupils and teachers, in settings where teachers have also allowed themselves change in relation to their perceptions and expectations of the children.

Contexts of learning

StoryBuilding is useful for children with a wide range of learning needs and can be developed and adapted for different levels of learning and language acquisition. The approach can also be used with storyboards for children with little language (Crimmens, 2006).

It is important to remember that there are some children who have great difficulty with processing sensory experiences, especially children with autistic spectrum difficulties (Emmons & Anderson, 2005). A gradual programme of sensory experience can be introduced with stories.

Cultural factors

Children feel affirmed when a story is used from their own culture and equally they can get a sense of surprise with a story that is totally different. My own answer is to create a balance between local traditions and new material. Therefore I may use a story version of *A Midsummer Night's Dream* or *Hamlet* with children in Kazakhstan but also use the *Bored Prince* or *The Foolish Bai* from their local tradition (Jennings, 2005).

Try it yourself

Top tips

- Use physical warm-ups and drama games to focus energy before focusing on the story.
- Choose a story that you know well and that has a clear structure with a resolution at the end.
- When helping to structure creative stories, use a whiteboard to write everyone's suggestions and then select them in different combinations.

Remember a story from your childhood and summarise it in your journal. Remember all the feelings that were associated with it. How has it affected your attitudes to storytelling now?

Where to go

Training courses are available in StoryBuilding and therapeutic storytelling (www.ndpltd.org) and from time-to-time similar courses are run by specialists such as Alida Gersie, Nancy Mellon (www.healingstory.com), Sharon Jacksties (www.sharonjackstories.co.uk) and Nicola Grove (www.drnicolagrove.com).

Resources

Margot Sunderland has a range of specially written picture books addressing emotional issues with children. Sunderland, M. (2001). *Using story telling as a therapeutic tool with children: Helping children with feelings.* Milton Keynes: Speechmark.

Jennings, S. (1999). *Introduction to developmental playtherapy: Playing and health.* London: Jessica Kingsley.

Note

1 For the full text of this story see Jennings, S. (2004/2017). *Creative storytelling with children at risk.* Abingdon: Routledge/Speechmark, or email drsue@ndpltd.org.

References

Cozolino, L. (2002). *The neuroscience of psychotherapy.* London: W. W. Norton.

Crimmens, P. (2006). *Drama therapy and storymaking in special education.* London: Jessica Kingsley.

Emmons, P. G. & Anderson, L. M. (2005). *Understanding sensory dysfunction.* London: Jessica Kingsley.

Gersie, A. (1991). *Storymaking and bereavement.* London: Jessica Kingsley.

Gersie, A. (1992). *Earthtales: Storytelling in times of change.* London: Green Print.

Gersie, A. & King, N. (1990). *Storymaking in education and therapy.* London: Jessica Kingsley.

Grove, N. & Park, K. (1996). *Odyssey now.* London: Jessica Kingsley.

Heathcote, D., Johnson, L. & O'Neill, C. (Eds). (1991). *Collected writings on education and drama.* Evanston, IL: Northwestern University Press.

Holmwood, C., Jennings., S. & Jacksties, S. (Eds). (2022). *International handbook of therapeutic stories and storytelling*. Abingdon: Routledge.

Jennings, S. (1973). *Remedial drama*. London: Pitman.

Jennings, S. (1999). *Introduction to developmental play therapy: Playing and health*. London: Jessica Kingsley.

Jennings, S. (2017) [2004]. *Creative storytelling with children at risk*. Abingdon: Routledge/ Speechmark.

Jennings, S. (2005). *Creative storytelling with adults at risk*. Abingdon: Routledge/Speechmark.

Jennings, S. (2010). *StoryBuilding: 100+ ideas for developing story and narrative skills*. Buckingham: Hinton House.

Jennings, S. (2011). *Healthy attachments and neuro-dramatic-play*. London: Jessica Kingsley.

Jennings, S. (2018). *Working creatively with attachment difficulties with school-aged children*. Buckingham: Hinton House.

Polkinghorne, D. (1988). *Narrative knowing and the human sciences*. Albany, NY: State University of New York Press.

Spolin, V. (1963). *Improvisation for the theater*. Evanston, IL: North Western University Press.

Spolin, V. (1986) *Theater games for the classroom: A teacher's handbook*. Evanston, IL: North Western University Press.

Stanislavski, C. (1950). *Building a character*. London: Methuen.

Sunderland, M. (2001). *Using storytelling as a therapeutic tool with children*. Abingdon: Routledge/ Speechmark.

Vygotsky, L. (1973). *Thought and language*. Cambridge, MA: MIT Press.

Chapter 4

What can teachers learn from the stories children tell?

The nurturing, evaluation and interpretation of storytelling by children with language and learning difficulties

Beth McCaffrey

Background

Stories and storytelling have an influence far beyond their use in literacy lessons. Whilst they are indeed powerful tools in the development of language they are also crucial to the emotional development of children and to the formation of their social and ethical identities. In this approach most of the storytelling contexts start with a story, usually a picture-book tale. Ideas are then explored and developed through a range of playful and creative activities, and they all end with a story – this time the children's own.

This is not a pre-created standard intervention, but one guided by a set of principles. There is no formula for the creation of the different storytelling contexts provided. They are developed from that ingrained habit of teachers of looking out for and copying the best ideas of others and adapting them to best suit their own teaching preferences and the needs of their current class.

Theories and principles

Dahlberg and Moss (2005: 99) discuss '[a] pedagogy of listening where teaching is responsive to the perceived needs and interests of the children'. All teachers are acutely aware that mindful listening – 'listening that requires a deep awareness and at the same time a suspension of judgments' (Rinaldi, 2001, quoted in Dahlberg & Moss, 2005: 99) – is incredibly difficult to achieve in classrooms with competing demands on their attention. For this reason I allocate one-to-one time for each child in order to listen to their storytelling. In the first instance these are equivalent amounts of time, but can later be differentiated in the interests of equality (e.g. if a child needs more time to express themselves because of particular language difficulties).

An integrated curriculum with opportunities for multimodal representation

This enables children to make connections across learning experiences and to express themselves in diverse ways. Children with special educational needs do not necessarily need a specialised curriculum, but one that offers opportunities to learn and consolidate in a wide range of imaginative ways and that is deeply enriched and memorable. In developing the contexts for storytelling (which may last for a week or more), use is often made of a range of expressive arts including painting, collage, clay work, mime, dance, music, and puppet play.

DOI: 10.4324/9781003159087-4

The concept of 'playful work' (where adult interaction within variably structured settings extends and challenges learning)

This concept fully acknowledges the essential role of play (and in this context particularly, fantasy play) in the holistic development of all children, and hopes to harness the engagement and intrinsic motivation that free play inspires. In playful work, however, the role of the adult is pivotal – both in modelling ways to play alongside an exploration of alternative possibilities, and in gently challenging and extending children's language and thinking. A consistent theme is that play may need to be modelled for some children as it will not be a spontaneously occurring activity. One of the activities frequently used is Gussin-Paley's dramatisation technique where: 'The dictated story … to fulfil its destiny is dramatized on a pretend stage with the help of classmates as actors and audience and the teacher as narrator and director' (Gussin-Paley, 2004: 5). The children tell an adult their story, this is scribed and the children then choose their classmates to become the different characters in the dramatisation. The other drama strategies most frequently used are either interactive storytelling (where the teacher tells the story but encourages group or individual responses throughout) or the use of a 'prescribed drama structure' (see Sherratt & Peter, 2002: 77).

Spaces for therapeutic play

All children need some respite or therapeutic space within the busy day of the classroom, and some activities (e.g. the use of sandplay and clay) can provide possibilities for healing and integration that are equally as powerful as a 'taught' curriculum of social and emotional development. Therapeutic play provides opportunities for adults to respond to children 'as they are', fostering an atmosphere of acceptance and trust that is not conditional upon learning or improvement. The sandtray and miniatures I use to provide both therapeutic play and as a storytelling medium are set up in accordance with the guidance of Lois Carey (Carey, 1999: 188). They include as wide a range of items as possible, including models of living creatures, people (as varied as possible), buildings, scenery, transportation, and natural objects.

The final principle is one that relates most closely to the practitioners (Grove, Gussin-Paley, Edmiston, and Fox) who were the inspiration for my storytelling approach (and whom I would highly recommend the readers of this chapter seek out and read in detail) – the principle of giving stories and storytelling prominence in the lives of all children.

Work in practice

There is no set sequence of repeated activities that I can describe, and the suitability of any sessions will vary from class to class. The following are two different story contexts I have used on several occasions with different groups of children with language and learning difficulties, aged 6–9 years, in a special school (McCaffrey, 2009).

Story context 1: sandtray stories

Introduction to storytelling activity

- The sandtray and miniatures available for use are shown to the children.
- The teacher demonstrates the telling of a story using some miniatures of their choice.

- Teacher-chosen objects are cleared away and each child chooses one object to place in the sandtray and is encouraged to make a suggestion towards the telling of a group story.

Context for storytelling

- Children are each given 15 minutes of individual play time with the sandtray and free choice of the number and type of objects to use. They are made aware that at the end of this time they will be asked to select some miniatures and to tell a story using them.
- Teacher watches and scribes the stories as told (including as much non-verbal action as possible).

The sandtray is usually a highly motivating play experience and when first used the children are often reluctant to formalise their play into a story – they just want to continue with the action! Once children have had regular access to the sandtray, however, and have become familiar with the routine of storytelling, they can combine the two tasks fluidly. It just takes some perseverance.

CHARLIE'S STORIES

The following are examples of two stories told using the sandtray by the same child at the start and end of the school year.

> The princess was walking. They came back to her house. Then the lion came and woke her up and that fell and then the lady on the camel went found a fairy and saw her and fly back to her house.
>
> (Charlie, aged 7 years, in September)

> It's a magic land and things get big and small and the snake is getting biggest and eating up the small things. It eats the little boy and all the balls and the baby zebra. It eats the polar bear. But the cheetah is the fastest animal in the world and it runs away and the snake turns round to eat the frog. But the frog is magic and is very big and there is a giant lizard dinosaur and they try to eat each other up and the frog jumps on the snake's head. Then the magic queen takes her wand. It's all different colours and hits the snake hard on the head and the snake is dead and it goes small again. And all the things go back to being small and they don't go back again.
>
> (Charlie, aged 8 years, in June, a few weeks after a dramatisation of *Alice in Wonderland*)

Story context 2: using existing picture-book stories – The Bad-Tempered Ladybird by Eric Carle

Introduction to storytelling activity

- Mathematics sessions about time – using the story of *The Bad-Tempered Ladybird*.
- Class act out the story using the repeated phrases and action mimes for each of the creatures encountered.

- Pictorial list of minibeasts shown to group and each child asked to act as one of these for the creation of a new story (e.g. *The Angry Wasp*).
- Group story created through dramatisation.

Context for storytelling

- Children draw a storyboard for their individual version of the story, with separate events happening at different times, as in the original text. The complete story is then told to an adult scribe.
- Each story is then dramatised using Gussin-Paley's technique, with the children choosing the actors for their characters.

POPPY'S STORY

> At 2 o'clock the happy ladybird was playing in the garden. At 3 o'clock it met a little cat with his friends. At 4 o'clock it meets a sleepy ladybird and a wake-up hopper. 'Hey you! Do you want to play basketball and dance all around to the music and then drum all the way home?' 'Yes please.' And they played Ring-a-Ring-a-Roses and The Farmer's in his Den.
>
> (Poppy aged 6 years)

This story contains one of my favourite images from all the stories I have collected – that of the sleepy ladybird and the wake-up hopper. This creativity may have been forced upon Poppy because she did not have the word 'grasshopper' fully integrated into her vocabulary, but it is nevertheless a powerfully contrasting image. The story was written for dramatisation and Poppy ensured that all the class would want to take part. She included basketball to tempt the boys and Ring-a-Ring-a-Roses because it was the favourite game of her best friend. Such inclusivity and cooperation is exactly what we like to celebrate in the classroom and it is important to note that this would not have been achieved if I had insisted that the main character in Poppy's story should replicate the bad-temperedness of the original ladybird.

Outcomes and evidence: what we look for

Assessment framework

The multi-perspective analysis grid that forms the assessment framework for this storytelling approach was integral to the research because it supported the development of a holistic understanding of the different strands of each child's development. Scribed stories and reflective notes are used to complete the assessment, and for everyday classroom use it can be adapted to focus on whichever elements from the list below teachers are most interested in at the time (full details of the framework are provided in McCaffrey, 2009).

- *Context*: Details about the child and the context of the story; number of words used.
- *Language analysis*: Number of words, sentence level (Knowles & Masidlover, 1982), T-units (Fox, 1993, pp. 53–54) and P[1] and National Curriculum Level Descriptors (Department for Education and Science, 2001).

- *Structure*: Aspects of character, predicament, climax, resolution, and setting (Fox, 1990, pp. 105–106, and Grove, 2005, p. 74). These are the elements which allow the child to construct a coherent narrative that is causally and temporally related.
- *Rhetorical*: Use of language for effect; figurative language and story language (Grove, 2005, p. 74, and Fox, 1993, p. 73). These are poetic elements which can help to involve the audience and bring the story alive.
- *Aesthetic*: Creativity and impact – the shape and beauty of the story form (Grove, 2005, p. 97).
- *Social*: Source of story material and cultural codes (Barthes, 1970, quoted in Fox, 1993, p. 172).
- *Reflections:* Personal reflections on any elements in a story that do not easily fit into any of the other sections on the grid. However thorough an assessment or evaluation procedure is thought to be, stories can never easily be reduced to component parts because there is almost always something more important to say.

Outcomes

During the research, progress was measured using the existing framework in schools for England, based on levels of the National Curriculum, and allocating points per level. As a rough guide, level P4 (4 points) equates to a child who is functioning at a very early level of development, using a few single words, whereas level 1A (11 points) equates to a child who is doing well for a five-year-old in the first year of school.

It was apparent that the children made far greater than expected progress against the recent National Progression Guidance (Department for Education, 2009). The average level of the first set of stories was 5.8 (range 4.6–7.2) and for the second set of stories 8.6 (range 7.1–11.3). On average, the children gained 2.8 points during the intervention, ranging from 1.8 to 4.1 (see Table 4.1).

It is important to note, however, that whilst the trend was upward for everyone this was not straightforwardly linear. All the children made frequent regressions to a lower level before attainment at the next level was secured. The individual pathways also highlighted the effect that different story contexts had on individual children and served to emphasise the importance of assessing the work of children over a period of time and across contexts rather than the now generally discredited practice of summative assessment of single pieces of work at a single point in time.

Table 4.1 Comparison of mean National Curriculum level of stories 1–5 and stories 17–21

	Mean level of stories 1–5	Mean level of stories 17–21	Amount of progress
Charlie	7.2 (P7)	11.3 (1A)	+4.1
Emily	6.6 (P6.5)	9.9 (1B/1A)	+3.3
Poppy	4.6 (P4.5)	7.1 (P7)	+2.5
Joshua	5.5 (P5.5)	9.3 (1C)	+3.7
Tessa	5.6 (P5.5)	7.3 (P7)	+1.8
Lauren	5.2 (P5)	7.3 (P7)	+2.1
James	6.1 (P6)	8.0 (P8)	+1.9

The story of Emily

Emily was 6 years old at the start of the year and had been diagnosed with moderate learn-ing difficulties and global developmental delay. Whilst she was able to speak in short sen-tences, her verbal responses were always significantly delayed owing to her difficulties with processing language. Over the period of the study she made significant progress in speaking from P6[2] to L1C,[3] which can partly be explained by her increased self-confidence. The underlying language skills may have already been present but lying dormant and unused in previous learning contexts.

Emily blossomed from being a somewhat anxious and serious girl into someone who could take a leading role in entertaining and amusing the class. She seemed to be exploring a new identity for herself through her stories and the way that she told them. Throughout the research period, Emily's exploration of identity was revealed in two ways. The first example of this was her attempt at bravery through stepping into the unfamiliar, which was evidenced in the very first story that she told. Emily desperately wanted a spider to be in her sandtray story and whilst she was clearly nervous about handling this large rubber toy, persevered with it in order to tell her tale.

A second exploration of identity was revealed in Emily's consistent creation of a 'perfect' world without disharmony. So persistent was she in this desire that she replaced retelling with complete inversion when telling her own story in the style of *The Bad-Tempered Ladybird*. Her story of *The Hungry Ant* is nothing less than an exemplar of good behaviour and politeness: 'Would you like to share my ham sandwiches?', 'Oh yes please!' Emily herself was a perfect exemplar in school, but her behaviour at home was very different and conflicts with her younger brother could be particularly intense. It is as if she projected her wishes into stories of how the world 'should be', and how she herself wished she could consistently be within it.

It was completely unexpected therefore when, at the end of the year, Emily left the safety of her storytelling world and laid bare her home life with all its arguments and fears. In a whole-class dramatisation she directed a re-enactment of an argument with her brother, which included a great deal of shouting and banging. Her plea at the end of the story: 'Brother, please can we both stop fighting' seemed testament to Emily's sincere wish that all at home could be harmonious, even if she herself did not always help such a cause. This sudden revelation of previously concealed concerns was immediately accepted and drama-tised with relish by her peers, for whom nothing extraordinary had happened. Neither was there any sense that Emily felt uncomfortable about this disclosure; she had come to it in her own time and through her own form of storytelling.

Contexts of learning

Issues to consider

When I wrote the 'story' of my research project it involved the analysis of 21 stories told by 7 children (aged 6–8) over a school year. This small class of children was supported by me as the teacher and two teaching assistants. This high staff-to-pupil ratio indicates that this storytelling approach may be most suited for use with small groups in either special schools or mainstream settings. It was particularly formulated for use with lower primary-aged chil-dren, although the selection of stimulus stories can adapt it to become age- and interest-appropriate for older or younger year groups. Whilst the approach was devised for children with learning difficulties (and does require that they have at least minimal verbal or other communicative skills) it is equally appropriate for mainstream children. However, it may require some ingenuity on behalf of the class teacher to dedicate this level of curriculum time to the creation of storytelling contexts. These can take variable lengths of time and some could easily become part of independent learning sessions, whilst whole-class dramatisation or interactive storytelling sessions usually take between 30 minutes and 1 hour.

Cultural factors

The school in which I work is predominantly White British and for all pupils the first language is English. I am not able to definitely assert therefore that this storytelling approach would be suitable and meaningful in a multicultural setting, although I am cautiously optimistic that this would be the case. The choice of stories would obviously need to reflect all cultures and the highly visual and kinaesthetic modes of expression and communication within the storytelling contexts would hopefully benefit any children for whom English was not a first language. Importantly, one element of the assessment process is a reflection upon the cultural codes revealed in the stories told by the children, and these could highlight both similarities and differences between cultures and provide important and meaningful points for exploration within the class.

Try it yourself

Top tips

- Develop opportunities to listen to the stories that the children want to tell you – and only ask questions to which you genuinely want to know the answer. Enjoy listening and forget your anxieties about whether or not the stories are meeting any objectives!
- Produce individual collections of all the stories that the children tell. They will feel valued as storytellers and the collections will be invaluable as a record of their development – however you choose to analyse and assess them.
- Start developing storytelling contexts with stories that you love and approaches you feel secure with – then start to experiment and have fun.

Acknowledgements

To Professor Brahm Norwich and Professor Elizabeth Wood – for keeping faith.

Notes

1 P-scales in the National Curriculum are a framework for assessing pre-formal levels of pupil attainment. They are to be replaced in 2022.
2 Early language level.
3 Level 1(C to A) is (broadly speaking) the level expected of mainstream children in Year 1in the UK (5–6 years).

References

Carey, L. (1999). *Sandplay therapy with children and families.* New Jersey: Aronson.

Dahlberg, G. & Moss, P. (2005). *Ethics and politics in early childhood education.* London and New York: Routledge.

Department for Education (2009). *Progression Guidance 2009–10: Improving data to raise attainment and maximize the progress of learners with special educational needs, learning difficulties and disabilities.* London: DfE.

Department for Education and Science (2001). *Supporting the target setting process.* London: DfES.

Edmiston, B. (2008). *Forming ethical identities in early childhood play.* London and New York: Routledge.

Fox, C. (1993). *At the very edge of the forest: The influence of literature on storytelling by children.* London and New York: Cassell.

Fox, R. (1990). *Language and literacy: The role of writing.* Exeter: University of Exeter.

Grove, N. (2005). *Ways into literature: Stories, plays and poems for pupils with SEN.* London: David Fulton.

Gussin-Paley, V. (2004). *A child's work: The importance of fantasy play.* Chicago, IL: University of Chicago.

Knowles, W. & Masidlover, M. (1982). *The Derbyshire Language Scheme.* Updated manual available at: www.derbyshire-language-scheme.co.uk.

McCaffrey, B. (2009). A story of stories: What can teachers learn from the stories children tell? PhD thesis, University of Exeter.

Sherratt, D. & Peter, M. (2002). *Developing play and drama in children with autistic spectrum disorders.* London: David Fulton.

Chapter 5

Lis'n Tell: live inclusive storytelling

Therapeutic education motivating children and adults to listen and tell

Louise Coigley

Background

Lis'n Tell: live inclusive storytelling[1] is a way of telling a story that includes what is happening in the moment. It is an approach to communication development that sets out to promote curiosity, encourage wonder, facilitate joy and invite responsibility – leading to 'spontaneous intentional participation'. This term was coined 18 years ago, to describe outcomes seen in inclusive storytelling sessions I was developing. Some children taking part started to respond, verbally or non-verbally, without cues or prompts, for the first observable time in group situations.

Once spontaneous intentional participation is achieved, Lis'n Tell addresses speech, language or communication needs, incorporating educational or therapeutic targets. Sounds, words and linguistic structures can be introduced and reinforced through Lis'n Tell. Social skills can be modelled, encouraged and strengthened. Lis'n Tell supports literacy skills and educational topics.

In Lis'n Tell there is a key teller: a teacher, therapist, parent or assistant who strives to include any responses from participants. These may be involuntary or deliberate exclamations, gestures, looks or words from the participants. The key teller uses '5Rs': 'Rhythm and Role, Rhyme, Repetition and Ritual'. A participant may change the *rhythm*, actions or words of a story-chant being shared. These shifts are included and expanded by the key teller (R1). There are many *roles*, according to abilities and interests, such as: keeper of objects, scribe, illustrator, musician, narrator, director, character, eye gazer (R2). Parts of the story that sound the same (*rhyme*) might be *repeated* (R3 and R4). Activities related to the theme, such as lighting a candle, forming a procession or passing an object might begin, weave through and/or end the story. This brings a kind of ritual, or meaningful pattern to the story (R5) (Coigley, 2011).

Props (significant objects attractive to participants) are shared. Iconic pictorial gestures, signs, pictures or symbols are used to accompany the storytelling. Musical instruments may also be played.

History

After qualifying as a speech and language therapist/pathologist (SLT/P) in 1982, I longed to work creatively. Most intervention was table based. We sat and taught words with pictures of verbs and objects.

Searching for a more practical and inspired way of life, in 1983 I moved to an intentional community, part of the Camphill Movement. I lived and worked there with children with

DOI: 10.4324/9781003159087-5

autism and/or intellectual disabilities (IDs) as a volunteer SLT/P and caregiver for five years. It was there that I was first asked to tell a story. This terrified me at first, then my interest overcame my fear. I witnessed the positive effect it had on children's attention levels and engagement. This began my journey as a storytelling SLT/P. Then I lived in other Camphill communities for six years with adults with autism and/or ID. Their responses continued to inform my understanding and practice of therapeutic educational storytelling.

Camphill communities aim to honour everyone for their unique contribution, tapping into what positively interests each individual. Co-workers adapt to those with ID, and lead them to develop new skills (McKanan, 2020). Life, in part, revolved around festivals, poems, songs, plays, puppet shows and grace before meals. Even daily tasks became explorations in storytelling, and sometimes mini dramatic or poetic processes to engage children's attention and motivation. Sweeping the floor became an adventure in catching dust, a tea towel transformed into a sail of a ship while washing up.

I left an adult rural Camphill community in 1990, to co-found a small urban community, and develop SLT through storytelling in more conventional settings: NHS clinics and schools. Storytelling was then a very unusual approach! I didn't know of anybody else working in this way. I was invited to work and train the staff at Beverly School for the Deaf in Middlesbrough, England, an area of high socio-economic need. I was then asked to run early language development groups, and train my SLT/P colleagues. I did this for four years. Regular evaluations from parents/SLT/Ps and teachers were extremely positive, in terms of pupil's memory for the stories and their increased 'levels of engagement' (Mundy-Taylor, 2013), within and beyond the sessions.

Two writer-practitioners particularly encouraged me at that time. In *Teacher* (1986), Sylvia Ashton-Warner describes how particular words hold dynamic power for children. This gave me more confidence to work with children's interests. Dorothy Heathcote's method of education through drama, *Mantle of the Expert*, builds contexts for children to act as experts. (Wagner, 1979). This resonated with my longing to see children as powerful collaborators, not as 'dis-abled'. In Camphill, children and adults with disabilities are seen as having as much to teach as to learn. I was fortunate to visit Dorothy repeatedly, talk about my work and receive her insights. From 1994–1998, full-time courses in storytelling, speech and drama taught me deeper skills to convey the power of the relationship between voice, gesture and the imagination. The title of my approach: Lis'n Tell: live inclusive storytelling was launched in 2001, whilst I was working at a special school.

Theories and principles

Children need imaginative activities with an emotional content to support their learning. They often relate to images and experience more easily than concepts (Ashton-Warner, 1986; Wagner, 1979; Steiner, 1966). They need social interaction to be able to learn (Dewey, 1897). Imagination is a powerful tool that can help us solve problems (Dewey, 1897; Mellon, 2003). Children who are given the opportunity to listen to, enjoy and retell stories have a better chance of developing literacy skills (Westby, 1985). Phillips, Bunda & Quintero (2018) locate 'Story' within 'everyday language' used by people from different ages, classes, disciplines and cultures whereas 'Narrative' comes more from academics. Narrative implies a linear, conceptual structure, useful for language assessment purposes. I have never heard a child say, 'Tell me a narrative', but plenty will ask to be told a story.

Lis'n Tell, which is a multi-layered approach, is more at home with the term 'storytelling'.

The underpinning *principles* include:

• Involvement of the skills and interests of everyone present, be they child or adult participant, carer, teacher, assistant, family member or therapist.
• Respect, trust and recognition that each has a valued and equal contribution to make, whether verbal or non-verbal.
• Commitment to creating contexts and situations where participants become experts. The space is protected to ensure the least able are given time to respond.

Storytelling is recognised in the Arts as a human necessity (Okri, 1997), and in Science as a core human behaviour that helps to make memories and meaning and build emergent literacy (Isbell et al., 2004; McCabe & Rollins, 1994; Westby & Culatta, 2016). Storytelling fosters communication development, learning and well-being in children and adults, improving the capacity to imaginatively recall and use complex language (Isbell et al., 2004). It supports communication and social integration of people with autism (Sahin, 2016) and maximises potential and improves mental health for individuals with learning/intellectual difficulties (LD/ID) (Olsen, 2015). Live oral storytelling, contrasted with story reading, has been found to result in the largest gains in receptive target-vocabulary and best story comprehension. Additionally, children were found to be less restless and more attentive during live oral storytelling (Lenhart et al., 2020).

Increasingly research related to Lis'n Tell key ingredients is published. For example, the importance of gesture in semantic development (McGregor, 2008), the effects of storytelling on comprehension (Isbell et al., 2004), the influence of role (Whit et al., 2016) and oral storytelling (Lenhart et al., 2020).

Work in practice

We work with 'wonder tales' such as Grimm's, creation myths and modern stories, involving the children's personal interests. Sometimes, I work through spontaneous storytelling. For example, an agitated 13-year-old boy with attention and cognitive problems was talking rapidly and incessantly about horror videos. I edged in and offered him a postcard of Uccello's picture the *Battle of San Romano*. He immediately composed a tender story of love, death and reconciliation, then announced, 'I'm calm now' (Coigley, 2014).

We strive to reverence the essential individuality of participants. A girl with Rett's syndrome was beyond storytelling. We narrated and related to her being the princess of the tale. We regularly, gently chanted her name. When her father read the sessions report, he wept. He said that no one, apart from him, had ever seen his daughter as a princess.

Working with groups of up to 10 children, with staff support, we use the same story at weekly intervals for up to 12 weeks, or over 3 days or for just 1 day, depending on the needs of the children and the organisation.

Before a typical session

• An appropriate story is chosen and adapted for oral telling.
• Rapport building may begin before the session, for example while accompanying children in from the playground, or mirroring a child's particular way of greeting from afar e.g., whistling, while approaching the Lis'n Tell space.

During the session

- The key teller 'edges in' using significant objects (Coigley, 2007) and/or rhythmical chants/a leading question.
- There is an 'intro' at the beginning, involving story specific rituals, to build and release attention, and reinforce auditory and visual memory.
- After initiating spontaneous intentional participation, SLT/educational aims and targets are woven in.
- The children's unique ways of communicating are honoured, through noticing subtle nuances and overt forms of behaviour and including these in the story, when possible.
- Participants become 'co-tellers', taking on different roles.
- With children with profound and severe difficulties, all members of staff and/or family are invited to take on roles.
- The more disruptive or withdrawn a listener is, the more responsibility they are invited to take. Destructive behaviour by the students is managed appropriately by the staff present.
- The session finishes with the 'outro': acknowledging everyone's involvement and/or recapping key elements of the story.

The story of a group in a special school

An 8-year-old boy, dressed in gold-coloured silk pantaloons, strides around emphatically saying, 'Never!' A girl asks him his name. He walks beside a long, narrow, blue strip of shiny satin. The girl leans over and puts a slinky slim object (the 'snake') onto the silk. The boy jumps, yelling: 'I freezing!' We chant: 'Freeze like ice; burn like fire'. The girl asks him again, 'Name?'

The boy is autistic and the girl has severe IDs. They are taking part in the Egyptian creation myth, a struggle for power between the sun god Ra and his wise daughter Isis. A girl with Williams syndrome and myself tell the story in turns, leaving gaps for action and dialogue, adapting it when something unexpected happens. It has taken us six 40-minute weekly sessions to get to this point.

The boy playing Ra, initially kept interrupting. He now waits and listens before appropriately joining in. He refuses to move on at one point, until Isis wraps his foot in a bandage after the magic snake has 'bitten' him. I had forgotten to tell that part and he has remembered. Isis, who used to sit and pretend to sleep for nearly the entire session, now enthusiastically participates on cue. In the class there's also a girl with Apert syndrome. We know, from assessing her comprehension and observing her use of 2–3 sign combinations, that she has good everyday understanding and some inner language. However, she is reluctant to sign with her conjoined fingers. Her needs may also have been overly anticipated previously. We want to motivate her to communicate. Given an array of mixed props that she likes, she reaches towards them, sorts them and offers them in the correct sequence. She tells the story in her way, as keeper of the objects.

Another boy, with Down syndrome, refused to take part. I discovered his love of reading. I bare-boned the story to 20 verbs and nouns, printed them on separate pieces of card, and enlisted his help in ordering them. He does so for six sessions, listening intently, lining up the words. In the seventh session, he gets up and spontaneously *tells* the entire story, progressing from scribe to narrator role.

Outcomes and evidence: what we look for

We aim to accept each other as we are, and for some level of engagement from all. When this happens, we are in the flow of 'life-affirming energy' (Whitehead, 2018). Participating colleagues and parents often remark on this. We also aim to allow participants to 'show what they know', as Dorothy Heathcote often said. Then, educational/SLT/P targets are addressed.

From observations and feedback collected over the last 18 years, in 7 special schools; 4 UK paediatric SLT/P departments, 2 care homes and from tours and sessions undertaken in Malta, Canada, France and Greece the following selected ranges of outcomes from using Lis'n Tell have been reported by teachers and SLT/Ps including increased levels of:

- staff spontaneity with students with severe physical disabilities
- attention, sequencing and memory, in comparison to story reading with children with language disorders
- attendance and involvement of parents of young children with speech and language delays
- motivation of teenagers who stammer
- engagement, turn taking, showing imagination, sharing of ideas and development of narrative skills with children and adults with autism and IDs.

Assessment frameworks

These include:

- *Expression, Reception and Recall of Narrative Instrument* (ERRNI) (Bishop, 2004)
- *The Pragmatics Profile of Everyday Communication Skills* (Dewart & Summers, 1996)
- Lis'n Tell-trained SLTs in Lambeth, Jane Trevor and Sue Maughan, developed simple target and outcome forms looking at Engagement and Attention; Feelings; Thinking and Language, with relevant subcategories, based on a framework developed by Grove (2005)
- SLT/P Rebecca Eastburn developed a Lis'n Tell coloured chart, showing progress from before development of targeted social/comprehension/expressive language skills, through intermittent development of the skills to frequent use within and beyond the sessions. Parents have found this visual way of recording progress particularly useful.

Contexts of learning

These include individual therapy sessions using Lis'n Tell as a bridge to generalising specific skills such as phonological processes or linguistic structures; integration of children with additional needs into mainstream classes; classes in special schools; provision for children with emotional behavioural difficulties.

Issues to consider

The USA National Youth Poet Laureate's book: *Change Sings* (Gorman, 2021) is a beautiful, rallying call. However, change can sound a threatening tune for children with autism and/or social emotional and mental health (SEMH) problems. They may have problems with being able to cope with differences of routine, and interpreting others' rapidly shifting social cues, incurring acute anxiety. Working with such children is a deep and complicated area of Lis'n Tell. This is partly why the first part of the training takes a full two days. Some of the wisdom and genius of Gorman's work moves in the rhythms of her words. It is the rhythmical techniques of Lis'n Tell: chanting and call/response, which have shown some success with motivating such challenged children, individually and in groups. This includes children who present as antagonistic, obsessional or show 'apparent disengagement' (Gersie, 1997).

Four additional Lis'n Tell techniques which are particularly helpful here are: edging in with the right question with children with higher verbal skills, using objects or actions of significance, role play – especially with dressing up, and referring to the expert. All of these are threaded and re-threaded into the storytelling.

Cultural factors

It is etiquette amongst storytellers to acknowledge the provenance of a story, where or from whom it was first heard.

I have encountered fear existing between some cultures. Stories about Akbar, the sixteenth-century Muslim Mogul emperor, renowned for his religious tolerance, and his wise advisor Birbal, a Hindu, are deep, witty teaching tales. However, when introducing this story, I encountered anxiety from one group of Muslims, who had difficulty in incorporating a Hindu name. I have worked with an Arabic woman who feels that her ancestors' stories have been appropriated by a neighbouring culture. She regards this as an act of suppression.

In many story cultures, e.g., from Africa, Russia and Europe, we find a poor boy, girl or 'fool' who becomes the hero or heroine. This can represent the value of people in our societies who have skills, not of conventional intelligence, but of hands and heart. They may be mavericks of many kinds, who reveal deep truths. Each character in a wonder tale can depict different aspects of human nature (Meyer, 1995). Storytelling, emerging out of our deepest human experience, reveals a world of 'magical thinking' (Warner, 2011), of transformation, and our ability to overcome.

Try it yourself

Begin with children you think may be amenable! Tell a story that you like and that you think the children will enjoy. Compose story-based chants. Use them as call–response. Tell the story freely without referring to a book. Interact more dynamically with children with behaviour/attention challenges, giving them responsibilities. Watch and listen for *any* responses. Respectfully include them as they emerge. Explore a problem that the story poses, like an obstacle on a journey. Begin and end with some special words or actions. Use unusual, textured props that move, light up and/or make a sound, offer them around in a structured way. Do not correct the children; accept and reflect what they offer. Model more mature alternatives, in interesting inviting ways. Make a few deliberate verbal and physical mistakes. See if they correct you or at least are amused!

Top tips

- Include the interests of your students *and* relevant colleagues in your storytelling.
- Practise telling stories until they become second nature. You will then have more capacity for observing and including participants' responses.
- If it is too challenging to include responses from many children, start by including just one child.
- Remember, the reason for doing this is to increasingly surrender your telling to theirs.

Where to go

Contact me at lfc@lisntell.co.uk, @lisntell on Twitter and Facebook.

Resources and websites

www.lisntell.co.uk; www.schoolofstorytelling.com.

Acknowledgements

Deep thanks to the children and adults I've lived and worked with. My thanks also to the (SLT/Ps) and teachers working with Lis'n Tell: in the UK at Treloar School and College for Students with Physical Disabilities, Alton, Hampshire; Beacon Hill Academy for Students with Severe and Complex Learning Difficulties, Thurrock; the Loddon School for Children with Autism, Hampshire; to Speech Pathologist, Yannis Martinis and his Lis'n Tell work with dysfluent teenagers in Athens, Greece; SLT Team Calais, for their Lis'n Tell work with refugee children in France; Prof. Sue Roulstone, at the UK Bristol Speech and Language Therapy Research Unit, for her advice on observing 'process to outcome' and Dr David Crooke at the Research Department, Brighton Sussex Medical School, for overseeing my session evaluations. Lastly, I would like to thank my husband, Peter Sollars, for his invaluable insights.

Note

1 © Louise Coigley 2001.

References

Ashton-Warner, S. (1986). *Teacher*. New York: Touchstone Press.

Bishop, D. (2004). *Expression, reception and recall of narrative instrument (ERRNI)*. London: Pearson.

Coigley, L. (2007). *Lis'n Tell: Live Inclusive Storytelling*. Invited presentation at the Children & Families Research Centre, Macquarie University, Sydney, Australia. 5 June.

Coigley, L. (2011) *Lis'n Tell: live inclusive storytelling for all ages*. Invited presentation at 'Building Best Practice', The Association of Speech and Language Therapists in Independent Practice National Conference, 11 March.

Coigley, L. (2014). Lis'n Tell: Live inclusive storytelling with an 11 year old boy with cognitive problems. Available at https://www.youtube.com/watch?v=Gr01mDYNwKA.

Dewart, H. & Summers S. (1996). *The pragmatics profile of everyday communication skills in children*. Windsor: NFER Nelson.

Dewey, J. (1897). My pedagogic creed. *School Journal*, 54, 77–80.

Gersie, A. (1997) *Reflections on therapeutic storymaking. The use of stories in groups*. London: Jessica Kingsley Publishers.

Gorman, A. (2021) *Change sings*. New York: Penguin Random House.

Grove, N. (2005). *Ways into literature*. London: David Fulton.

Isbell, R., Sobol, J., Lindauer, L., & Lowrance, A. (2004). The effects of storytelling and story reading on the oral language complexity and story comprehension of young children. *Early Childhood Education Journal*, 32(3), 157–163.

Lenhart, J., Lenhard, W., Vaahtoranta, E. & Suggate, S. (2020). More than words: Narrator engagement during storytelling increases children's word-learning, story comprehension, and on-task behavior. *Early Childhood Research Quarterly*, 51, 338–351.

McCabe, A. & Rollins, P. (1994). Assessment of pre-school narrative skills. *American Journal of Speech Language Pathology*, 3, 45–56.

McGregor, K. (2008). Gesture supports children's word-learning. *International Journal of Speech–Language Pathology*, 10(3), 112–117.

McKanan, D. (2020) *Camphill and the future: Spirituality and disability in an evolving communal movement* (pp. 1–2). Oakland, CA: University of California Press.

Mellon, N. (2003). *Storytelling and the art of the imagination*. Cambridge, MA: Yellow Moon Press.

Meyer, R. (1995). *The wisdom of fairy tales*. London: Floris Books.

Mundy-Taylor, J. (2013). *Storytelling engagement in the classroom: Observable behavioural cues of children's story experiences*. Doctoral thesis, Newcastle University, Australia. Full text available http://hdl.handle.net/1959.13/939911.

Okri, B. (1997). *The joys of storytelling, A way of being free*. London: Phoenix House.

Olsen, A. (2015). "Is it because I'm gormless?" A commentary on "Narrative therapy in a learning disability context: a review". *Tizard Learning Disability Review*, 20, 130–133.

Phillips, L., Bunda, T. & Quintero, E. (2018). *Research through, with and as, storying*. London: Routledge.

Sahin, A. (2016). *Storytelling and Asperger syndrome: A key for social integration*. https://137.122.9.184/bitstream/10393/35364/1/Sahin%20%282016%29.pdf (Accessed 18.8.21).

Steiner, R. (1966). *General education course: Lecture 2, 1919* (pp. 26–40). Forest Row, E. Sussex: Rudolf Steiner Press.

Wagner, B. J. (1979). *Drama as a learning medium*. London: Hutchinson Press.

Warner, M. (2011). *Stranger magic charmed states and the Arabian Nights*. London: Chatto & Windus.

Westby, C. E. (1985). Learning to talk: Talking to learn. In C. S. Simon (Ed.), *Communication skills and classroom success* (pp. 181–218). San Diego, CA: College Hill Press.

Westby, C. & Culatta, B. (2016). Telling tales: personal event narratives and life stories. *Language, Speech & Hearing Services in Schools*, 47, 260–282.

White, R., Prager, E., Schaefer, C., Kross, E., Duckworth, A. & Carlson, S. (2017). The "Batman Effect": Improving perseverance in young children. *Child Development*, 88(5), 1563–1571.

Whitehead, J. (2018). *Living theory research as a way of life*. Bath: The Brown Dog Press.

Chapter 6

Interactive storytelling

Keith Park

Background

A Swahili story, *Meat of the Tongue* (Carter, 1991), tells of a sultan whose unhappy wife grows leaner and more listless every day. The sultan sees a poor man whose wife is healthy and happy, and he asks the poor man why this is. 'Very simple', answers the poor man, 'I feed her meat of the tongue.' The sultan immediately orders the butcher to buy the tongues of all the slaughtered animals of the town, and feeds them to his wife. The queen gets even thinner and more poorly. The sultan then orders the poor man to exchange wives. Once in the palace, the poor man's wife grows thin and pale. Eventually the sultan learns that 'meat of the tongue' is story — the poor man tells his wife of his daily experiences, sings her songs and tells her legends.

Storytelling, it seems, is a vital ingredient of human experience. This being so, it is relevant for everyone. Jean Ware (1994: 72) suggests that in choosing activities for people with profound and multiple learning difficulties (PMLDs) our aim should be 'to enable the child to participate in those experiences which are uniquely human'. Storytelling seems to be one of these uniquely human experiences. Whether it is legend, myth, folk tale, fairy story, poem, novel, film or play, the principle is the same: everyone everywhere enjoys stories. According to *Meat of the Tongue*, we all *need* them.

History

Around 20 years ago, a teacher asked, 'When we are in a circle saying good morning, by the time Tony (dual sensory impairment, PMLD) realises it's his go, his turn has passed. Can you think of a way they can all do it together?' I took inspiration from the scene in *Casablanca* where 'Knock on Wood' is sung using call and response at Rick's café.[1] I developed the first story using Red Riding Hood knocking on the door of the cottage with the wolf asking 'Who's there?' Interactive Storytelling grew from these small beginnings. It can be used with anyone and has been implemented with children and adults with and without learning disabilities across the UK.

The method used with all the stories is call and response; this approach is many thousands of years old and is used in various forms throughout the world. For example, the storyteller calls out a line and the other participants respond either by repeating the same words or by calling out a different line, and so on throughout the story. This rhythmic exchange between the storyteller and the group provides a powerful momentum. It is very simple and very effective.

DOI: 10.4324/9781003159087-6

Theory and principles

Within this approach, it is rhythm, response and repetition that are emphasised as a means of developing social communication. The story aspect is the narrative structure that acts as the framework within which this interaction takes place.

The rhythm is the basic four-beat, which Trevarthen (2005) suggests is fundamental in mother–infant communication worldwide. Hence Interactive Storytelling is drawing on the earliest movement and sound responses, which we could think of as the two valves of the heart opening and closing. For example:

> *If* we *sha*dows *have* of*fen*ded
> *Think* but *this* and *all* is *men*ded
> *That* you *have* but *slum*bered *here*
> *While* these *vi*sions *did* appear
>   (Shakespeare, *A Midsummer*
>   *Night's Dream*)

We use a variety of poetry, plays and novels, which communicate through the musical nature of the text. When traditional stories (such as folk tales) are used, these are written up in metrical form such as the Egyptian legend *The Well of Truth* or a South African tale, *Tokoloshe Man*. The same metrical technique is applied to Aesop, Homer, Chaucer and adaptations of classic texts such as Dickens' *A Christmas Carol* and *Oliver Twist*.

The following principles reflect the fact that the beginnings were with groups of either children or adults with severe and profound learning/intellectual disabilities. Nevertheless, they apply equally to anyone and everyone, irrespective of ability.

Apprehension precedes comprehension

Introducing their adaptation of Homer's *Odyssey* for individuals with severe and profound learning disabilities, Grove and Park (1996) ask:

> How necessary is verbal comprehension to the understanding of poetry and literature? We know that people with profound learning disabilities can enjoy music, so why not the music of words? Do we have to *comprehend* before we can *apprehend*? Does the meaning of a poem or story have to be retrieved through a process of decoding individual words, or can it be grasped through a kind of atmosphere created through sound and vision?
>
> (p. 2)

A good illustration of this 'atmosphere created through sound and vision' is provided by Samuel Taylor Coleridge's *Kubla Khan*, which has been described (by the poet Swinburne) as the supreme example of music in the English language. When read aloud, the poem can seem to be a mysterious and magical incantation (readers are recommended to try it). Is this the right formatting?

> I would build that dome in air,
> That sunny dome! Those caves of ice!

And all who heard should see them there,
And all should cry, Beware! Beware!
His flashing eyes, his floating hair!
Weave a circle round him thrice,
And close your eyes with holy dread,
For he on honeydew hath fed,
And drunk the milk of paradise.
  (Samuel Taylor Coleridge, *Kubla Khan*)

A second example from twentieth-century literature is *Finnegans Wake* (Joyce, 1971), the monumental novel by James Joyce, the first word of which is 'riverrun'. The storyline of the book is nightmarishly complex, large parts of it are unintelligible, and yet when it is heard it has poetic prose of great beauty and power. Joyce suffered from eye problems for all his adult life and was nearly blind during the 17 years it took him to complete *Finnegans Wake*. Large parts were dictated by him, and in a language that is not really English, but a dreamlike combination of many languages. The following extract, constructed out of the last and first sentences of the book, contains a mixture of rhythm and timing that is easy to do, although harder to describe on paper: 'riverrun' is three short beats, while the intervening lines are slower. The music of words should become apparent on reading it aloud. It has been used many times as part of a poetry workshop.

riverrunfrom swerve of shore to bend of bayriverruna way a lone a lasta loved a long theriverrunfrom swerve of shore to bend of bayriverrun

(James Joyce, *Finnegans Wake*)

The writer Samuel Becket once said of *Finnegans Wake*: 'it isn't about anything — it just *is*'. A first step towards any construction of meaning is to provide opportunities for the *apprehension* of text that involves active participation. Instead of just hearing and seeing a piece of literature, we can explore the possibilities of acting it out and then see how people respond. For all readers of *Finnegans Wake* (not only those with special needs) the starting point is the feel and sound of the text – meaning emerges through our interaction with it.

Affect and engagement are central to responses to literature

In her discussion of using literature with individuals with severe and profound learning disabilities, Grove (2005) suggests that:

Meaning is grounded in emotion, or affect, which provides the earliest and most fundamental impulse for communication ... It follows that we can take two routes when adapting literature for students with language difficulties. We can build rich affective associations, using stretches of text as script, emphasising the feel of the meaning. This can be regarded as a 'top-down' approach. The second approach is 'bottom-up', and involves decoding meaning through simplification and explanation. The starting point for the top-down approach is to generate an emotional response to the text.

(pp. 15–16)

Recital and performance are valid means of experiencing stories, drama and poetry

'For most of human history, "literature" has been narrated, not written — heard, not read' (Carter, 1991: ix). Fiction and poetry have existed in oral form around the world for many thousands of years, long before the development of comparatively recent (and more passive) forms: writing, printing, radio, TV, cinema and the internet. The oral narration of stories was, and often still is, a social event where the story is sung, spoken or chanted – in other words, performed (Pellowski, 1990). Storytelling may be far more important than reading and writing: our starting point for literature may therefore be, using Grove's terminology, 'the physicality of text' (Grove, 2005: 11), in performance and recital.

Work in practice

Sessions are generally weekly and last about 30–45 minutes for teenagers, and around 15–20 minutes for very young children. We encourage young people to take over and lead the sessions once they are familiar with the routine.

Introduction The session begins with one or more name games. This activity is a semi-improvised interactive song using four-point rhythm that includes everyone's name in sequence around the circle. This enables those who are blind or partially sighted to be aware of everyone present. The games encourage people to point at each other – not as requests but to single each other out. Tiny poem stories may be made up for each person, perhaps reinforcing their own 'social story'.

> On Monday Calvin slammed the door
> We said Calvin what's that for?
>
> Don't be sad, don't get mad
> It's OK to make mistakes
>
> On Tuesday, Margaret broke a plate
> She got in a right old state
>
> Don't be sad, don't get mad
> It's OK to make mistakes

Main section This is a performance of a story that we repeat three or four times, depending on the length.

As an example, *Tokoloshe Man* was written in 2011 by Izanne van Wijk, then a teacher at the Bridge School in Islington, London. Izanne is from South Africa and her first language is Afrikaans; as a child, she had heard the story from her grandmother, who in turn had heard it from her own mother, and so on back down the generations. Izanne wanted to use Interactive Storytelling as a means of sharing her language and culture with her group of children with profound and multiple learning disabilities.

The main part of the story is in English, and the chorus is in Afrikaans. The Tokoloshe is a malevolent spirit or goblin who walks at night. Children are warned that they must build up their beds on bricks so that the Tokoloshe can walk underneath the bed and go on his way. Otherwise it's big trouble! Izanne explained that many houses are built in a circular shape so that the Tokoloshe cannot hide in corners.

Chorus
In de middel
Van de nag
De Tokoloshe
Vir jou wag[2]

Tokoloshe
Zombie Man
He will get you
If he can
Chorus

Tokoloshe
Bite your toes
Tokoloshe
Scratch your nose
Chorus

Make sure you build
Your bed up high
So Tokoloshe
Walk on by
Chorus
Close the curtains
Lock the door
You think you're safe
But are you sure?
Chorus

Close A closing 'goodbye' or 'finish'. No props are used in the session apart from drums or bongos that help accentuate the rhythm of the interactions.

Combining with music and song

Storytelling and song/music have always gone together; and are a natural pair in Interactive Storytelling. An example of this is 'Bound for South Australia' where the usual chorus line of 'Heave Away, Haul Away' is replaced by someone's name, for example:

In South Australia I was born
Peter!
In South Australia round Cape Horn
Peter!
Heave away you rolling winds

Peter!

etc.

Each subsequent verse can include a new person's name.

Outcomes and evidence: what we look for

The approach is primarily aimed at enabling interaction – that is awareness and response to others, turn taking, anticipation, gaze alternation, showing objects, seeking physical proximity. These are all aspects of very early communication (Bates et al., 1979). We also look for clear evidence of enjoyment and confidence; awareness of others in the group; familiarity with and increased control over poetic language.

Assessment frameworks have been many and varied over the years. One approach is video diaries. Sessions are filmed and then analysed in staff meetings to discover what was most effective in promoting communication and interaction. Engagement profiling is also widely used.[3]

The story of Nicole

Nicole was 12 years old. She was deafblind, had profound and multiple learning disabilities and complex health needs. At school she had one-to-one support.

One day we decided to experiment. We took Nicole and her group to the school hall, which has a wooden floor, and placed her carefully on it in the middle of a circle of people. Then, as we performed the poems and stories in call and response, we stamped on the wooden floor, which resonated and caused an immediate effect. To our surprise, Nicole began to move from side to side on the floor and smile. This was a significantly different behaviour from her usual repertoire, which was an impassive facial expression and total silence.[4]

Over a period of several years Nicole was one of the group that visited many famous London venues to perform workshops: the Globe, the National Maritime Museum and the National Theatre. Her mother perhaps spoke for us all when she said, 'I have no idea what is going on inside her head. But it is clear that she is part of a group and is gaining from being a member of a group.'

Contexts of learning

Interactive Storytelling is used in classrooms, at home, in the high street and in the theatre. Within the school curriculum it is mostly included within the English, drama or performing arts sessions. In some schools, the speech and language therapist will provide language and communication aims, or the physiotherapist and occupational therapist will advise on optimal positioning of participants for the sessions.

Outreach is also a significant aspect of Interactive Storytelling, which lends itself to short performances in significant cultural spaces. This often results in increased levels of engagement and awareness of these special environments. To achieve this focus, it is critical that site staff are fully committed and involved – and if they can join in, young people get a chance to interact with new people, leading the way.

Various groups have performed Shakespeare on stage at London's Globe theatre as well as at the National Theatre, Middle Temple, a BAFTA (British Academy of Film and Television Awards) ceremony and the House of Commons; Bible stories in cockney rhyming slang at Westminster Abbey, St Paul's Cathedral, Rochester Cathedral and the church of St Mary-le-Bow; sea shanties in the National Maritime Museum and the Docklands Museum, London;

Chaucer at Canterbury Cathedral and street theatre in south-east London, when we discovered that if you are not raising money you can get a street performance licence for free: the group chose to do pantomime in the street.

Working with interactive stories during the pandemic

Virtual storytelling and music sessions have worked well one-to-one – notably, a WhatsApp using Norman Lindsey's poetry with one 16-year-old student and his mum (in one frame), me in another, his teacher in the third – all of us being in London – and, thanks to wonders of technology, his occupational therapist who was in lockdown in South-Eastern Australia. However, Interactive Storytelling with groups on Zoom was not as successful, because of the time lag.

Issues to consider

Managing anxieties is an issue that sometimes arises, either in relation to group participation, or to the storytelling.

The participants will often be chosen by the school staff. Some people may find it challenging to be in a group, even more so if there is a public performance. In such cases it is often more appropriate to start in a small group or one-to-one in school.

One day I was running a workshop on *Macbeth* with a group of teenagers with severe learning disabilities. We turned off the lights, closed the curtains and recited the witches' spell in a whispered call and response:

> Double, double toil and trouble
> Fire burn and cauldron bubble
> Fillet of a fenny snake
> In the cauldron boil and bake
> Eye of newt and toe of frog
> Wool of bat and tongue of dog
> (Shakespeare, *Macbeth*)

After the final line, one girl shivered and said 'light on'. Her teacher asked her why 'Scary', she said. Fears and anxieties can come to the fore as we tell stories. Rather than ignoring these feelings, they can be safely integrated into the proceedings, by validating, responding and reassuring. In this case, we asked the group what to do, and they supported her to turn the lights on. Make sure the person concerned feels okay, acknowledge the feeling, if necessary follow up with the teacher.

Cultural factors

The standard format of a one-day workshop in Interactive Storytelling is divided into two parts. The first part is an interactive demonstration of various story scripts. For the second part, participants divide into groups and write their own story or poem. People of dual or multiple heritage are encouraged to think of a poem or story from their non-English heritage and rework that into an interactive framework. This celebrates the multicultural and multilingual society of the school and the community. Examples include:

- *The Well of Truth* is a traditional folk tale from Egypt. It was brought to one of the sessions by a parent of a pupil with severe learning disabilities – whose first language is Arabic – and reset as an interactive call and response version, using Arabic words and phrases with English (Park, 2010).
- *Tokoloshe Man* (see above).
- *Grama Afabet* (i.e. Grandma's Alphabet) is a poem written by a member of staff from Jamaica, which can be performed in patois (Park, 2010).

Prior to the pandemic, a UK-wide tour of 'Folk Tales from Around the World' had been planned to encourage inclusion, diversity and respect. This was a response to many reports of disturbing instances of verbal abuse directed at members of staff from various special schools in the wake of the Brexit referendum.[5] People were told to 'go home' or 'go back to where you belong' and various other unprintable insults. One member of staff was spat on in a bus. So to celebrate multiculturalism, and to try and demonstrate that we are better than this, a free 45-minute storytelling workshop was developed using stories from Africa, Australia and Europe. The school would host the event and, in lieu of payment, give a donation to Refugee Action. Two workshops were given before lockdown and more are planned once travel is possible.

Try it yourself

Top tips

- *The circle* This may sound very simple but we have found that one of the most important aspects of the activities is the position in which participants are arranged. Sitting in a single-line circle formation, with no second row, reinforces the group identity and focuses the energy and attention of the participants upon each other. If you try the same activities with everyone arranged in a semicircular formation you may find, as we did, that it is much harder work and that the atmosphere and feeling of the group is quite different.
- *Know the script* Storytelling sessions are far more likely to succeed if the group leader knows the lines by heart and does not need to refer to notes. Sometimes it may be necessary to look at a script, but wherever possible it is best to learn the lines before you start. It is also important to feel comfortable with the words – if Shakespeare feels very foreign, for example, then it will be much better to try something else. There are plenty of other choices – Spike Milligan's poetry is a great favourite in many schools.
- *Fun* Storytelling activities should be enjoyable. If no one is engaged, think about a change of content or a change of activity.

Acknowledgements

Thanks to Izanne van Wijk for permission to share *Tokoloshe Man*.

Notes

1 Can be found easily on the Internet. Dooley Wilson is the pianist.
2 Translation: In the middle/of the night/the Tokoloshe/waits for you.

3 https://www.gov.uk/government/publications/the-engagement-model (Accessed 3.5.21).
4 Resonance boards, designed originally by Lilli Nielsen, were then introduced https://www.lilli works.org (Accessed 11.5.21).
5 When the UK voted to leave the European Union in 2016.

References

Bates, E., Benigni, L., Bretherton, I., Camaioni, L. & Volterra V. (1979). *The emergence of symbols: Cognition and communication in infancy*. New York: Academic Press.
Carter, A. (1991). *The Virago book of fairy tales*. London: Virago Press.
Grove, N. (2005). *Ways into literature*. London: David Fulton.
Grove, N. & Park, K. (1996). *Odyssey now*. London: Jessica Kingsley.
Joyce, J. (1971). *Finnegans wake*. London: Faber & Faber.
Park, K. (2010). *Interactive storytelling* (2nd ed.). Bicester: Speechmark.
Pellowski, A. (1990). *The world of storytelling: A practical guide to the origins, development and application of storytelling*. New York: H. W. Wilson.
Trevarthen, C. (2005). First things first: Infants make good use of the sympathetic rhythm of imitation, without reason or language. *Journal of Child Psychotherapy*, 31, 91–113.
Ware, J. (1994). *The education of children with profound and multiple learning difficulties*. London: David Fulton.

Chapter 7

Speaking and Listening Through Narrative

Bec Shanks

Background

Speaking and Listening Through Narrative is a structured, multisensory, flexible and adaptable approach to teaching children how to tell stories. As an intervention it follows the developmental pattern that children move through in their acquisition of narrative skills – working on the individual components that make up a story and gradually combining them, using a structured framework that children are then taught to use for themselves. Research shows us that typically children aged 4–5 years without language difficulties, given the right context, are able to convey adequate information, taking into account the listener's knowledge and organising the content of what they say to demonstrate that they have some knowledge of story structure (Botting, 2002).

From this perspective, *narrative* is considered to be the way in which we coherently convey information to others about what has happened or what is going to happen. Our ability to do this is influenced by our linguistic competence, our world knowledge and our pragmatic (social) understanding.

A *story* is viewed as the framework that we use to structure and organise that information. As such, it needs to comprise key components in order that the information given has a context and makes sense to the listener: namely (in its simplest form) when, who, where, what *happened* and an *ending*.

History

This approach was originally developed in 1999 in response to primary teachers' concerns about the numbers of children entering school with unidentified speech, language and communication needs. They presented with difficulties in attending and listening to teachers' instructions, poor vocabulary, limited receptive and expressive language skills. Teachers were also concerned about the lack of focus on developing oracy in the classroom and how this was reflected in the children's limited ability to express their ideas on paper. The original Bercow report addressed this area of unmet need (2008). Given the already demanding task of delivering the curriculum, teachers were seeking an intervention that complemented rather than added to everyday classroom teaching.

The result was a jointly funded pilot project (1999–2001) between the local education authority (LEA) and Stockport speech and language therapy (SLT) department, targeting children aged 5–7, based in six local schools in areas of social deprivation. Following its success the LEA funded a roll out of the programme to all the local primary schools. A

DOI: 10.4324/9781003159087-7

further project, aimed at differentiating the original intervention for children aged 3–5 years in Nursery and Reception, was delivered by SLT Judith Carey as part of a wider regeneration initiative (2001–2004).

Theories and principles

Speaking and Listening Through Narrative follows the principles of Applebee's stages of narrative development (Applebee, 1978). Between the years of 2 and 7, children develop concepts of character and setting, and a gradual understanding that events tend to follow a central theme and are linked both causally and temporally. Initial teaching focuses on understanding the significance of setting ('who', 'where' and 'when') before embarking on the 'what happened' part of the story. Once they are able to link events together, children then learn to appreciate that what happens in the story is dictated by the motivations and goals of the characters, hence developing their understanding of problem-solution-type episodes.

These components are a simplified form of *story grammar* (Stein & Glenn, 1979), acting as a story blueprint within which to organise people, settings, actions and events. This process of unpicking a story facilitates children's ability to recall, link and understand events in the story, which in turn supports inferential understanding. For example, in order for a child to identify a character's goal (what the character might do), the child first needs to recognise and identify that there is a problem that needs to be solved. Hence the development of inference and children's understanding of story grammar go hand in hand. (Filiatrault-Veilleux et al., 2015). There is also a direct link between structure in oral narratives and written narrative competence since the majority of children cannot put down on paper what they are not able to verbally order and recount (Pinto, Tarchi & Bigozzi, 2016).

The approach also acts as a tool for facilitating social use of language. Narrative ability is integral to our ability to create and maintain social relationships as children, into adolescence and beyond into adulthood (Wetherell, Botting & Conti-Ramsden, 2007). Academic success is one outcome of education but social competence could be considered to be just as important, if not more so.

A final principle of the approach is that it is collaborative – between the SLT and education professionals. Not only is the intervention effective in boosting speaking and listening skills in targeted children but those schools able to release a member of staff to work alongside the SLT are also investing in an adaptable whole school intervention. The collaboration can raise staff awareness, and consequently confidence in identifying and meeting the language and communication needs of their pupils. Used as a pre-referral intervention, this may mean that the direct involvement of speech and language therapy services are unnecessary.

Teaching and learning framework

Resource packs (see below: 'Resources') are designed for chronological ages 3–14 years, with consistent features. Each story element has its own colour, sign and symbol. The signs are based on British Sign Language (Makaton Vocabulary[1]). The multisensory aspect to the approach is key, as it provides visual and kinaesthetic cues to support understanding and recall of the story elements. Initially, the concepts are taught individually to develop listening and attention skills, to support understanding and to extend key vocabulary. In subsequent sessions, children learn how to combine the various elements to support the retelling of familiar events and well-known stories, before using the complete framework to generate and retell stories of their own.

Work in practice: a typical session

The following is a description of a typical session aimed at a group of up to six children aged 5–7, using one of the resource packs and focusing on the concept 'where'.

The session starts with a recap of 'good listening' rules with their corresponding cards. These are really helpful visual cues, particularly for those children who need more frequent reminders for taking turns, putting their hands up or just trying to stay in their seat!

The SLT then recaps all the five story components with their colours and signs before introducing the focus concept 'where'. The therapist shows the 'where' card, models the 'where' sign for the children to copy and asks each child a simple 'where' question linked to their experience; for example, 'Where do you live?' or 'Where do you go to buy food?'.

The therapist emphasises that 'where' words are all places that you can go and the children then have to think of their favourite place. Answers may range from 'the park' to 'Disneyland', depending on experience. Given more time, this task can be extended: the children can draw their chosen 'where' on a worksheet provided. Some children may be able to write a sentence about it. Each child is then given a preselected book to see how many 'wheres' they can find and share with the group.

Using the 'where' pictures from the resource pack or other sourced pictures of typical locations the children might then be split into two teams for a 'where' quiz. This activity usually highlights those children who struggle to wait their turn, and also demonstrates gaps in vocabulary.

The next activity involves a feely bag containing items linked to specific places, such as *goggles: swimming pool/sea; football: garden/pitch/stadium*. The focus is on attention and listening as well as supporting vocabulary and categorisation. The children take turns at taking an item out of the bag, naming it and then saying where they might see it or where it goes.

The SLT then recaps any new vocabulary from the session and finishes with a story with a strong focus on 'where' (from the resource pack, a made-up story or an actual text). The therapist highlights all the story components and reinforces these when reading the story. There are extension activities for each week that can be used depending on the time available and the range of ability within the group. As the weeks build up then the concepts are combined in activities such as 'who goes where'. Once the concepts of *who, where* and *when* have been covered, a range of consolidation activities can be used to reinforce these concepts before moving on to the *what happened* section.

For this age group, the 'who' and 'when' sessions follow a similar format to that described above. The quiz games really help to focus the children's listening skills and develop cooperation – as soon as they learn that shouting out means that their point goes to the other team, children soon start to take their turn and put their hand up if they think they know the answer! It is always surprising how many gaps in vocabulary are identified in these first sessions, and the amount of *non-specific vocabulary* (vague terms such as 'this' or 'thingy') that some children rely on. Learning and over-learning new vocabulary within the sessions supports children's recall of these words outside of the session. All the children really enjoy the feely-bag game. Not only does it bring the element of surprise but there is often more than one right answer. It affords children who are less confident or those who would typically be reticent about joining in, the chance to have a go without the fear of getting it wrong.

By the time the children have completed week 4 (intro, 'who', 'where' and 'when') it is clearly possible to see an improvement in their attention and listening; they are starting to be more specific in their use of vocabulary and even children who were shy to begin with are willing to take part in all the activities and are showing their enjoyment in participating.

Application to different types of story

Rather than being limited to specific story types, this approach can be applied as a framework to most genres of narrative. With young children in Nursery and Reception (3–5 years), the most common narratives are personal – based on events that they have experienced themselves. Traditional tales and nursery rhymes are also used. From Year 1 (5 years) onwards, the story framework can be used and applied to traditional tales and fictional stories as well as to facilitate children's recounts of actual events. For example, using a story planner as a visual prompt to support recall of what happened at the weekend. In the resources aimed at older children (aged 11–14) the approach is adapted to incorporate factual accounts and recounts, scripts and persuasive texts, with the aim being that the narrative templates can be used across the curriculum to support pupils' ability to plan, recall and structure their responses, both verbal and written.

Outcomes and evidence: what we look for

All children involved in the original and subsequent pilot studies were assessed for both narrative skills (Renfrew, 1997b; Leitao & Allan, 2003) and language skills (descriptive information and grammatical complexity, Renfrew, 1997a, 1997b). For more detailed information regarding the original pilot study, assessment methods and outcomes see Davies et al. (2004).

Following a term's intervention with a group of Nursery children, carried out by Judith Carey and using the *Nursery Narrative* resource pack (see 'Resources'), the following findings were reported by staff and evidenced on reassessment. It is important to note that these findings are typical of both the qualitative and quantitative outcomes from using this approach with all piloted age groups ranging from 3–11 years.

Post-intervention assessment revealed:

- Increased attention and listening skills
- Increased linguistic confidence (expressive language age increased by 14 months in a 6-month period)
- Increased vocabulary
- Use of non-specific vocabulary reduced from 15.3 per cent to 5.2 per cent
- Use of specific verbs increased from 6.8 per cent to 21 per cent

For example: *Pre-intervention*: 'It doing that', *Post-intervention*: 'A big goose flapping its wings'

- Increased staff awareness and increased focus on language within curriculum areas

- Teachers reported that sessions were practical and easy to manage, leading to gains in confidence and esteem, and enabling children to utilise new knowledge and make relevant verbal contributions.

A subsequent study carried out by Judith Carey in Stockport in 2011 where all the children from one Nursery class were screened pre- and post- intervention showed similarly impressive outcomes. Post intervention assessments at the end of a term revealed:

- Information scores improved by 86 per cent
- Grammar scores improved by 20 per cent.

The story of Kamil

At the time of his pre-intervention assessment Kamil, aged 5;5, was in Year 1 and was acquiring English as an additional language. His teacher reported that he was very quiet in the classroom, struggled with vocabulary and sentence structure and rarely contributed verbally to discussions. Three months later, his teacher reported greater linguistic confidence in the classroom, both in the use of more complex sentence structures and a wider range of vocabulary. Kamil was reported to be more willing to contribute to classroom discussions and to volunteer information. His post-intervention transcription of the *Peter and the Cat* narrative (Leitao & Allen, 2003) demonstrates improved coherence and a definite use of story structure (clearly identified characters and setting, stated problem and solution for 'what happened' and an ending).

Pre-intervention

> Peter.
> When he was walking home, he climbed a tree 'cos he heard a meow
> He looked behind him
> When he got to the top, he sawed it was really high
> The man heard the boy saying help
> Then he quickly got the ladders and rescued the boy
> The boy said can we keep the cat? said the little boy
> Yes said Mum

Post-intervention

> Peter loved animals
> Once he was walking home from school
> He heard a cat saying meow
> And he looked behind him
> And it wasn't there
> And the cat meowed again
> And then he saw the cat was stuck up the tree
> The boy climbed up the tree
> But when he got to the top, he saw how high the tree was and then he holded on to the branch

And then he said Help!
Then a man was watering his trees
And he heard Help!
And then the man got a ladder, to get Peter and the cat down
Peter said thank you to the man to get the ladder
Then he went home
And Mum said you are late
And Peter explained to Mum and said can we keep this cat?
And Mum said yes

Equally important observations by teachers of the Year 1 and 2 children who received the group narrative intervention for a term ranged from: adding increased detail when describing a picture, providing reasons for possible actions or events, increased use of connectives to link ideas in their oral narratives, overall increased confidence in class and improved story writing.

Contexts of learning

This approach can be delivered with individuals, groups or adapted for a whole class. It is primarily intended for children within a mainstream setting but has also been adapted for children and young people in special schools and for children with Developmental Language Disorder (DLD). A qualified SLT should always be involved in supervising the intervention. The approach would not be considered appropriate for children and young people functioning developmentally below 3 years in language and cognition. Because it is not prescriptive, it is up to the person delivering the intervention to adapt the approach to individual needs. For example, within a mainstream environment a teacher may spend a week on the concept of 'who' but a special school teacher may take half a term, with appropriately differentiated resources. Similarly the Nursery and Reception resources are designed to follow the relevant UK curriculum and so the concept of 'who' may span a term, covering different topics – family, people who help us, mini beasts, etc. Children with DLD require a more intensive approach for a longer period of time. Their narratives often contain less developed setting information, fewer causal and temporal relations to tie events together and fewer complete episodes. For these children, the intervention needs to be tailored to the individual's language profile determined by a qualified speech and language therapist.

The pack for older children has the specific remit of using the principles of narrative to provide teachers with cross-curricular templates that can be used to support pupils' ability to plan, recall, organise and recount information whether for Science, English or History.

Cultural factors

This approach has been found applicable to children from a range of cultures. A large percentage of children taking part in the original pilot study had English as an additional language and they benefited equally when compared to their monolingual peers.

Try it yourself

Top tips

- Think multisensory: all children, not just those with speech, language and communication needs, benefit significantly from additional cues to support their story learning and are more engaged when they can see and 'feel' the story as well as simply hearing it.
- Don't be afraid of repetition: as practitioners we tend to think that children will be bored the second time around. However, evidence shows that the more opportunities children have to listen to the same story, the deeper their understanding and subsequently the better their recall of all the story elements (see Locke & Locke, 2006).
- Remember to move at the child's pace and don't be tempted to move to the next level without consolidating current knowledge and understanding. The beauty of this approach is that within a group each child can be working at their own level.
- Take time to plan – work with the school prior to starting intervention to agree a *who, where* and *when* (staffing, room and agreed time) and to ensure a shared understanding of the benefits.

Where to go

- For training courses in using the Nursery, Reception and Key Stage 1 narrative packs please contact Judith Carey, Speech and Language Therapist, at: carey.judith@yahoo.com.
- For advice on implementing any of the narrative resources, setting up a whole-school approach, problem solving and training please contact Bec Shanks, Speech and Language Therapist at: becshanks@ hotmail.com.

Resources

The following resources and narrative assessments are available from Black Sheep Press at: www.blacksheeppress.co.uk.

Ages 3–4 Nursery
Carey, J., Broughton, H., Shanks, B. & Rippon, H. (2002). *Nursery narrative.*

Ages 4–5 Reception
Carey, J., Shanks, B. & Rippon, H. (2002). *Reception narrative.*

Ages 5–7 (KS1)
Shanks, B. & Rippon, R. (2003). *Speaking and listening through narrative: A pack of activities and ideas* (2nd ed.).

Ages 7–11 (KS2)
Apparicio, V., Shanks, B. & Rippon, H. (2007). *From oral to written narrative.*

Ages 11–14 (KS 3–4)
Shanks, B. & ICAN (2011). *Secondary talk narrative resources.*

Assessment resources

Leitao, S. & Allan, L. (2003). *Peter and the cat, narrative assessment.*
Carey, J., Leitao, S. & Allan, L. (2006). *Squirrel story narrative assessment.*

Note

1   https://www.makaton.org.

References

Applebee, A. (1978). *The child's concept of story*. Chicago, IL: University of Chicago Press.

Bercow, J. (2008). *The Bercow report: A review of services for children and young people (0–19) with speech, language and communication needs*. Available at: https://dera.ioe.ac.uk/8405/7/7771-dcsf-bercow_Redacted.pdf (Accessed 27.4.21).

Botting, N. (2002). Narrative as a tool for the assessment of linguistic and pragmatic impairments. *Child Language Teaching and Therapy*, 18(1), 1–21.

Davies, K., Davies, P. & Shanks, B. (2004). Improving narrative skills in young children with delayed language development. *Educational Review*, 56(3), 271–286.

Filiatrault-Veilleux, P., Bouchard, C., Trudeau, N. & Desmarais, C. (2015) Inferential comprehension of 3–6 year olds within the context of story grammar: A scoping review. *International Journal of Language and Communication Disorders*, 50(6), 737–749.

Leitao, S. & Allan, L. (2003). *Peter and the cat, narrative assessment*. Keighley, W. Yorkshire: Black Sheep Press.

Locke, A. & Locke, D. (2006). *One step at a time: A structured programme for teaching spoken language in nurseries and schools*. Gosport, Hants: Ashford Colour Press.

Pinto, G., Tarchi, C. & Bigozzi, L. (2016) Development in narrative competences from oral to written stories in five to seven year old children. *Early Childhood Research Quarterly*, 36(3), 1–10.

Renfrew, C. E. (1997a). *Action picture test*. Milton Keynes: Speechmark.

Renfrew, C. E. (1997b). *The bus story test*. Milton Keynes: Speechmark.

Stein, N. & Glenn, C. (1979). An analysis of story comprehension in elementary school children. In R. Freedle (Ed.), *New directions in discourse processing* (pp. 53–120). Norwood, NJ: Ablex.

Wetherell, D., Botting, N. & Conti-Ramsden, G. (2007) Narrative in adolescent specific language impairment: A comparison with peers across two different narrative genres. *International Journal of Language and Communication Disorders*, 42(5), 583–605.

Chapter 8

Using narratives to enhance the language, communication and social participation of children and young people with speech, language, and communication needs

Victoria Joffe

Background

This chapter describes the Enhancing Language and Communication in Secondary Schools (ELCISS) programme based on a research project funded by the Nuffield Foundation.

The adolescent period is a significant transition, typified by changes in all aspects of development, including language (Moshman, 1999). Even though most children have acquired the basic foundations of their target language by the age of 3 years, language development does not stop at this point but develops in complexity throughout adolescence, when growth is more subtle and gradual, but no less significant (Nippold, 2007). As children move from primary to secondary school, their interactions typically become more peer-focused, and they are required to negotiate the many new challenges of secondary school: multiple teaching styles, an increasingly complex education curriculum, an understanding of more complex vocabulary and grammar, the need for abstract reasoning and idiomatic understanding, heavy reliance on the written word, the ability to take the perspectives of others and a greater need for independent working and self-reflection.

These are challenges for all young people, but for those with speech, language and communication needs (SLCN), they can present as insurmountable barriers to educational success and social and emotional stability.

There is limited specialist support available in secondary school, with reduced or no services available to young people with SLCN (Bercow, 2008; I CAN & RCSLT, 2018). This reduction in support may lead one to believe that early SLCN are remediated, or independently improve once children reach secondary school. Whilst this may be the case for some, consistent research has shown that for many children, their SLCN are persistent and continue into adolescence and even adulthood (Johnson et al., 2010; McLeod & McKinnon, 2007; Snowling et al., 2001). Some research suggests that 10 per cent of young people will show some problems in school with language and/or communication (Nippold, 2010a). Furthermore, the language and communication difficulties they encounter can lead to problems with literacy, educational attainment, behaviour, self-esteem and social and emotional functioning (Conti-Ramsden et al., 2013; Durkin & Conti-Ramsden, 2010; Joffe & Black, 2012; Johnson et al., 2010; Snowling et al., 2006; Snowling et al., 2001).

However, it is not too late to support the older child with SLCN (Nippold, 2010b). The challenge is to find the right contexts, partnerships and materials to do so.

DOI: 10.4324/9781003159087-8

History

My interest was ignited by the students themselves, and by their parents and teachers. I became aware, as my clients progressed through preschool and primary, how little support they were given in their secondary schools. As their parents and teachers looked to me for advice, I became increasingly aware of the chasm that existed in the literature, research and resources for the older student with SLCN. The unsuitability of many of the areas targeted for therapeutic intervention, their apparent lack of relevance to the lives of the young people and the juvenile nature of the materials encouraged me to explore a different mode of support for this group.

In 2005, we conducted a pilot intervention study with secondary school students with SLCN targeting narrative and vocabulary enrichment. We wanted to address areas that would facilitate access to all subjects of the curriculum, as well as support students in building friendships. Stories and words are prominent across the curriculum and our observations suggested that the skills that distinguished successful students were the ability to weave words together creatively and tell a coherent story, to hold the attention of their peers and adults and express themselves as confident communicators. These appeared to be the very same skills that our students with SLCN were struggling to master.

The work on this initial project helped us recognise the need for resources specifically targeted at this older age group, and the importance of engaging them in intervention, as active collaborators. We also wanted to support the generalisation of new skills to the classroom and home, and to do this we needed to widen the therapeutic partnership and invite school staff to deliver the intervention in collaboration with speech and language therapists (SLTs). These insights and experiences shaped the development of the ELCISS programmes to develop narrative (Joffe, 2011a) and vocabulary (Joffe, 2011b) skills.

Theories and principles

The ELCISS narrative programme creates awareness of the role of narratives and supports students through a graded and developmental set of 21 session plans, to be active listeners to stories and to become powerful, reflective and engaging storytellers. It is through the process of storytelling that language, communication and social interaction skills are enhanced.

The principles are drawn from intentional, explicit and student-centred learning, where the students play an active and influential role in the development and progression of the intervention, are made explicitly aware of its aims, and set and evaluate their own learning objectives (Freebody et al., 1995; Edwards-Groves, 1998).

The narrative intervention is a flexible multidimensional approach. It includes a range of strategies and frameworks to support the students during the storytelling process (Vygotsky, 1978). The pictures and tasks have been developed to be appropriate, relevant and engaging for older children.

Each participant is encouraged to start wherever they feel most comfortable. For some, this may involve no storytelling at all, but active listening to the stories being shared, evaluating them and asking appropriate questions. For others, their storytelling journey may begin with retelling a picture story sequence, moving to retelling a story from a favourite film or book and then to generating their own story – first told in tandem with another group member and then recounted on their own.

Emphasis is placed on the key features of active listening and storytelling, and the act of storytelling is viewed as an interactional two-way or group process. The component skills of listening and storytelling are identified, broken down and made explicit to the participants in order to support their own mastery of the process.

Narratives and stories are used interchangeably in this programme and are viewed as an organised framework through which the young people can express themselves, both verbally and non-verbally. Stories have a definite structure and are sequentially organised into related units (Naremore et al., 1995). This organisational framework is used as a key support tool to help shape the production and evaluation of stories. Stein and Glenn's (1979) story grammar framework is adapted in this programme through the use of a story planner consisting of the following story grammar elements: *beginning* – setting (character, time, place); *middle* – episode (what happens?, immediate response, action, reaction) and *end* – outcome (result, message).

Storytelling draws upon a range of complex cognitive and linguistic skills (Naremore et al., 1995; Nippold, 2007), and the programme supports the expansion and development of language at the level of phonology, morphology, syntax, semantics, vocabulary and pragmatics. The intervention highlights for students the power and fun of language through stories and characterisations. Robust discussions, for example, are held about the famous Dahl characters Augustus Gloop and Verruca Salt, from *Charlie and the Chocolate Factory*, and intriguing debates ensue about the connection between names, characters and personality and the power of language to create stark and deeply ingrained images. The themes of the programme are drawn from subjects in the curriculum as well as the interests of the participants.

Narrative ability plays a significant role in the social and emotional development of students (Boudreau, 2008). Stories can act as a means of connecting students to their peers, the development of new friendships and a greater understanding of world events (Dickinson et al., 1993; Mello, 2001). The programme encourages students to evaluate the world around them and to express how they see themselves in this world.

One activity, for example, involves students sharing past, present and future autobiographies, which provide opportunities for increasing awareness of family, culture and heritage, self-reflection and realistic future goal planning. One boy changed his future story from being a professional footballer to working in maintenance at his favourite football club, the latter more realistically matching his ability level. Thus, the programme has an important socio-emotional component.

The approach is collaborative, being delivered by teaching assistants (TAs) and supported by SLTs. Participants are given a homework task, which they themselves called 'Mission to Achieve', involving teachers and families.

Work in practice

A typical session starts with a group greeting and revision. Students then share their 'Mission to Achieve' task and the trainer provides feedback and facilitates discussion. Every session finishes with a summary, revision and preparation for their next 'Mission to Achieve'.

The following is a description of a midway session focusing on characterisation, with activities listed in order.

1   Revise components from the story planner covered in the previous session.
2   Identify students' heroes, with reasons for their choices and discuss with group.

3 Describe their hero. Students are encouraged to provide rich and detailed descriptions using the character word map, including details about physical appearance, personality, mood, thoughts, feelings, use of language and behaviour.

4 Share the biographical story of their hero using the story planner. Students have already covered the differences between fiction, non-fiction and biography.

5 Develop three questions to ask their heroes. This task enhances their use of appropriate questioning.

6 Share a personal narrative. Students tell a personal story about something difficult in their lives and can change one aspect of the story to get a different outcome.

7 Provide biographies of curriculum-based characters to support generalisation of new skills to the classroom.

8 Revise the session.

9 'Mission to Achieve': Develop a biographical portrayal of a character the student is learning about in class using the story planner and character word map.

Outcomes and evidence: what we look for

Our findings from the ELCISS randomised control intervention study of 358 12-year-old students with SLCN showed that the narrative intervention was effective in improving storytelling. Students receiving the narrative intervention performed significantly better on a standardised storytelling test compared to the control group (who received no training) post-intervention. Significant improvements were also noted on non-standardised narrative measures in the narrative group, but not in the control or vocabulary groups, both in the active process of storytelling as well as in the explicit understanding of narratives.

Assessment frameworks

The research programme incorporated both standardised and non-standardised assessments of language and storytelling. It is important to use a combination of the two, as standardised tests provide information on how the student is performing in relation to their peers, but are not always sensitive enough to pick up subtle changes in performance.

We used a range of tasks to identify progress in both the linguistic and narrative quality aspects of storytelling. Materials used to generate stories included sequence stories, picture descriptions and objects which the students were required to use to tell their story. We also devised a 'narrative checklist task', which investigated explicit understanding of stories; for example, key components of a story, requirements for active listening and examples of story genres.

The story planner was also used to assess storytelling by identifying the key components of the story that the child has included. Language can be measured through mean length of utterance, type token ration and counting the number of adjectives, adverbs or more complex sentences used.

It is also important to get the perspective of the students, their teachers and parents through interviews, discussions and questionnaires. The programme incorporates 'My Learning Profile', which students complete, and captures their perceived strengths and areas of need.

Feedback collected from students, SLTs, TAs and teachers reflects the strengths of the programme in developing the language, educational and social and emotional abilities of young people with SLCN.

The students reported benefits in language: 'I really liked the storytelling best, it helps me with my talking and I hope we are going to do it again' and 'It helped me to bring out my language properly and I enjoyed it too'; and self-esteem and social skills: 'I felt confident and started socialising more'. Other students reported that 'I used to feel nervous but now I can express myself much more', 'it taught me to concentrate and listen more' and 'now I am able to understand more and have more confidence when I am talking to people'.

The teachers' comments reflected positive impacts on the students, TAs and the school; for example, an assistant head teacher observed:

> The ... students ... have made outstanding progress in their literacy skills which has impacted in their attainment across all curriculum areas ... The TA trained to deliver the speech and language interventions has benefited in terms of her ability to impact on the learning of students in addition to progressing in her own professional development.

Another deputy special educational needs coordinator noted:

> Each student has absolutely loved being part of the project and they often come and ask when it is their turn again ... The strategies taught in the small groups ... were useful and easily applied in all their lessons. The parents have fully supported this project and we have received excellent feedback from all of them ... They have all commented on the confidence their children have gained and the enjoyment they have experienced throughout each session.

All the TAs reported feeling significantly more empowered to support students with SLCN in the classroom; for example, 'The training has given me the knowledge and understanding to effectively support students with language and communication impairments' and 'Not only has this project helped the children taking part I feel it has helped all the children I support in lessons'.

The story of Himansu

Himansu, in year 7, was 12.3 years. He was eligible for free school meals and was exposed to three languages at home: English, Urdu and Punjabi. Himansu presented with mild receptive language difficulties and more pronounced expressive language difficulties. He participated in the narrative intervention, and was required to tell a story using at least three of the following: mobile phone, handcuffs, car, camera, horse, feather.

Pre-intervention

> The story is about um police are on horses just taking the horses around and then er they catch a man which is driving too fast, speeding and then they find out his number plate then they take a picture with this camera and then um they use phones to call the taxi people if like they're going the other way and then um they the people get out the car and then the police run after them. They handcuff them then the car's just there because it was stolen from somebody and the feather was and the feather just dropped from the sky.

Post-intervention

> On one rainy day there was a man called Jack. Jack was very rich. He had a wife and three kids. One day he was off to work. He was very fed up because there was a lot of rush and he could not get through all the cars so when he got to work he phone his wife and said I'm coming back early because there was a lot of rush. So it was time for Jack to go home and he drove off really fast down the motorway when a horse came out of nowhere and Jack had to swerve his beautiful car away from the horse. His car got damaged and the horse was in very much pain. When his wife heard about this she was very sad and she told him not to drive very fast on the motorways. So they took the horse away and the horse finally got better after a few days. Jack had earned a lot of compensation and he thought to himself and said I could never drive a car again.

The two stories show the improvements made in narrative quality and language. Narrative quality was assessed through a profile based on the story planner and he obtained a score of 14 at pre-intervention and 37 at post-intervention. This improvement is reflected in his characterisation of Jack, use of story components, consideration of the emotional state of his characters and use of descriptive words. His mean length of utterance increased from 8.08 at pre-intervention, to 11.06 at post-intervention, giving an indication of grammatical improvement.

Contexts of learning

The original programme was devised for secondary school students with SLCN. The programme is suitable for all students in secondary school as well as the older primary school years, from around 8 years of age. The programme is detailed enough in plans, teaching notes and explanations to be delivered by assistants with support and guidance. It is written up as 21 separate intervention sessions that form a coherent and progressive programme for narrative development. In the original project the sessions were delivered three times per week, and TAs reported that they felt this intensity was positive for the child as it maintained momentum. The programme can be delivered in full in one month, one term and even across a year, depending on the abilities of the group and the level of discussion undertaken. The intervention was delivered in small groups of between two and six students. The programme is designed to be flexible and to meet the different needs of the students and your own needs too!

Issues to consider

There may be times when students share highly emotional and difficult experiences, and it is essential that support is provided to them, if needed, outside of the session. Students should feel comfortable sharing their stories and understand the importance of trust and confidentiality. Trainers may also need to seek guidance, on occasion, to ensure student safety and well-being.

It is important to ensure the appropriate level of support is provided to assistants when they are conducting the programme.

Cultural factors

Students from a range of socio-economic, cultural, ethnic and religious backgrounds have taken part. Storytelling proved to be a powerful leveller, providing opportunities to learn about the cultures and beliefs of others.

Try it yourself

Top tips

- Make sure everything you do is relevant to students' own lives and experiences.
- Share your own stories and experiences, as this will encourage participants to share theirs with you.
- Encourage ongoing reflection and evaluation.
- Just do it! Dive in and have a go – you have nothing to lose and everything to gain.

Where to go

For further information, advice and training, see www.elciss.com and contact Victoria Joffe at: v.joffe@essex.ac.uk.

Resources

Joffe, V. L. (2011). *Narrative Intervention Programme: Using narratives to enhance language and learning across the secondary school curriculum.* Milton Keynes: Speechmark.

Acknowledgements

The research underpinning the narrative intervention programme was funded by the Nuffield Foundation (Grant No: EDU/32220).

References

Bercow, J. (2008). *The Bercow report: A review of services for children and young people (0–19) with speech, language and communication needs.* Available at: https://dera.ioe.ac.uk/8405/7/7771-dcsf-bercow_Redacted.pdf (Accessed 27.4.21).

Conti-Ramsden, G., Mok, P. L. H., Pickles, A. & Durkin, K. (2013). Adolescents with a history of specific language impairment (SLI): Strengths and difficulties in social, emotional and behavioral functioning. *Research in Developmental Disabilities,* 34, 4161–4169.

Dickinson, D., Wolf, M., Stotsky, S. & Gleason, J. (1993). Words move: The interwoven development of oral and written language. In J. Gleason (Ed.), *The development of language* (pp. 369–420). New York: Macmillan.

Durkin, K. & Conti-Ramsden, G. (2010). Young people with specific language impairment: A review of social and emotional functioning in adolescence. *Child Language Teaching and Therapy,* 26(2), 105–121.

Edwards-Groves, C. J. (1998). *The reconceptualisation of classroom events as structured lessons: Documenting changing the teaching of literacy in the primary school.* Unpublished doctoral thesis, Griffith University, Australia.

Freebody, P., Ludwig, C. & Gunn, S. (1995). *The literacy practices in and out of schools in low socio-economic urban communities.* Canberra, Australia: Commonwealth Department of Employment, Education and Training.

I CAN & Royal College of Speech and Language Therapists (RCSLT). (2018). *Bercow: Ten years on.* Available at: https://www.bercow10yearson.com (Accessed 10.12.20).

Joffe, V. L. (2011a). *Narrative intervention programme: Using narratives to enhance language and learning across the secondary school curriculum.* Milton Keynes: Speechmark.

Joffe, V. L. (2011b). *Vocabulary enrichment intervention programme.* Milton Keynes: Speechmark.

Joffe, V. L. & Black, E. (2012). Social, emotional and behavioural functioning of mainstream secondary school students with low academic and language performance: Perspectives from students, teachers and parents. *Language, Speech and Hearing Services in Schools,* 43, 461–473.

Joffe, V. L., Rixon, L. & Hulme, C. (2019). Improving storytelling and vocabulary in secondary school students with language disorder: A randomised controlled trial. *International Journal of Language and Communication Disorders,* 54(4), 656–672.

Johnson, C. J., Beitchman, J. H. & Brownlie, E. B. (2010). Twenty-year follow-up of children with and without speech-language impairments: Family, educational, occupational, and quality of life outcomes. *American Journal of Speech Language Pathology,* 19, 51–65.

McLeod, S. & McKinnon, D. H. (2007). Prevalence of communication disorders compared with other learning needs in 14 500 primary and secondary school students. *International Journal of Language & Communication Disorders,* 42, 37–59.

Mello, R. (2001). The power of storytelling: How oral narrative influences children's relationships in classrooms. *International Journal of Education and the Arts,* 2(1). Available at: www.ijea.org/v2n1 (Accessed 5.21).

Moshman, D. (1999). *Adolescent psychological development: Rationality, morality and identity.* Mahwah, NJ: LEA Publishers.

Naremore, R., Densmore, A. & Harman, D. (1995). *Language intervention with school-aged children: Conversation, narrative and text.* San Diego, CA: Singular Publishing Group.

Nippold, M. (2007). *Later language development: School-age children, adolescents, and young adults.* Austin, TX: Pro-Ed.

Nippold, M. (2010a). *Language sampling with adolescents.* San Diego, CA: Plural Publishing.

Nippold, M. (2010b). It's NOT too late to help adolescents succeed in school. *Language, Speech and Hearing Services in Schools,* 41, 137–138.

Snowling, M. J., Adams, J. W., Bishop, D. V. M. & Stothard, S. E. (2001). Educational attainments of school leavers with preschool history of speech-language impairments. *International Journal of Language and Communication Disorders,* 36(2), 173–183.

Snowling, M. J., Bishop, D. V. M., Stothard, S. E., Chipchase, B. & Kaplan, C. (2006). Psychosocial outcomes at 15 years of children with a preschool history of speech-language impairment. *Journal of Child Psychology and Psychiatry,* 47(8), 759–765.

Stein, N. & Glenn, C. (1979). An analysis of story comprehension in elementary school children. In R. Freedle (Ed.), *New directions in discourse processing* (pp. 53–120). Norwood, NJ: Ablex.

Vygotsky, L. (1978). *Mind in society.* Cambridge, MA: Harvard University Press.

Chapter 9

Creative use of digital storytelling

David Messer and Valerie Critten

Background

Storytelling has probably existed in some form since we started as humans to use language. In contrast, digital storytelling has only been possible in the last decade, a very recent innovation in human history even when compared to writing and print. Even so it is clear that digital technology can be harnessed to open up different forms and contents when storytelling (Kucirkova et al., 2014).

History

We have been involved in developing and using the Our Story app widely in schools. By describing it, we can outline what we mean by creative digital storytelling, and its possibilities. This free app for smartphones, tablets and iPads (to download search for Our Story 2 in App Store or Google Play) can be used with many different formats of digital storytelling (Kucirkova et al., 2014). In this way, the app does not narrow the choices made by anybody using it. What they choose to do can be their own ideas and a means of self-expression, especially important for people with communication difficulties. Because of this approach we are less concerned with focusing on a particular type of story (fictional, traditional, descriptive, etc.); instead, we emphasise the flexibility in what is told and how it is told. The aim is for children and adults to express their own voice in a story format that has a 'professional' look.

Our Story enables photographs on digital devices to be put into a sequence to make up a story on what we term a storyboard (see Figure 9.1). The photographs or videos can be existing ones or those specially taken for the story. Once a photograph has been dragged onto the storyboard, then tapping on the picture will allow users to add text, sounds or speech to the photo. In other words, what is being created is a digital picture book with photographs that can have text and sound added to them. A finished story can be played on the device or sent to other people to view with the app; it can also be printed out or sent by email in the form of a purely visual PDF file.

Theories and principles

The Our Story app draws on theories in education and psychology, especially socio-cultural theory, to provide an easy-to-use interface and activities that can encourage communication and interest in literacy. Important principles are that digital technology can offer new possibilities for learning and education, and in addition, that technology can powerfully engage and motivate (Flewitt, Messer & Kucirkova, 2015). We also wanted to provide an app that could encourage

DOI: 10.4324/9781003159087-9

Figure 9.1 A screen shot from Our Story, photographs can be dragged onto the storyboard at the bottom to make up a digital picture story. Video recordings can be included.

children's interest in communication and literacy, by making possible the creation of stories that are personalised around children's own interests and culture. This is an important part of the process of using Our Story as the user can insert their own personal information such as their friends, places they like to go or things they like to play with or do, which is thought to increase their sense of empowerment and raises self-esteem (Kucirkova & Cremin, 2018).

Work in practice

In many ways an issue with digital storytelling is that it is very open ended, this means a lot of choices and decisions are needed especially when the storyteller is new to the process, but this also can be an advantage as exploration and modification are possible rather than following a set format of say stories having a beginning, middle and end. Indeed, digital storytelling as we conceive it can be contrasted with a written or even oral story where there is often an established format, to one that is more like acting out a story so that a range of skills and expressions can be brought into the service of communication.

Both stories and narratives can be used in digital storytelling, with stories involving more emphasis on fiction and entertainment, while narratives involve more description, for example a topic like 'My holiday' or 'What I like doing'. Consequently, our interest in digital storytelling covers many different forms, and fundamentally it concerns a sequence of events and images that communicate information that a person wants to give others.

Because of this we do not have detailed recommendations about the use of Our Story, rather the app can be adapted to the needs and interests of the users. This flexibility can be off putting, but we believe it also means that digital storytelling can be used to achieve many different aims in many different circumstances. Hopefully, this becomes clearer when we discuss examples of use.

Outcomes and evidence: what we look for

Digital storytelling is a valuable activity in itself, it provides storytellers with a platform to voice issues of concern and interest to them, and the information they provide can be useful to carers and families (Clark & Moss, 2011). Additionally, the experience of storytelling develops abilities such as organising information, presenting information in a way to interest the reader and learning to use different forms of communication. Furthermore, Karmiloff-Smith (1992) suggests that re-representing information in a new format is likely to result in new understandings and insights for the storyteller.

There also is a wealth of evidence that most children are highly motivated to use digital technology (Flewitt et al., 2015), and as a result will engage and be motivated to use digital storytelling. In the examples below, the storytellers were engaged and motivated by the idea of creating a digital story and were very proud of their achievements.

Research studies provide evidence that personalised stories can make new vocabulary more likely to be remembered, and that engaging with creative apps can result in higher levels of speech than other types of app especially those with closed content (Flewitt et al., 2015). Our examples below also resulted in other outcomes. In the first example, there was a meeting with a speech and language therapist before and after the project to identify communication-related learning objectives. It was found that each of the children had met their targets through enacting and telling the story. The use of the iPad, especially the functions of the camera and the video that were used in the app, and the attachment of the iPad to the smartboard motivated, excited and enthralled the children. It was a special time in the class when drama, storytelling and technology married together to produce a class story.

Children and families are usually proud of the stories that are produced (Kucirkova et al., 2014). In our second example, both of the male students practised telling their stories with the teaching assistant (TA), recognising or reading some of the words in the captions and they communicated their stories to their class. In post-project interviews with the class teacher and the TA, they said that the families appreciated the work completed by the students: 'Technology gives a good outcome to their work; it looks like the kind of work completed by children in mainstream schools' (Critten & Kucirkova, 2015: 5).

The story of a class of children

Val (second author) taught in a special school for children with physical and associated learning and communication disabilities. She organised a storytelling activity with nine children aged between 7 and 9 years in her class, most of whom had some form of communication difficulty and used Alternative and Augmentative Communication (AAC) devices such as a communication book with images (low tech) or an electronic device (high tech).

The final stories were digital picture books, each screen consisting of a picture chosen by the storytellers and put in the sequence that made most sense to them. These pictures could be swiped forwards and backwards on the device just like turning pages and could be printed out. Text was often added to the pictures, and sounds, music or speech also could be recorded with each picture.

The class were first introduced to a range of stories such as fairy tales, myths and legends through listening to and looking at books. Val and her support staff decided to write a story as part of a whole class project 'The Great Outdoors' and the children chose to tell a story based on a visit to the local spinney which had entranced them. It had been a magical visit as the spinney was covered in blossoming trees, there was a stream and many insects were flying or crawling around.

Figure 9.2 The spinney story: the spider is going to weave her cobweb around the flowers near to the stream.

All of the children were encouraged to express their ideas about the spinney, so the staff raided the dressing-up box, and brought in costumes from home so that the children could dress up and relate to an aspect of the spinney visit that was important to them. Everyone used iPads to take photos and filmed the children dancing or acting a part. The staff were able to attach the iPads to the smartboard in the classroom and show all the photos and video clips, and a number of the photos that the children particularly liked were printed. From these photos and clips they were able to put together a sequence which was the basis of a story.

Next to the classroom was a sensory room, and everyone decorated it as the spinney. The bubble tubes became the stream, paper flowers made by the children were hung up and the wind machine provided the breeze that was integral to the story. Photos of the children were taken in their costumes acting the story in the sensory room (see Figure 9.2). Once the story was completed the children enacted their story in the sensory room, narrated by two children who were good readers.

'The Story of the Spinney' was put together on the app by the children choosing photos of themselves and everyone added captions to tell the story. The story and photographs were printed out and made into a booklet for each of the children to take home to show their parents and families.

The story of Jimmi and Aaron

One of the key considerations is to inspire storytellers with ideas or a starting point, e.g. the title or the subject matter. Sometimes it can be extremely difficult to have a starting point which resonates with or motivates people with severe learning difficulties/cultural differences/different life experiences, or people living with dementia. One important consideration is the difficulties with the communication of ideas: either because an individual had little or no speech or because they are unable to understand others. In these circumstances, how can you inspire a story that is meaningful for them?

Two male students (Jimmi, 16 years old and Aaron, 18 years old) both with severe learning difficulties (SLD) attended a transition class in a special school. Both of the students had emigrated from different countries in Africa in challenging circumstances. Both were physically strong and active and were well over six feet tall. They were constantly challenging each other in the class and their teacher felt that if they could express their emotions it would encourage them to communicate positively with each other and with others in the class. An intervention in the form of an action research study was organised with the teacher and a TA and monitored and recorded by Val. There were five sessions over five weeks each consisting of: aim, progress and evaluation (Critten & Kucirkova, 2015).

In the initial session the two students were taught to use the camera on the iPad which they both found straightforward, and they enjoyed looking at the photos they had taken. To start them off on their stories, the teacher encouraged them to take photos around the school while separately accompanied by the TA: Aaron chose to take photos of the staff especially the reception staff who greeted him every morning; Jimmi chose to take photos of his favourite classrooms. Each week the teacher and the TA helped the students to choose the order of their photos and to choose and type captions for each photo on the app. They were able to build up their stories on the iPad with one-to-one help. They chose their own pictures and the order of the pictures. It was important that the narrative was their own although others might have put the photos in a different order.

Contexts of learning

The advantage of the app is that it can be used in a group or a class situation where members of the group can make individual choices about parts of a story, or by individuals who have a personalised story. The Our Story app can also be used with adults who have communication difficulties. We carried out a research project with adults living with dementia who had deteriorating speech and language abilities, and memory loss. In common with the children in our case studies, the adults had difficulties with a starting point to their stories, however once they started a story they found that the process initiated other reminiscences and promoted communication (see Critten and Kucirkova, 2019). In another project digital stories have been created about growing and eating vegetables, these can be downloaded and used with Our Story to encourage healthy eating (https://www.seeandeat.org/ebooks).

Issues to consider

Our approach to digital storytelling grew out of the possibilities offered by the Our Story app and our experiences of using the app with individuals who had a range of abilities and needs. Some common features of the examples we have provided are:

- Finding a starting point which excites and motivates the storyteller/s
- Teaching the storyteller to become familiar with the functions of the technology so that they have more agency
- Encouraging the storyteller/s to review and amend their work
- Encouraging the stories to be shown to friends and family.

The main limitations for the children and adults we have worked with came if they were unfamiliar with digital technology and both the use of iPads and the Our Story app had to be taught to them. This meant that they needed one-to-one help to enable the stories to be produced.

Be aware that families may need support when taking part in projects. Jimmi and Aaron's teacher did a home visit to ensure the family understood the research and to gain their consent.

Try it yourself

Top tips

- Gradually build up the technical skills of the children/adults to sequence their own photographs. If needed show how to make a story, but make sure you scaffold, and give help when it is needed. Adapt to the pace of your storytellers. Also, support the storyteller's motivation and inspire them to express their own ideas by making the experience fun.
- Remember that the content of the stories can be very flexible – photos of the storyteller (often very popular), drawings, screenshots from the internet, photographs of pictures from books or magazines (remember about copyright), photos of toys that are characters in a story and videos. In this way storytellers can choose aspects of their own culture. Storytellers often like to hear their own voice or make sounds related to the story.
- Encourage the children/adults to communicate their stories with others by: showing it on the digital device, using a printed copy or by emailing the story to others.

Training and resources

Make sure you are reasonably confident about using any digital story-making app. For Our Story there are help screens when using the app, and general advice about using the app (tap on Get Started on the opening page of the app, e.g. the delete button can be disabled so there is little risk of losing a story).

Acknowledgements

Professor Natalia Kucirkova was involved in the creation of the Our Story app, involved in the research projects mentioned in this chapter and has made a major contribution to research and theory about digital storytelling.

References

Boudreau, D. (2008). Narrative abilities: Advances in research and implications for clinical practice. *Topics in Language Disorders*, 28(2), 98–114.

Clark, A. & Moss, P. (2011). *Listening to young children: The mosaic approach*. London: National Children's Bureau.

Critten, V. & Kucirkova, N. (2015). Digital personal stories: A case study of two African adolescents, with severe learning and communication disabilities. *Journal of Childhood & Developmental Disorders*, 1, 1–9.

Critten, V. & Kucirkova, N. (2019). 'It brings it all back, all those good times; it makes me go close to tears': Creating digital personalised stories with people who have dementia. *Dementia*, 18(3), 864–881.

Flewitt, R., Messer, D. & Kucirkova, N. (2015). New directions for early literacy in a digital age: The iPad. *Journal of Early Childhood Literacy*, 15(3), 289–310.

Karmiloff-Smith, A. (1992). *Beyond modularity: A developmental perspective on cognitive science*. Cambridge, MA: MIT Press.

Kucirkova, N. & Cremin, T. (2018). Personalised reading for pleasure with digital libraries: Towards a pedagogy of practice and design. *Cambridge Journal of Education*, 48(5), 571–589.

Kucirkova, N., Messer, D., Critten, V. & Harwood, J. (2014). Story-making on the iPad when children have complex needs: Two case studies. *Communication Disorders Quarterly*, 36, 44–54.

Chapter 10

Storytelling in sign language for deaf children

Rachel Sutton-Spence

Background

Deaf literature is the body of creative language work of deaf communities. It is produced by deaf people, for deaf people, about deaf people, and it is in the language (sign language) of deaf people. It includes storytelling, poetry, jokes and other creative pieces, fiction and non-fiction. Deaf literature introduces deaf children to their deaf identities, as individuals and as members of social and language communities. All deaf children have the experience of being deaf in a world where most people (if not everyone) they know is hearing. However, very few deaf children know about the experiences of *other* deaf people. Original stories by deaf people, aimed directly at deaf children, provide what Ben Bahan (2006) calls "deaf world knowledge" and helps them make sense of their deaf world experience.

We know that storytelling is essential for the development of all young children. Andrews and Baker (2019, p. 7) list some of the benefits for deaf children of seeing stories and other forms of language play in sign languages: "motor development, communication, social-emotional skills, world knowledge, cognition, language, and literacy", and enjoyment. Promoting deaf children's literacy in sign language also supports their spoken/written language literacy skills. My focus here is on sign language literacy and how we can foster it with original deaf stories in sign language.

If we tell deaf children the story of the *Three Little Pigs* in sign language, they access their shared cultural heritage with other children. There are good examples on the internet of translated children's stories from books. Many of these are beautifully told and provide good sign language role models, but the *content* doesn't reflect who deaf children are as deaf people.

We can adapt classic stories. If we make the pigs deaf (and why not?), it gives the child an immediate bond with the characters. If the deaf wolf signs so fast that his windmilling hands create a wind to blow down the straw and wooden houses (Mourão, 2011), we privilege sign language and show its potential for creativity (and it is funny).

But we can go further. What if, as well as translating and adapting existing children's stories for young deaf audiences, we start with *deaf norms* for literature and teaching, and create and tell original deaf stories in sign language? We did this in our "Didactic Literature" project, as a group of deaf teachers and students[1] in the Department of Brazilian Sign Language (Libras) at the Federal University of Santa Catarina in Brazil created stories for very young children and novice signers.[2]

Barry (2017) distinguishes between the sequence of events (the story), and the way these are ordered, packaged and presented. In deaf literature the story's facts relate to deaf

DOI: 10.4324/9781003159087-10

people's experiences and knowledge of the deaf world, and the way of telling it follows what deaf storytellers know about appealing to their audiences – how to make it a satisfying, understandable, highly visual experience. Narratives for very young deaf children are important for *how* they are told and for *what* is told.

Deaf pedagogy (Ladd & Gonçalves, 2012; Gonzales, 2017) is an educational philosophy and practice that highlights the importance of deaf adults passing on to deaf children what it means to be a deaf person, in terms of sign language, deaf traditions and visual deaf culture. As part of deaf pedagogy, deaf teachers tell narratives of personal experience – "This happened to me and here is what I learned from it, so you can learn from it too". For younger children, however, we also want to encourage their imagination and their sense of the absurd, while introducing basic sign language input and encouraging simple responses from them. For this reason, we focused on creating fictional vignettes.

Theories and principles

We start with the principle that deaf children should have fun with stories in sign language. In deaf literature, we can play with sign language, making it do new things, breaking it apart, taking it to its limits and beyond, just to see what will happen. Sometimes we forget about play to focus on mediating deaf children's difficulties and many deaf adults tell us that learning was a serious affair when they were at school. However, research has repeatedly shown that children learn better when there is laughter and humour (Jonas, 2009). In sign language storytelling, children can have fun, but *directed* fun, where they can easily make sense of what they see, play with their own signs, draw on their own knowledge and develop their language, world-knowledge and social skills.

I set up the "Didactic Literature" project after over 20 years of researching sign language literature in the adult deaf community (Sutton-Spence & Kaneko, 2016), and becoming increasingly aware of the importance of deaf teachers for teaching stories and teaching through stories (Sutton-Spence & Ramsey, 2010). Talking to deaf friends, colleagues and other researchers in the field, it became clear that as deaf children are increasingly educated in the mainstream, they may have some understanding of "hearing people's stories", especially if they are translated into sign language, but not of *deaf* storytelling, and this is especially true for the very young.

Storytelling for very young deaf children is based on different assumptions than for learners who have already acquired a language or for those who cannot easily acquire it because of additional difficulties, because deaf children can easily acquire sign language and the insights it brings, so long as they are exposed to it.

About sign languages

Sign languages, like spoken languages, have an underlying structure of simple units that we can combine to produce new and different signs (*handshapes, locations, movements* and *orientations* of the palm and fingers). While hearing children enjoy discovering rhymes and repetition of other sounds in their spoken language, deaf children (when given the chance) are delighted to discover that certain signs share the same handshape or can have double meanings, and that repeated movement in signs creates a rhythm.

Sign languages, *unlike* spoken languages, are fundamentally visual and deaf children need to learn how the visual world they see around them is transferred into their visual language.

When stories are presented in sign language alongside pictures of what they represent, deaf children understand how to make these transfers using the linguistic resources available in their own sign language.

Sign language literature

Any unwritten story is performed as well as told and the usual medium for sign language literature is live, embodied, performed signing (even if it is captured on video). Because these stories only exist in the telling, good-quality performances suitable for young audiences are essential and exaggerated facial expression in these performances is especially engaging.

Ideally, we would hope for a deaf adult who can tell engaging, high-quality sign language stories to every deaf child, but we can't expect that to happen any time soon, because most deaf children have hearing families, are educated in mainstream or other settings and usually have a hearing teacher. Additionally, we can't expect all fluent deaf signers to have the gift of storytelling. Although they can learn explicitly how to tell stories, most deaf teachers start behind the curve in comparison to hearing teachers, because their schooling and teacher training rarely includes deaf literature. In the absence of the ideal, then, we can use videos of teachers and storytellers who *do* have the talent and training. Then the teacher simply needs to know how to use these stories to the best effect.

The American Deaf storyteller Stephen Ryan listed some of the key characteristics of good signed storytelling (Ryan, 1993). He suggested that storytellers should aim to create powerful visual images through their signing, especially through mixing signs with acting out the role of characters (sometimes called "constructed action") (Smith & Cormier, 2014). When telling stories for very young children, this way of acting is the most engaging and easiest for them to understand (essentially saying "I am a cow/ant/banana/whatever"; "and here is what I do and how I do it"). However, stories are also a good opportunity to learn sign language vocabulary.

Creating original deaf narratives for very young children

Our stories provide good-quality sign language models, highlight the structure of the language, are short (about one minute), visual and as funny as we could make them. Every story has illustrations that are large and brightly coloured, some of them animated. We pay careful attention to the placement of signs within the signing space, the signer's gaze direction, facial expression and body movement and the rhythm and timing of the signs. They were recorded in a professional studio, and it is worth saying that even the most skilled storytellers needed a lot of practice and several takes to get each one right.

The stories have a single character (which is linguistically easier to follow than multiple characters), who is understood to be deaf, to increase engagement with the child: "deaf like you".

We all find humour in seeing human traits in non-humans (Bergson, 1911), and anthropomorphism appeals especially to children. We chose animals and objects for characters (such as a cow, a dog and a bat). These and the things they do (such as playing basketball, going on a bus or wearing high heels) should be familiar to the children, through everyday experience, or through films or books.

As we expect children in this age group to find incongruity, slapstick and bodies funny (Luckner & Yarger, 1997; Boldo & Sutton-Spence, 2020), we made sure the stories covered these aspects. Incongruously, the cow is in high heels, the dog is playing basketball, the bat is on the bus, and so on. Also, the cow in her high heels repeatedly falls over; a monkey playing different musical instruments (all of which he plays enthusiastically but throws away because they don't "work" because he's a deaf monkey) is horribly smelly and an ant realises she is naked.

Bergson (1911) also notes that we laugh at exaggeration, where smaller things are made larger and larger things made smaller. As children find exaggeration especially funny, we took care to exaggerate facial expressions and sign movements.

Our stories are also based on traditional "handshape" games that are part of deaf folk-lore around the world. In particular, we created stories that use the same handshape for every sign. Linking handshape stories with incongruous ideas came from Smith and Jacobowitz (2006). Their book asks, "Have you ever seen?" using images such as a horse painting, an elephant cooking or an ice-cream riding a motorbike. These simple "nonsense" pairings arise because both signs share the same handshape in American Sign Language (ASL). We chose similar ludicrous pairs of noun and action that share hand-shapes in Libras. For example, the signs for "cow" and "high heels" both use the Y handshape (see Figures 10.1–10.4: The story of the grumpy cow).

Figure 10.1a, b The cow is standing in her high heels and falls over as her heels slip

Figure 10.2 The cow (shown on the body and face and head) in her high heels (shown on the left hand) looks up at an aeroplane (shown on the right hand)

Figure 10.3 The cow (shown on the body and face and head) looks at her mobile phone (shown on the left hand) and signs "Hello!" (shown on the right hand)

Figure 10.4 The combination of facial expression, the sign for cow and the accompanying picture provide the illustration for the story.

We extended this so that *all* the signs in any story use the same handshape creating an equivalent effect to rhyme in spoken languages. For example, in the story of the cow in high heels, the same handshape occurs in the signs for cow, walking-in-high-heeled-shoes, aeroplane and mobile phone. (Imagine a parallel effect in English of "A cat. What's that? Splat! A cow pat …"). When the cow answers the phone, she signs "Hello" (it is a video phone call because she is a deaf cow) and a playful adjustment of the handshape of the sign makes it fit in with all the others. It is still understandably "Hello" but looks silly after changing it to make it "rhyme". (Think of Ogden Nash's poetic offer: "Who wants my jellyfish? I'm not sellyfish!")

Figure 10.4 The combination of facial expression, the sign for cow and the accompanying picture provide the illustration for the story.

Work in practice

How to run a session

The stories are designed to be watched with a teacher or other adult who will help the child's learning. We recommend that you don't start with the story, but by introducing its content. For example, show pictures or a film (even better) of ants or cows (or whatever is in the story), and find out what the child already knows about them. Make sure they know the central signs, such as "ant" or "cow" or teach them if necessary. Use matching picture games, prepare models or bring in toy replicas for the children to play with and learn the signs. This helps them to focus on the visual characteristics of the animals.

Then, watch the video together and observe the child's reactions, checking for understanding and what interests or amuses the child. Then watch it again and ask the child to copy the story as it is signed. Children enjoy mirroring what they see and the feel of producing the signs. Then ask the child questions about the signs in the video, drawing their attention to the handshapes used in the story and engage them in two-way conversation. If there are two or more children in the group, they can then tell the story to each other, or tell it back to you. More advanced students can suggest other signs that use that handshape, add them to the story or create a new story.

Outcomes and evidence: what we look for

There are currently no formal assessment frameworks for deaf children learning sign language literature in Brazil, though one is in the process of development (see for an example in ASL, Ashton et al., 2012). An assessment of British Sign Language (BSL) skills, using a narrative task, is available and is being adapted for some other sign languages (Herman et al., 2004). This does not assess signed stories as literature, however.

Mirus and Napoli (2018) suggest outcomes to look for, with *interest* being fundamental. Deaf children enjoy and show especial interest in signed stories told by skilled tellers, for example: mimicking the stories as they watch them repeatedly; telling the child next to them about the story; retelling the stories and varying them, exaggerating certain parts to show feelings or personal interests. Children will retell the stories together, as a game; one will elaborate on the other's sentence, building off each other's elaborations of the story that leave them laughing. As they play with the signs in the videos and transform them, the children are claiming language ownership, They appropriate the stories as their own, sometimes explaining them to their teachers. This suggests that the children are delighted that these stories are designed for and belong to them, as deaf people. Teachers, student teachers and other colleagues using our stories have seen similar positive responses with children and adults in different settings across Brazil. One teacher found that the lure of these stories increased "attendance" and encouraged children who frequently missed online sessions to log on to lessons during the Covid pandemic.

Another, working one-to-one in remedial education, showed them to an 11-year-old deaf boy with a cochlear implant who had resisted learning sign language because he believed that his implant meant he was no longer deaf. He laughed at the cow who fell over, the naked ant and the smelly monkey, and his teacher reported it was the first time he had shown interest in the potential for sign language.

The story of Josemara

Josemara is a 10-year-old autistic deaf girl at a bilingual school for deaf children in the Amazon region. Her teacher showed the stories to a group of five girls of a similar age, who had more advanced signing skills and were easily able to pay attention to their teacher and to the video playing on the screen. On the first viewing, Josemara's classmates copied the signs they saw on screen although not fluently because they hadn't yet understood the linguistic features underlying the story. During this part of the lesson, Josemara wouldn't look at the screen, rarely looked at the teacher or her classmates (although she was clearly aware of them in her peripheral vision) and randomly moved her hands occasionally. When the teacher had explained the significance of the handshapes, they watched the video again and the other children copied the signs with confidence and clarity, enjoying understanding what they were seeing and signing, adding their facial expressions of the animals. Josemara also began copying the signs, sometimes looking at the screen, sometimes looking at her classmates. When faced with a more complex sign, she looked at her own hands and at those of her classmates, trying to produce it correctly. When she signed "cat", she recognised what she was signing and understood that she was signing it correctly, repeating it several times with confidence, looking at her teacher and classmates with obvious satisfaction. Throughout this second viewing, she was smiling to herself. Her teacher reported that this sort of engagement was unusual for her.

The story of Vinicius and Arturo

Vinicius is 10 and Arturo is 12, deaf boys with intermediate level signing skills. Their teacher reported that they were immediately interested in the stories because they were different from the signed texts they usually saw. They were particularly intrigued by the idea of signs sharing the same handshape. Their teacher devised games for them, based on the stories such as a multiple-choice game of images of different animals. This stimulated further discussion about how animals can be described in sign language, engaging the students and improving their Libras skills. At first, they didn't notice the handshapes, but once the teacher had drawn their attention to it in the first story, the two boys quickly attuned to the task of spotting the selected handshape in each story and offering the different signs that used that handshape. The teacher then used "lucky dip" to choose a different handshape, and the boys worked together to create a new story, of a battle between dinosaurs. Their story had a simple plot, as each boy "acted out" his own dinosaur, showing creative and imaginative use of classifiers and constructed action. There was plenty of exaggeration and strong facial expression as they performed their piece. The recording of this lesson shows the boys laughing and the teacher smiling as he watches.

Contexts of learning

As described above, these activities can be used effectively with children who have a range of learning needs. We think they could also be adapted for use with hearing children using key word signs, where teachers are often unsure how to promote creative communicative use of the modality (see Parkhouse & Smith, 2019).

Issues to consider

Most importantly, story performers should be recognised within the deaf community as model children's storytellers. Non-deaf people must be ready to engage on deaf cultural terms. It is all too easy for people immersed in the "hearing" tradition of what makes a good story for small children to apply these criteria to judge deaf stories. Everyone needs to respect and accept that deaf adults know what deaf children need to see – after all, those deaf adults were children once!

Cultural factors

Our stories are tailored to the Brazilian deaf community, and teachers around the world should make sure that their stories reflect the daily experience of their own deaf children. That said, animals doing silly things are appreciated in most places. It is worth trying to find performers who fit different gender, ethnic and other profiles.

Try it yourself

If you are a fluent native signer, skilled in creating and telling deaf stories to deaf children, try creating short, single-handshape stories like these. Use a single (deaf) character and try to make them as silly as possible. Remember to exaggerate the facial expression and use illustrations if you can.

If you don't have these skills, find someone recognised in your local deaf community as a good deaf children's storyteller. Show them these stories and invite them to adapt them or create equivalents in your sign language.

If you make the stories freely available on the internet, it will contribute to the whole community.

If you don't have those contacts and can't make them, find stories performed by skilled deaf storytellers and show them to deaf children. Ideally, they should be original deaf stories, but these are still rare. You can still go through the steps of showing the children objects and pictures first, working with them on signs and talking about the story content, before copying and developing the stories. Remember to encourage production as much as reception.

Choose a handshape and list signs that share the same handshape. Introduce these to the child. Ask the child for more signs with the same handshape. Play with the signs to make a silly story.

Play the "How silly!" game of two incongruous signs that share a handshape in your sign language and draw a picture of the silly thing.

Top tips

- Prioritise the visual in simple stories to stimulate awareness of sign language structure for children.

- Letting the child produce signs is as important as watching them.
- Make it fun!

Where to go³

Libras stories are at: https://vimeo.com/showcase/6241328.

Original deaf "songs" for the very young in ASL are available from Hands Land, an excellent ASL resource. Its introductory video explains the importance of these language games: https://www.youtube.com/watch?v=zKrpkBY23eg.

Good storytelling models in translated stories for children in BSL: https://everydaybsl.wordpress.com/2020/05/24/childrens-stories-in-bsl.

Children's storytelling at: https://www.youtube.com/playlist?list=PLmUSUOO1Mlu2wTHRo5I-miKRVEZ3BsUPh.

BSL sign poetry at: https://www.youtube.com/channel/UCfO_GnnCDuaWLbigOBj3S_w.

Acknowledgements

My thanks to the "Libras Didática" project team: Marina Teles, Aldenisa Peixoto, Helio Alves do Melo Neto, Anna Luiza Maciel, Jaqueline Boldo, Juliana Tasca Lohn, Martin Haswell and Donna Jo Napoli, and to the students and teachers who tested the stories.

Notes

1 See acknowledgements.
2 https://vimeo.com/showcase/6241328.
3 All accessed 28.4.21.

References

Andrews, J. F. & Baker, S. (2019). ASL nursery rhymes: Exploring a support for signing deaf children: Early language and emergent literacy skills. *Sign Language Studies*, 20, 5–40.

Ashton, G., Cagle, K., Brown Kurz, K., Newell, W., Peterson, R. & Zinza, J. (2012). *Standards for learning American Sign Language: A project of the American Sign Language Teachers Association.* Accessed from https:// aslta.org/ wp- content/ uploads/ 2014/ 07/ National_ ASL_ Standards. pdf (Accessed 20.8.21).

Bahan, B. (2006). Face-to-face tradition in the American deaf community. In H.-Dirksen Bauman, J., Nelson & H. Rose (Eds.), *Signing the body poetic* (pp. 21–50). Berkeley, CA: University of California Press.

Barry, P. (2017). *Beginning theory: An introduction to literary and cultural theory.* Manchester: Manchester University Press.

Bergson, H. (1911) [Trans. 2003]. *Laughter: An essay on the meaning of the comic.* London: Macmillan & Co.

Boldo, J. & Sutton-Spence, R. (2020). Libras humor: Playing with the internal structure of signs. *Sign Language Studies*, 20(3), 411–433.

Gonzales, M. (2017). Being and becoming a deaf educator: The construction of deaf educators' roles and pedagogies in Chilean deaf schools. PhD thesis, Graduate School of Education, University of Bristol.

Herman, R., Grove, N., Holmes, S., Morgan, G., Sutherland, H., & Woll, B. (2004). *Assessing BSL development: BSL Production Test (Narrative Skills)*. London: City University.

Jonas, P. (2009). *Laughing and learning: An alternative to shut up and listen*. New York: Rowman & Littlefield Education.

Ladd, P. & Gonçalves, J. (2012). 'A *final frontier? How Deaf cultures and Deaf pedagogies can revolutionize Deaf education*. In L. Leeson & M. Vermeerbergen (Eds), *Working with the deaf community: Deaf education, mental health and interpreting* (pp. 9–33). Dublin: Interesource Group Ireland Limited.

Luckner, J. & Yarger, C. (1997). What's so funny? A comparison of students who are deaf or hard of hearing and hearing students' appreciation of cartoons. *American Annals of the Deaf*, 142, 373–378.

Mirus, G. & Napoli, D. J. (2018). Developing language and (pre)literacy skills in deaf preschoolers through shared reading activities with bimodal-bilingual ebooks, *Journal of Multilingual Education Research* (8), Article 10, 75–110.

Mourão, C. (2011). Literatura Surda: produções culturais de surdos em língua de sinais. In L. Karnopp, M. Klein & M. Lunardi-Lazzarin (Eds), *Cultura Surda na contemporaneidade* (pp. 71–90). Canoas, Brazil: Editora ULBRA.

Napoli, D. J. & Sutton-Spence, R. (2019). Deaf children, humor and education policy. *Revista Educação Especial*, 32, 1–27.

Parkhouse, C. & Smith, G. (2019). 'Yes, no, maybe': A call for a paradigm shift in attitudes towards key word signing. In N. Grove & K. Launonen (Eds), *Manual sign acquisition in children with developmental disabilities* (pp. 315–334). New York: Nova Science.

Ryan, S. (1993). Let's tell an ASL story. In Gallaudet University College for Continuing Education (Ed.), *Conference Proceedings, April 22–25, 1993* (pp. 145–150). Washington, DC: Gallaudet University Press.

Smith, A. K. & Jacobowitz, E. (2006). *Have you ever seen…? An American Sign Language handshape DVD/book*. Cave Spring, GA: ASL Rose.

Smith, S. & Cormier, K. (2014). In or out? Spatial scale and enactment in narratives of native and non-native signing deaf children acquiring British Sign Language. *Sign Language Studies*, 14, 275–301.

Sutton-Spence, R. (2005). *Analysing sign language poetry*. Basingstoke: Palgrave Macmillan.

Sutton-Spence, R. & Kaneko, M. (2016). *Introducing sign language literature: Creativity and folklore*. Basingstoke: Palgrave Press.

Sutton-Spence, R. & Ramsey, C. (2010). What we should teach deaf children: Deaf teachers' folk models in Britain, the U.S. and Mexico. *Deafness and Education International*, 12(3), 149–176.

Chapter 11

Literature and legends

Working with diverse abilities and needs

Nicola Grove and Maureen Phillip

Background

Many of the chapters in this book reference works of written fiction, used as a basis for retelling or performing (see *inter alia* Dowling, Chapter 1). The multi-sensory story books described by Fornefeld (Chapter 12) and Lambe, Miller and Phillip (Chapter 17) also illustrate how boundaries are blurred between the act of reading aloud and the act of telling. The world of stories and storytelling is hybrid and fluid. This chapter will provide a summary of some 30 years work on developing access to literature for people who find it hard to read or to follow a complex written text (even if read aloud). Children and adults with profound intellectual and multiple disabilities (PIMD) are our starting point for an inclusive approach. We define literature broadly as any text of cultural significance: novels, plays, poetry and non-fiction genres such as biography or essays. Any of these can contain a "story", which we consider flexibly as an account of a significant experience.

History

We were both voracious readers as children and studied English literature at university.

Nicola was working in a special school in 1988 when the National Curriculum was launched in England and Wales. Originally, special education was exempt, and it took the civil servants in charge by surprise when teachers actually demanded access for this population, on the grounds of a right to inclusion.[1] The 1990s saw an explosion of creativity in expanding topics and subjects to all children. The intervening years have seen something of a backlash against subject-based teaching, and here is not the place to rehearse arguments about whether we should be returning to a narrower curriculum, focused more on needs than access. Nonetheless, gains were made that have enabled learners of all abilities to participate in some of the same culturally important topic-based learning as their peers in mainstream. With enough imagination, richly inclusive curricula can be designed to address learning and developmental needs within stimulating contexts of experience (Grove & Peacey, 1999; see also McCaffrey, Chapter 4; Park, Chapter 6; Grace, Chapter 15).

For Nicola, using literature as a source for teaching emerged from exploring the use of narrative frameworks to deliver communication objectives (Grove & Park, 1996, 2001; Pulli, Chapter 16). At that time, two types of story were used with pupils with severe learning disabilities: highly structured accounts designed to teach independence skills – of

DOI: 10.4324/9781003159087-11

the *Peter Learns to Clean his Teeth* variety – which have a place, but are not much fun to be honest – or the reading and dramatisation of stories aimed at younger children, and deemed appropriate because of the "mental age" of the learners – for example, reading *Who Sank the Boat* to a group of 16–18 year olds.[2] It must be emphasised that if the story is good enough, there is really no problem about age appropriateness (we yield to no-one in our admiration and love of *Where the Wild Things Are*). The problems are the lack of range and opportunity, the low expectations and the mismatch between what is on offer and the chronological ages and experiences of the young people. The school had an ambitious drama programme, and the school leavers put on *West Side Story*. The two leads were in a romantic relationship, but knew they faced separation, with little prospect of seeing each other ever again, because of family pressures, location and their own inability to connect.[3] Frankly, *Who Sank the Boat* wouldn't have had a lot to offer, but in *West Side Story* they were able to act out some of their passion and their loss.

Through working with teachers and pupils and exploring different frameworks, a format for adapting texts was designed which proved successful enough for schools to take on board, with the result that it is common now to see teachers prepared to work with many classic works of fiction (Lawson et al., 2012). Subsequently, the charity Openstorytellers[4] began to run multi-sensory book clubs with classic literature (*Treasure Island, Christmas Carol, Far from the Madding Crowd*). Maureen and Promoting A More Inclusive Society (PAMIS) have also spent years researching both fictional and personal multi-sensory storytelling, based on Fuller's work (see Chapters 13 and 17).

Theories and principles

The basic principles relate to how we understand literature, partial participation, the nature of language and cultural access.

The nature of literature

Literature is not the same as *literacy*. You do not need to be able to read or write to enjoy or indeed create stories, plays and poetry. Literature should be seen as a creative art form, overlapping with drama, dance and music.

Literature comes alive in the mind of the "reader"/experiencer (see Beach, 1993). Canonical literary theory maintained that the meaning of a text resided literally in the words on the page; a moment's reflection is enough to falsify this premise. You only have to take part in a reading group to marvel at how differently people respond to the same book. Meaning goes beyond text, and our experience of literature is strongly coloured by how we receive it, for example particular performances or adaptations. This gives us a lot of freedom to explore and change the way we develop texts for audiences who have diverse language skills.

Partial participation

The term was coined by Baumgart and colleagues (1982). Essentially what this means is that you can enjoy and understand *something*, without having to understand *everything*. The key is to find the hooks within a text to which your students will respond (and these will vary with individual preferences and abilities).

Language: communication and aesthetics

It is all too easy to think that because a person's cognitive and language skills are at an early level of development, all language addressed to them should be stripped down and simplified. This is of course both necessary and useful in many contexts – for example when you are instructing them, or giving them information about what is going to happen (see Gray, Chapter 18). However, language is also used to communicate feelings, atmosphere and as an art form – in song, and poetry. People can and do respond to and enjoy the sound and feel of language (Trevarthen, 2009). For example, one teenager with a very short attention span loved to recite long words ending in "-ion" like "situation", "exclamation" and "aspiration". She collected them like pebbles from a beach. (If I had known then what I know now, we would have encouraged her to perform rap poetry. So you need to work on two levels at once – language that moves the plot along or explains the text, and language as sensation – music, recitation, movement. Changes in the tone, pitch and volume of the voice help people to engage with and follow the story. The use of the voice in a story is also beneficial for those supporting someone with PIMD.

Cultural access

Books remain hugely popular. Book groups and clubs, literary events and festivals have all mushroomed. Festival communities in Scotland are now beginning to actively include multi-sensory storytelling into their standard festival programmes. Literary and storytelling for people with PIMD can be variable, fun and exciting, weaving together to create a variety of experiences that add culture, colour and vibrancy to the lives of people with PIMD and their support networks. For example, *Felix After the Rain* (Jogan, 2020) explores friendship and sadness. People with PIMD rarely get opportunities to explore emotions, and literature can provide these opportunities within a safe framework. For the Edinburgh International Book Festival 2020, people with PIMD chose to be actively involved in the creating and performing of a multi-sensory version of the book at the festival, visible to an international audience.[5] This gave them a sense of pride and achievement and the event helped raise awareness of emotions and responses related to friendship and sadness.

Work in practice

Teaching and learning framework: the text

Adapting literature is about what you leave out as well as what you keep in!

- Follow a simple logical storyline that feels true to the original; leave out subplots unless there is a very good reason to keep them in.
- You can leave out whole sections as long as there is a narrative flow and time to establish characters and the key elements of the plot.
- Don't avoid the dark aspects of a story, but treat them gently and lightly, de-emphasise terror and despair, and always end with a positive message of hope and empowerment. Feeling a bit scared in a safe environment is a very important learning experience, but must be contained, and de-briefed.

Steps in adaptation

1   Read the book! Have a notebook and pencil to hand. Have two columns, one for epi-sodes, characters, events, plot lines, chunks of text that you intuitively think will work particularly well; the other for aspects you think should be omitted.
2   Jot down all your great ideas.
3   Think through *why* these will work/not work. Having a strong argument will really help you draw up your framework.
4   Consider responses you will be looking for in learners.
5   Make a plan. The following can be useful headings:

Genre: what kind of book is it (this helps you decide on atmosphere and can be really good for selecting musical accompaniment, or scenic projection, e.g. ghost stories, romance, pirates, detective).

Themes: make a note of the main themes and messages in the text, e.g. *Pride and Prejudice* – "don't judge by first impressions". Themes help you to identify topics for discussion.

Plot: plan out the major episodes. In general, we find that for a novel, eight episodes works well, with an introduction and closing session making for a ten-session project (which can of course be extended or shortened as required).

Characters: we tend to stick with main characters (unless a minor character has a particular appeal). Think of ways in which each can be associated with a prop, item of costume, catchphrase.

Settings/scenes: contrast works well, e.g. *court* vs *wood* in *Midsummer Night's Dream, ship* vs *island* in *Treasure Island*. Don't use so many different scenes that you confuse people.

Text selections: for each episode, find sections of text that you can read out loud, dramatise, project onto the wall, cut up and play around with. We regard this as the one absolute non-negotiable in accessing literature. Just paraphrasing and acting out bits of story is great fun but it's not engaging with the wonderful mind and words of the authors, which is what we really want to offer our students.

Props and resources: for each episode, draw up a list of sensory resources, bearing in mind that too many of these will distract from what you are doing and can lead to overload.

Teaching and learning framework: the learners

The next task is to bring together the text and your learners. As an example, Maureen offers an approach to a classic story.

Alice's Adventures in Wonderland

Not only does literature entertain and teach but it can be a powerful tool to support people through challenging times in their lives. This story offers a multi-sensory, multi-faceted adventure that is colourful, varied and full of amazing characters, which makes it a safe and fun way to explore people and emotions. Tenniel's illustrations are integral to the story, and can be projected, or made into large pictures.

Jenny is a young school leaver who is fearful about entering adult services. The theme of bravery is perfect for exploring her anxieties and fears alongside Alice. There are so many scenes in the story where Alice shows courage, and over time Jenny's fear lessens and her confidence grows in the role of the character By the end of the programme Jenny wants to continue the work and creates a personal story that reflects her own bravery.

The script is prepared with the theme of bravery in mind and Alice's courageous moments are celebrated. Alice meets many strange characters, most of whom make no sense at all, but Alice resolutely continues her journey, getting stronger and more assertive as her adventure progresses.

1   Identify the theme.
2   Identify the group.
3   Together, choose the story roles and characters they will portray, with Jenny as Alice.
4   Profile how each individual communicates. Include sensory likes and dislikes as this helps to select stimuli to allow everyone to gain maximum benefit from their interactions (see Flo Longhorn's *The Sensology Workout – Waking Up the Senses*[6]). Incorporate functional assessments (e.g. vision and hearing).
5   Use this information to refine the text to include anything that will enhance the experience of the individuals involved.
6   Pull out all the words or signs of Alice's brave actions in the text as emphasis of the theme of bravery in the story and relate them to Jenny as the main character where appropriate.

Alice choosing to explore new places

- Down the rabbit hole – create tunnels and the sensation of going down, down, down: "burning with curiosity ... down went Alice after the White Rabbit, never once considering how in the world she was to get out again" ... "curiouser and curiouser".
- Through the little door with the golden key into the beautiful garden – among the bright flowers and cool fountains: "Now I'll manage better this time".

Confronting and coping with characters who challenge

- The caterpillar's probing questions "Who are you?" force Alice to reflect on her new identity.
- The Red Queen "Off with their heads" with the screaming baby is scary, but Alice is strong enough to outface her.

After 8–10 weeks the story will be familiar to the group and you could continue the transition work with Jenny by creating a personal story. This would incorporate Jenny's anxieties in relation to change, linking her feelings, actions and courage with those of Alice.

Working with legends

Similar approaches can of course be used with the legends, folktales and myths that inform our cultural identities. Handed down through generations, they are part of our heritage. They are in the landscape all around us, in the hills, forests, seas and mountains and villages and cities. The essence of the story should not be lost in the adaptation, but the expansive freedom to create a magical experience allows artistic freedom to flourish. Legends also allow learners to share in other cultures – work in Japan, South Africa and Canada revealed many stories that featured characters who were different in some way, and whose stories could motivate and inspire (Grove et al., 2016).

Outcomes and evidence: what we look for

We aim for engagement, enjoyment and response to the text – its meaning, themes, characters – the sound of the language and some level of recognition of *what this means to me*. One young woman, responding to Sergeant Troy's manipulative behaviour in Thomas Hardy's *Far from the Madding Crowd*, actually started to say *no* in the role of the heroine, and to generalise this at home (she had previously been acquiescent). You know when literature has been understood when the group want to create a follow-on story. After working on Roald Dahl's *Charlie and the Chocolate Factory*, one group created their own multi-sensory story – *Life After Charlie's Chocolate Factory*. In doing so, they demonstrated their knowledge of the original, which turned out to be substantial, as well as considerable knowledge of the type of stimuli suited to each individual.

For a more detailed account of outcomes based on observations, see the account of Grove and colleagues (2015) of responses by a mixed ability class in a special school to Dickens' *Oliver Twist*.

Contexts of learning

Places and spaces

Literature, storytelling and learning can happen anywhere, and do not have to be confined to the classroom. Walks, visits to parks and heritage sites, museums and galleries offer perfect spaces for storytelling. In fact, taking literary experience to communities is an excellent way of simultaneously raising awareness of people with PIMD and encouraging organisers to be more inclusive. Festivals are rich, vibrant cultural celebrations that are varied and exciting. There are book festivals, nature festivals, folklore festivals, music festivals and many more. They all offer opportunities to weave multi-sensory storytelling and literature into their existing programmes, making them an ideal day out for families and a wonderful way to engage people with PIMD in stories, and indeed in civic and global issues (Gersie et. al., 2014). There is nothing more rewarding than erecting and decorating an accessible story yurt, at a festival, ready for an experience that transports people to the magical world of stories.

Creativity for supporters

If the story captivates the supporter too, they are more likely to continue the practice themselves with story sessions. For example, mothers attending a storytelling group with their children have gone on to develop their own multi-sensory stories. The ability of literature and stories to open a creative space is powerful, as the following quote from a parent illustrates:

> The last time I wrote anything was many years ago when I was still in Uni. The last few weeks have been incredibly enjoyable for me. Every time I sat down with pen and pencil

in my hand, I felt this warm, comforting feeling inside my chest. Ever since I was a child, I loved drawing and writing but somehow as it usually happens in life, I disconnected from it. Thank you again for bringing this exciting light back into my life. I used to have a dream when I was a child, that one day I would write something in English.

Issues to consider

Choosing books

When pupils are choosing books the following factors should be taken into account:

- What their peers are reading and enjoying
- Classic stories giving access to valued culture
- Their own interests – What films and television programmes are they watching? What does this tell you about themes that engage them?
- Stories to challenge and stretch the imagination
- Stories for managing problems and human relationships, e.g. loss, change, arguments
- Stories that address issues they will certainly encounter, through exposure to news and current affairs, e.g. racial discrimination, immigration, asylum seekers, climate change, but also positive stories of achievement
- Stories that feature familiar experiences, and characters like themselves.

Age appropriateness: young people and adults

In early years and primary stages it is generally very easy to use the range of excellent children's books available, where the language is simple and direct. Of course these can continue to be used as favourites to share at older ages. For teenagers, writing is often more complex and challenging. We are beginning to explore contemporary literature, searching out writers with an interest in adapting their work for young people with special educational needs. The same principles apply, so if you find a book you love, have a go!

Cultural factors

Look for books that are culturally diverse and that feature people with disabilities, to promote a sense of visibility and pride (Henderson et al., 2020; Short, 2018) https://www.children sbookacademy.com/blogonauts/the-importance-of-diversity-in-childrens-books (accessed 3.1.21).

Try it yourself

Top tips

- Choose books you really love and want to share.
- Run a taster – before embarking on a whole book try out a couple of episodes.
- Write the text sections you want to use clearly on separate cards on a key ring so that you can easily find them, and perform them (rather than just reading them out).

Where to go

PAMIS has a range of multi-sensory resources available on its website at: https://pamis.org.uk.
Stories from Japan and other cultures can be found at: www.drnicolagrove.com.
Detailed guidance for adapting texts along with several examples can be found in *Ways into Literature* (Grove, 2005).

Notes

1 In the UK it was only in 1970 that education was extended to include those with profound and complex needs, previously catered for in care institutions or hospitals.
2 Observed in 1992.
3 I know, right? Hard to imagine a time before mobile phones for all and social media.
4 www.openstorytellers.org.uk.
5 *Felix After the Rain: A Sensory Story from PAMIS* – Learning, Edinburgh International Book Festival. Available at: (edbookfest.co.uk) (Accessed 3.5.21).
6 https://sites.google.com/view/flolonghornsensorybooksfreedow/home (Accessed 3.5.21). This is a free download.

Acknowledgements

We gratefully acknowledge the support of funders and of the learners, families, teachers and therapists who have collaborated in adapting works of literature in innovative ways.

References

Baumgart, D., Brown, L., Pumpian, I., Nisbet, J., Ford, A., Sweet, M., Messina, R. & Schroeder, J. (1982). Principle of partial participation and individualized adaptations in educational programs for severely handicapped students. *Research and Practice for Persons with Severe Disabilities*, 7(2), 17–27.
Beach, R. (1993). *A teacher's introduction to reader-response theories*. Urbana, IL: National Council of Teachers of English.
Gersie, A., Nanson, A., Schieffelin, E., Collison, C. & Cree, J. (Eds). (2014). *Storytelling for a greener world: Environment, community and story based learning*. Stroud, Glos: Hawthorn Press.
Grove, N. (2005). *Ways into literature*. London: David Fulton.
Grove, N., Harwood, J., Henderson, E., Park, K. & Bird, R. (2015). Literature and stories in the lives of pupils with severe and profound learning difficulties. In P. Lacey, R. Ashdown, P. Jones, H. Lawson & M. Pipe (Eds), *The Routledge companion to severe, profound and multiple learning difficulties* (pp. 305–315). London: Taylor & Francis.
Grove, N. & Park, K. (1996) *Odyssey NOW*. London: Jessica Kingsley Publishers.
Grove, N. & Park, K. (2001). *Social communication through drama and literature for people with learning disabilities: Macbeth in mind*. London: Jessica Kingsley Publishers.
Grove, N. & Peacey, N. (1999).Teaching subjects to pupils with profound and multiple learning difficulties: Considerations for the new framework. *British Journal of Special Education*, 26(2), 83–86.
Grove, N., Takano, M., Udo, M. & Mitsudo, Y. (2016). Heroes with a difference: Legends and personal stories with Japanese school children. *SLD Experience*, Spring, 3–5.
Henderson, J., Warren, K., Whitmore, K., Flint, A., Laman, T. & Jaggers, W. (2020). Take a close look: Inventorying your classroom library for diverse books. *The Reading Teacher*, 73(6), 747–755.

Jogan, D. (2020). *Felix after the rain*. London: Tiny Owl Publishing.

Lawson, H., Layton, L., Goldbart, J., Lacey, P. & Miller, C. (2012). Conceptualisations of literacy and literacy practices for children with severe learning difficulties. *Literacy*, 46, 101–108.

Short, K. (2018). What's trending in children's literature and why it matters. *Language Arts*, 95(5), 287–298.

Trevarthen, C. (2009). The functions of emotion in infancy: The regulation and communication of rhythm, sympathy, and meaning in human development. In Diana Fosha, Daniel J. Siegel & Marion F. Solomon (Eds), *The healing power of emotion: Affective neuroscience, development, and clinical practice* (pp. 55–85). New York: Norton.

Chapter 12

Storytelling with all our senses mehr-Sinn® Geschichten

Barbara Fornefeld

Background

mehr-Sinn® Geschichten (multisensory stories) are stories which are not simply told but can be experienced with all our senses. They are stories to look at, listen to, smell and taste, feel and experience. They have their own way to be told and they are stored in story-boxes. Since they can be experienced by multiple senses and can be characterised by a simple but expressive language and inspiring music to evoke atmospheres and emotions, multisensory stories have developed into recreational options for families and educational options for institutions for people with profound intellectual and multiple disabilities (PIMD) and homes for elderly people.

Although mehr-Sinn® Geschichten were originally developed for children, adolescents and adults with profound and multiple disabilities, they can also give pleasure to people without any disabilities. They aim to eliminate the prejudice that people with profound disabilities are unable to understand fairy tales and other stories. Additionally, they aim to enable them to experience cultural participation.

mehr-Sinn® Geschichten have been developed in a common project between Cologne University and the association KuBus®.[1] Professionally supported students retell the contents of fairy tales,[2] myths,[3] legends[4] or tales from the Bible[5] and prepare educational versions. They elaborate non-fiction stories[6] with corresponding materials and put them into practice with people with PIMD. Subsequently, KuBus started to distribute them (see Figure 12.1).

An attractive wooden box stores sensory materials like soft rag dolls, glittering bowls, small boxes with odorous spices and many other inspiring things. The materials have been developed and compiled in cooperation with an institution for people with PIMD in Heisbergrucken, Germany. The story box contains a CD with appropriate music and sounds that have been specifically composed and recorded for each multisensory story by Hans Steinmeier, composer, arranger and director of the North-Rhine Westphalian Federal Police Orchestra, and his co-musicians. Each is also equipped with a director's booklet including the narrative texts and special hints for how to present and narrate the story, supported by its materials, in an easily understandable way. In the case of a fairy tale, a print of the original version is included. A handbook gives information about the development and the method of multisensory storytelling. See www.kubus-ev.de.

The underlying idea is that multisensory storytelling always addresses the person as a whole and not only her or his cognitive abilities. The sound of the narrator's voice, her or his activities, the sensory materials and the music awaken emotions and create images. In

DOI: 10.4324/9781003159087-12

Figure 12.1 Little Red Riding Hood in a box

experiencing through their different senses, comprehension is made possible for people with profound disabilities.

Theory and principles

The concept of multisensory storytelling combines elements of the storytelling method with the old tradition of narrating fairy tales. It systematically explores fairy tales, myths and legends from the German heritage – and those of other countries too.

Fairy tales originate from a time when only a few people were able to read and very few possessed books. It was an oral time, when stories were orally passed on from one generation to the next and were cultivated by all social classes. At that time storytelling was a means to relax, escape from everyday life and accompany the transition from waking to sleeping (cf. Wittenhorst, 2010: 28ff). These customs survive today.

In the eighteenth century, the brothers Jacob and William Grimm collected national myths and fairy tales in order to explore them scientifically, a work which has met with great approval in many countries. Today, the 'brothers Grimm' are known as the founders of German philology and their collection of fairy tales has become famous all over the world.

Fairy tales, myths, legends and other genres of narration represent a part of our culture that accompanies us while we are growing up. Who does not like to remember her or his childhood, being read to aloud at bedtime or other situations when stories carried us off into extraordinary, cosy or remote atmospheres? We were not always able to understand every word of the story immediately, but we always experienced the tension or the wit of the story and always felt touched by it. Most of us have happy memories of these narrative moments, with their special interpersonal relationships.

Stories and fairy tales touch us in a special way and lead us to 'the things themselves', to our fundamental experiences and emotions like fear, grief, hope or pride. They relate to basic needs of mankind, like appreciation or security. They concern 'man as she/he really is' (cf. Lüthi, 2004).

People with profound disabilities have fundamental experiences and needs. They have lived through fear, grief, hope, pride or defiance, and they long for security and appreciation. Parents, who are often closer to their children's emotions than others, are able to recognise these experiences and needs. But carers in institutions for people with PIMD, who usually express themselves only in spoken language, sometimes cannot imagine that understanding without language is also possible. People with profound disabilities express their understanding of the world by means of changes in behaviour. Carers who have not learned to look at such changes or to listen to them tend to miss these behavioural expressions and the basic experiences and needs of people with PIMD. Carers might also think that stories are simply told by means of spoken words and can only be understood on a rational level. But the narrator's voice, the prosody of her or his language and the special atmosphere also help people to understand a story. Barbara Senckel (2002), who researched the effects of fairy tales on people with profound disabilities, came to the conclusion that they are an appropriate genre of literature for these children and adults. Fairy tales not only represent a common cultural heritage where people with and without disabilities can meet each other, but also open up opportunities for them both to develop their personalities.

People with PIMD are able to understand the content of stories if the stories are told in a way they are able to understand. The concept of mehr-Sinn® Geschichten is based on cultural studies and educational science, and its method of multisensory storytelling is based on an educational theory. The story-boxes with their sensory materials stimulate aesthetic experiences that make it easier to understand the story as a whole. This idea was expressed by a carer in a workshop for people with PIMD, who was asked about the listeners' reactions to the storytelling: 'They were curious, interested, some were very alert. You could see their joy, tension and pleasure. The target to experience the story by multiple senses has been achieved.'

This statement shows that stories can be understood on a pre-narrative[7] or pre-verbal level, an aspect which up to now has been insufficiently explored by special education. Stories address people in a special way that refers to the person as a whole. They help to generate identity and bring people closer to each other.

mehr-Sinn® Geschichten are inspired by Nicola Grove's *Ways into Literature* (2005) as well as by Loretto Lambe and James Hogg's multisensory storytelling (Lambe & Hogg, 2011). They also go back to Chris Fuller's idea of 'Bag Books' (Fuller, 1999) and her method of telling a story in a simple way. However, mehr-Sinn® Geschichten differ from the approach of multisensory storytelling with regard to their theoretical principles, their intentions, the aesthetic composition of the story-boxes and materials and the method of storytelling.

The educational concept of mehr-Sinn® Geschichten results from a long-term scientific discussion about the education of people with PIMD. It started in the 1980s with practical experiences in the education of pupils with profound disabilities and with the effort to provide them with cultural and educational content. The discussion about a sense-oriented pedagogy by Langeveld and Danner (1981), a phenomenology of perception by Merleau-

Ponty (1966)[8] and an aesthetic experience by Waldenfels (2010) and Wiesing (2009) led to a pedagogic concept for people with PIMD by Fornefeld (1991, 2001), which concentrates on the philosophy of the *Leib* and postulates the comprehension and experience of cultural opportunities which are perceptible to the senses. Multisensory storytelling assumes that narrators and listeners share common experiences. The process of storytelling initiates a dialogue between them, which is based on intercorporeality[9] (cf. Fornefeld, 2009). This dialogue proves the importance of literacy experiences (cf. Groß-Kunkel, 2011), which help people with PIMD to understand the main plot of a literary text if it is edited and condensed to its essential elements (cf. Heinen, 2003).

Work in practice

Each mehr-Sinn Geschichte with its sensory materials is described in the manual provided in the box. 'The story-boxes are designed in such an inspiring way. You do not have to look for materials. Everything is immediately at hand', reported a speech therapist who was testing mehr-Sinn® Geschichten in her practice at an early stage of development of our project. One student who cares for an elderly lady in an old people's home relates that the old lady always asks her: 'You've got a box with you, don't you?' She particularly likes the fairy tale of *Little Red Riding Hood* because it reminds her of her childhood.

mehr-Sinn® Geschichten are not just suitable for people with profound disabilities but for everybody, because they turn the process of storytelling into an extraordinary experience. Each story is printed in a shorter and a longer version so that it can be adapted to the listener's level of comprehension. For fairy tales like *Hansel and Gretel* or legends like The Wolf and the Seven Little Goats a copy of the original version is also included. 'Due to the different versions of the story, the music and the materials all the children in a group can benefit from the storytelling process,' a kindergarten worker said after she had tried a mehr-Sinn® Geschichte with her heterogeneous group and all the children enthusiastically joined in. This shows that mehr-Sinn® Geschichten are inclusive, too.

Interviews with carers who have been working with mehr-Sinn® Geschichten in different institutions for people with PIMD prove that these people can benefit from these experiences. A remedial teacher working with a group of adults with profound disabilities said:

> First our residents were irritated when I put the story-box with *The Oriental Market* on the table. But after I had told the story once, they wanted to listen to it again and again and refused to stop. All were very attentive, even those I would have never expected it from. It gives me so much pleasure to tell stories in such a way.

Another carer told the mehr-Sinn® Geschichte *Hansel and Gretel* (according to the brothers Grimm) to children with PIMD and reported: 'The children have come closer to me'. Video recordings of single case studies about multisensory storytelling have revealed that people with PIMD listen to the stories, turn towards the narrators and react to them.

The story of Jens

In a school for blind children, Britta Sommer, a student, chose the religious mehr-Sinn® Geschichte *Jesus and the Storm* to work with 7-year-old Jens. This boy has profound intellectual impairments; he is blind and was born with tetraplegia. While his classmates were being taught he was just present in the room. Mrs Sommer was firmly convinced that Jens would be able to understand something if he was offered appropriate subject matter. Therefore she developed the religious story *Jesus and the Storm* for him. Jens showed by his body tension and smacking sounds that he always enjoyed it when she entered the class. He liked the story and wanted to listen to it again and again. Mrs Sommer commented on his reactions: 'It is my personal desire to create other multisensory story-boxes in order to let pupils with profound disabilities participate in religious education'. To tell and listen to stories connects people with each other. It connects adults with children, and people with and without profound disabilities. Storytelling has a social impact because it builds bridges between people.

Development of mehr-Sinn® Geschichten

In order to achieve the aim of promoting understanding, mehr-Sinn® Geschichten require a process of multidimensional development and analysis (Figure 12.2), which normally takes six months and tries to address the following issues:

1   At the beginning there is the story, the literary original or the so-called 'what', which undergoes a scientific and didactic analysis according to linguistic and educational classification, structure of language and content and educational implementation.
2   The question of 'how' to transmit the content and 'how' to dramatise the narration should be answered as follows:

 a   The plot should be told in precise words and simple sentences.
 b   The dramatisation of the story should also consider the decision on 'with what' and refer to all sensory materials and music.
 c   With regard to 'who' is involved, mehr-Sinn® Geschichten differentiate between two target persons, the listener and the narrator. Narrating and listening are closely linked to each other and have to be carefully harmonised.
 d   Next is the question of 'where'. An appropriate atmosphere of narration is important for the sensory–aesthetic process of comprehension, which means that we need to specify the appropriate time and place.
 e   The 'what for', which is the aim of achieving cultural and social participation, also has to be considered in relation to dramatisation, materials, situation and content.

When developing mehr-Sinn® Geschichten, special emphasis has to be put on the prosody of the language and the quality of the music because both support the process of sensory–aesthetic comprehension (cf. Brandstätter, 2008, Lampson, 2010).

Outcomes and evidence: what we look for

Once the process of developing a mehr-Sinn® Geschichte is finished, the quality of the story has to be tested in single case studies with regard to content, dramatisation, materials and music. Video analyses are carried out by means of criteria-based behaviour observations (Schnitzler, 2008; Lehmann, 2009; Wittenhorst, 2010; Schulte, 2011; Sommer, 2011; Naumann, 2011). Between September 2010 and January 2011 six new mehr-Sinn® Geschichten were tested in 25 institutions such as families, kindergartens, special schools for mentally disabled, physically disabled or blind people, homes for the elderly and homes for

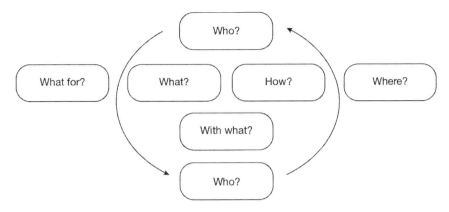

Figure 12.2 The multidimensional development of mehr-sinn® Geschichten

people with PIMD. All participants showed distinct reactions of attention, such as changed breathing frequency, a turn of the head, a smile or a vocalisation, when they were listening to the story for the first time. These reactions became increasingly distinctive, and the participants showed by their behaviour which parts of the story, which sensory materials and which music especially touched them. In all cases the listeners' behaviour corresponded to the special atmosphere.

The quality of the stories was evaluated by means of semi-structured questionnaires and narrative interviews. All feedback was positive, the innovative character of the concept was emphasised and its practicality was approved. Suggestions by the institutions were integrated into our concept; for example, longer versions of the texts for listeners with greater speech comprehension. So we developed a second plot, concerning logic and language, which fits into the first one. This new version now enables us to tell the new stories in mixed groups.

Since the method of multisensory storytelling is new to many people, we were asked to develop an educational programme which addresses parents, carers and students. This programme is based on three key aspects:

1 Getting to know the concept of mehr-Sinn® Geschichten.
2 Experiencing by one's own senses as a basis to understand and interact.
3 Getting to know and experiencing the basic methods of mehr-Sinn® Geschichten.

Although many people work with mehr-Sinn® Geschichten in various ways, the project is still a work in progress, and new stories are continuously being developed in many countries. In order to broaden the concept, we are observing what others do with the stories, listening to their experiences and paying attention to how people with profound disabilities react. Since everyone involved is attentively listening to each other, closer inter-relationships are being established between listeners, storytellers and researchers.

Notes

1 The Association to Promote Culture, Education and Social Participation for People with and without Disabilities.
2 For example, *Hansel and Gretel* or *Little Red Riding Hood*, after the brothers Grimm.

3 For example, *The Myth of the Giant Mils*.
4 For example, *The Little People from Cologne*, after August Kopisch.
5 *Jesus and the Storm* (Sommer, 2011).
6 *A Walk in the Wood* or *The Boxing Match*.
7 Pre-narrative refers to a philosophical dimension of interpretation.
8 The concept of mehr-Sinn® Geschichten is based on, among others, the *Phenomenology of Perception* (1945) by Maurice Merleau-Ponty. He defines phenomenology as the study of essences, including the essence of perception and of consciousness. He also says, however, that phenomenology is a method of describing the nature of our perceptual contact with the world. Phenomenology is concerned with providing a direct description of human experience. Perception is the background of experience which guides every conscious action.
9 A fundamental dialogue between people; their responsivity.

References

Brandstätter, U. (2008). *Grundfragen der Ästhetik. Bild – Musik – Sprache – Körper*. Cologne, Weimar and Vienna: Böhlau UTB.

Fornefeld, B. (1991). 'Wahr-nehmen' und 'Sinn-stiften' des (behinderten) Menschen. Anthropologisch-pädagogische Aspekte kindlicher Erkenntnisgewinnung. *Behinderte in Familie, Schule und Gesellschaft*, 14(3), 25–33.

Fornefeld, B. (1997). *Elementare Beziehung und Selbstverwirklichung geistig Schwerstbehinderter in sozialer Integration. Reflexionen im Vorfeld einer leiborientierten Pädagogik* (3rd ed.). PhD dissertation, University of Cologne. Aachen: Mainz Verlag.

Fornefeld, B. (2001). 'Wahr-nehmen' und 'Sinn-stiften' des behinderten Menschen. In K. Rühl & A. Längle (Eds), *Ich kann nicht … Behinderung als menschliches Phänomen* (pp. 27–39). Vienna: WUV-Universitätsverlag.

Fornefeld, B. (2009). Bei Leibe gebildet – Sonderpädagogische Impulse. *Zeitschrift für Heilpädagogik*, 60(3), 107–114.

Fuller, C. (1999). Bag Books tactile stories. *The SLD Experience*, 23, 20–21.

Groß-Kunkel, A. (2011). Literacy-Erlebnisse für Menschen mit und ohne Behinderung. Soziale Teilhabe durch gemeinsames Lesen. In B. Fornefeld (Ed.), *Mehr-sinnliches Geschichtenerzählen: Eine Idee setzt sich durch* [Multi-sensory storytelling: An idea gets through]. Berlin, Munster and London: Lit Verlag.

Grove, N. (2005). *Ways into literature*. London: David Fulton.

Heinen, N. (2003). Überlegungen zur Didaktik mit Menschen mit schwerer Behinderung: eine Zwischenbilanz. In Schulentwicklung. Gestaltungs(t)räume in der Arbeit mit schwerstbehinderten Schülerinnen und Schülern. In A. Fröhlich, W. Lamers & N. Heinen (Eds), *Texte zur Körper – und Mehrfachbehindertenpädagogik* (pp. 121–143). Dusseldorf: Verlag Selbstbestimmtes Leben.

Lambe, L. & Hogg, J. (2011). Multi-sensory storytelling: PAMIS' practice, experience and research findings. In B. Fornefeld (Ed.), *Mehr-sinnliches Geschichtenerzählen: Eine Idee setzt sich durch* [Multi-sensory storytelling: An idea gets through] (pp. 15–40). Berlin, Munster and London: Lit Verlag.

Lampson, E. (2010). Spiegelungen der Stille: Zwischen Hören und Denken. *Journal Phänomenologie*, 33, 20–26.

Langeveld, M. J. & Danner, H. (1981). *Methodologie und Sinn-Orientierung in der Pädagogik*. Munich: Ernst Reinhardt.

Lehmann, K. (2009). mehr-Sinn® Geschichten. Ein Mehr an kultureller Teilhabe für Menschen mit schwerer Behinderung. Examination paper, Cologne University.

Lüthi, M. (2004). *Märchen* (10th ed.). Stuttgart and Weimar: Metzler Verlag.

Merleau-Ponty, M. (1945). *Phenomenology of Perception*. Paris: Gaillard.

Merleau-Ponty, M. (1966). *Phänomenologie der Wahrnehmung*. Berlin: Walter de Gruyter.

Naumann, M. (2011). Freizeitpädagogik für Menschen mit Komplexer Behinderung? Mehr-sinnliches Geschichtenerzählen: Ein anwendungsbezogenes Schulungskonzept. Diploma thesis, Cologne University.

Schnitzler, M. (2008). Kulturelle Lebenswelten für Schüler mit schwerer Behinderung. Eine mehr-Sinn® Geschichte für Lea. Examination paper, Cologne University.

Schulte, I. P. (2011). Bildung mit mehr-Sinn®: Responsivität und Bildung. Examination paper, Cologne University.

Senckel, B. (2002). 'In den alten Zeiten, wo das Wünschen noch geholfen hat ...' Märchenstrukturen und die Struktur präoperativen Denkens. *Geistige Behinderung*, 41(2), 115–125.

Sommer, B. (2011). 'Jesus und der Sturm': mehr-Sinn® Geschichten als religiöse Teilhabe für Menschen mit schwerer Behinderung. Examination paper, Cologne University.

Waldenfels, B. (2010). *Sinne und Künste im Wechselspiel. Modi ästhetischer Erfahrung*. Frankfurt: Suhrkamp Verlag.

Wiesing, L. (2009). *Das Mich der Wahrnehmung: Eine Autopsie*. Frankfurt: Suhrkamp Verlag.

Wittenhorst, M. (2010). Geschichtenerzählen einmal anders: Märchen erleben durch mehr-sinnliches Geschichtenerzählen. Examination paper, Cologne University.

Chapter 13

Multi-sensory story-packs

Chris Fuller

Background

This approach to storytelling was designed for children, young people and adults who are unlikely to be able to appreciate regular stories because of their profound intellectual and multiple disabilities (PIMD), and it requires the stories to be in a particular physical format. The pages are individual A3 laminated cards or A4 for smaller hands, for children aged 1–2, with sensory objects and materials attached, for the listener to handle, hear, smell, look at and feel as the story unfolds. It is known as the multi-sensory storytelling technique (MSST).

Example: *Hide and Squeak* for children aged 1–2 years

Pages:

1   One day Nia heard a noise, a *squeak squeak* like this.
2   "I *think* it's coming from outside," said Gran, so they went into the garden.
3   "Perhaps it's in the shed," she said. So Nia opened the door. "*NO* ... only *rubbish* in here!" 4. "Maybe it's in the flowers? Ooooh the flowers smell *lovely!*"
4   Just then, a little bag fell off the washing line. "*Aah HA*, there's a lump in here ... a hairbrush. What's *that* doing in there!"
5   *Suddenly* ... tiny feet *sped* across the patio and over the lawn ...
6   And there, under the tree, was a little grey mouse and he was ... *squeaking! Action.* "*Oh*," said Gran, "he must have been in the house *all the time*. He's a *rascal*, Nia Rose ... *just... like... YOU!*" *The listener gets a tickle!*

Contents:

1   Furnishing fabric behind toy dog covered in glitter fabric and hanging on gold ribbon (toy dog only need a little pressure to squeak)
2   Fake grass
3   Hinged plywood door 3. Inside door: pleated polypropylene (IKEA bag)
4   Scented fabric flowers on sky blue felt
5   Bag front and brush
6   Canvas behind flapping string of beads
7   Cork tile tree, mouse (squeak inserted) in velvet pouch.

DOI: 10.4324/9781003159087-13

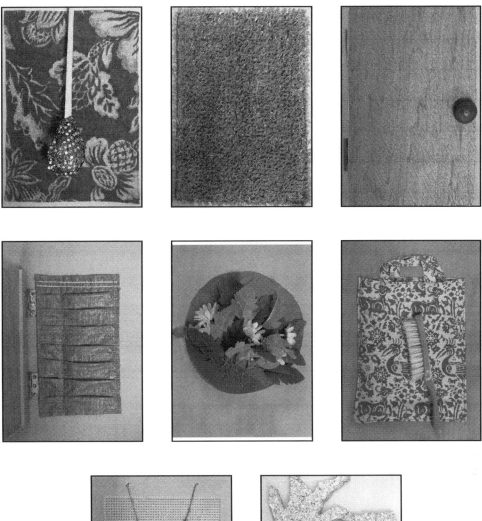
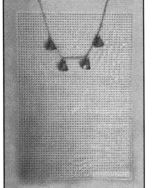

Figure 13.1 Example of a story-pack

In a story-pack every action required to make the page 'work' must cater for any physical disability, so size, shape – objects must be able to be grasped hand over hand with the storyteller – space between the object and the card and position on the card are all designed to be accessible and there is only one sensory experience per page. 'Look at' pages are clear, colourful, defined shapes which are glued to the page so that those with no sight or dual impairment can still feel them. Smells are absorbed into fabric or wafted from their original containers and can be pleasant but equally interesting and fun if they are not so pleasant! Materials for tactile pages need to be refreshingly different from everyday tactile experiences – sequined fabric, wire netting, chains, artificial grass, a squashy ball, vibrating toys – and sounds can range from the soft whisper of a toy dog with the squeaker removed to a metal spoon banging on a frying pan!

Most objects will be mounted on or tied to a page card with a length of cord or elastic so that there is a 'field' against which it is used and the storyteller can control a listener's action if necessary. This also gives listeners with no sight the confidence to explore a defined area close to their body. The large size of the card allows time for the brain to acknowledge what the hand is feeling and provides sufficient space to attach a moving mechanism such as a gate bolt or a letterbox so that the listener can experience a variety of actions. One or two objects will need to be unattached – a plant spray, a towel, a funny wig!

The stories are short and for each brief block of text, usually just one sentence, there is an accompanying page card, and a sound or a smell will be introduced at the point where attention may lag. The storyline carries the emotion of the story through the storyteller's voice, as the listeners will not necessarily understand the words, and it invites exaggerated voice tones, pitch and volume to create phrases of sound which will gradually become memorable. In this way it eventually offers the opportunity for sentences and page cards to be anticipated, the joy of a familiar story often told. The whole story, generally seven to ten sentences, is in enlarged print on a single A3 laminated sheet and placed on the floor. This allows the storyteller to have both hands free to help the listener to use the pages.

History

My own approach to multi-sensory storytelling began in 1989, when teaching a group of six 4 to 6-year-olds with PIMD who had been placed after lunch in a semicircle at one end of their classroom and looked just like any infant class waiting for a story.

On the shelf lay a box of 'tactile cards' made to encourage the pupils to look, listen, feel, reach for and grasp. Taking one with flapping bottle tops, another with a crinkled silver survival blanket, a third covered in bubble wrap and a fourth with a piece of nylon net over rustling polystyrene packing pieces, I told a simple story about a bookseller who travelled from house to house with his donkey (the bottle tops). He invited each child to feel the three pages of his 'book' (hand over hand with me) but no one had any money to buy it, so they asked him to try their friend next door and were then helped to touch the person next to them. The child who was last in the line had a bag of money – the class money for drinks! She bought it, and together we emptied the money into a shiny tin, which was then rattled vigorously around the group for fun.

The children appeared to empathise with the story, the cards were 'spot-on' for their interest value, everyone was actively involved in feeling each page, their turn came quickly and when the donkey sound flapped around the group it continually refreshed their attention. I wrote the story down so that it could be retold in exactly the same way, and repeated it every day. During the following weeks the children's enjoyment appeared to grow.

The success of this first story inspired a 'do-it-yourself' manual containing six stories and how to construct the corresponding multi-sensory story-packs (Fuller, 1990). Whilst teaching in special schools, I used multi-sensory storytelling for 9 years before establishing and heading Bag Books, a publisher of hand-crafted multi-sensory stories. During that time it became clear that 'having something to do', interacting with a member of staff who is repeating short dynamic pieces of text, and is physically close, enabled my pupils with severe and profound intellectual difficulties to focus their attention and be happily engaged throughout a 30-minute story session. The evidence available from research into developing literacy though multi-sensory storytelling in children with PIMD (Watson et al., 2002) indicates that the benefits are to the result of all the components of the stories, from the social context to the reinforcing stimuli, to the appropriate language. 'The packs do indeed hold the listener's attention and connect with the child in a meaningful and enjoyable way' (Hogg, 2004) and this is in accord with a research study commissioned by Bag Books:

> [I]t is clear from our research that Bag Books are considered to be an important tool for making English and literacy – as well as a wide range of other curriculum topics – accessible and for bringing significant pleasure to a large number of students.
>
> (Preece & Zhao, 2014)

Theory and principles

Underpinning the practice is the fact that every sensation is a form of information which feeds the nervous system and sensations come from every joint, muscle, area of skin and sense organ in the head, to send sensory input to the brain. The senses which give us most of our conscious awareness of the world are sight, sound, touch and hearing (Ayres, 1982). We therefore have many pathways through which we can reach children and adults with profound developmental delay, and give them a sensation.

Research into access to literature (Webb, 1992 quoted in Grove (2005) suggests that early response begins with a sensory experience that alerts us to what is there. Our feelings then assess the sensory experience and it is the bond between feeling and language that is the foundation of literature. Through our feelings, a story becomes a story and not just a list of events, and so the storyline must have a crescendo of happenings leading to a dramatic or significant middle. In tandem, the objects and materials in a multi-sensory story must also seek to generate appropriate feelings for the storyline: a bonfire can glow and crackle with red rustling material; a fairy laugh can be tinkling bells; scampering mice can be beads flapping against canvas, and the urgency of catching the school bus can be a loud horn!

So we now have relevant sensory input but what will enable the listener to focus on it? As children with PIMD have attention skills that are developmentally early, it is the joint attention and joint action which occur when storyteller and listener are using a page card or are engaged together in an action that support their ability to attend to their own actions (Charman et al., 2001).

Finally, we need to think about the delivery of the storyline. Research into early language development has found that babies need to hear multiple sound signals so that the brain neurons can map the sounds and look for consistencies. At this stage the brain is not concentrating on what the words mean but on segmenting the speech sounds and looking for consistencies (Tallal, 2004). We also tend to exaggerate our voice when speaking to a baby: 'Oh look at *you*!', which amplifies and enhances the acoustic information. The same research revealed that children with language delay have a slower auditory processing threshold. For listeners in the early stage of language development or on the autistic spectrum, repeating a story many times and using an exaggerated and slower style of delivery will give them the best possible chance of being alert to a phrase of sound and eventually learning it.

Any story can be delivered in this way – fictional, factual, traditional, personal – but the content and concepts of the stories need to be pared down to a limited number of short sentences and the end of a sentence should reflect the action to be taken on its corresponding page card. There are ready made story-packs available (Bag Books: see 'Where to go'), but anyone can make their own to deliver virtually any subject in the curriculum or purely for pleasure, with contents and storyline specifically designed for the chronological age of the listener(s).

Work in practice

In a typical session the storyteller sits opposite or close beside a single listener, but stands in front of a group, to help them to use the page card or make the action, and also to respond immediately to any reaction – an eye blink, involuntary gesture, change of facial expression or body position or the smallest sound.

Everyone sits on a chair, wheelchair or raised equipment such as a side-lyer, arranged in a semi-circle with the ends curving inwards and with their accompanying staff or carers sitting behind them. Listeners with challenging behaviour sit at either end with their support member beside them. This seating has several advantages. The page cards can travel uninterrupted from one listener to the next as the short piece of text is repeated, the pages are roughly at the same level and the curved seating gives everyone the opportunity to be aware of each other's reactions. Having a stable base helps listeners to focus their attention and stay in the group, and the storyteller can oversee the whole group at a glance.

When the storyteller is unfamiliar with the group, they introduce themselves by shaking each person's hand and this reveals the listeners' dominant hand. For someone who is tactile defensive, their hand is taken very briefly to feel or use the page contents and then released immediately. If this continues to be intolerable, each card is placed on their lap or activated by their foot or another body part. For a hand that needs time and help to unclench, the sentence is repeated until their grasp is successful and comfortable.

The sentences are said slowly and clearly for each listener, with pauses, pitch, tone and volume exaggerated to create that memorable phrase of sound and to engage the listeners in the emotional feel of the story: happy, funny, crazy, scary, charming, etc. Then the listeners 'tell' the story through their actions and at the end the storyteller will praise them: 'Give yourselves a clap, you're brilliant!', which is also the clue that the story is finished.

Outcomes and evidence: what we look for

Every listener accesses and enjoys the stories at their own developmental level which means that they can be used with a group of mixed intellectual ability. Outcomes can begin at the most basic stage, that of the listeners purely being exposed to the stories' range and variety of linguistic, physical, and emotional experiences, being able to tolerate the required physical interaction and displaying simple reflex responses. For someone with no voluntary movement, progress will be muscles relaxed and ready to make the aided movement for a familiar page, and increased attention skills. Others will learn to reach and grasp and in due course to make the action unaided. Some people will smile at the familiar phrases, others will look and enjoy their peers' reactions, and some listeners will be able to repeat or remember certain phrases and eventually be able to tell the story themselves.

When a story has been repeated many times there is evidence of increased alertness, anticipation, improved attention skills and real pleasure in hearing the expected (Fuller, 1991), and in factual personal stories, proof that a sequence has been learnt (Watson, Lambe & Hogg, 2002; Fenwick, 2005, 2007; Young et al., 2011). Progress is assessed by using video and regular recording on observation sheets that monitor focus of attention, attention span, anticipation, communication skills, social interaction, interaction with pages, behaviours indicating enjoyment or displeasure and, for more able listeners, comprehension and acquired vocabulary.

The story of Freddie

An example of one small person's progress is 5-year-old Freddie who, when he first came to his new special school, was scared of virtually everything. Developmentally around 18 months and tiny for his age, he would bottom shuffle his way into a corner of the classroom and screech if another pupil came near him. He never touched anything with his hands and kept his gaze down.

In his first term I told a multi-sensory story called *Desmond* three times a week, and as soon as he saw the story-pack box he would move himself round sideways on his chair and turn his head away. When it came to his turn I rested each page on his knee and he would squirm further round in his chair to get away from it. Then one day I noticed that after the page had left him he looked up and watched the other children using it. By the third week he was smiling at the cat sound when the other pupils laughed, but still facing sideways and hiding when it was his turn.

He needed help to be brave and join in, and so the following week I took his left hand and rested it on the nylon cat fur page and we stroked downwards just once. The hand shot back out of my grasp but he turned his face forward for the cat sound and laughed. It took only two more weeks before Freddie could sit straight in his chair and would allow his hand to be taken to use every page. By the end of the half term he could do it himself and would flap his hands excitedly when the first page came out of the box. At first a new story-pack would mean his reverting to hiding until he was familiar with it by watching the others, but eventually a new story was exciting.

The story of Omar, a young adult

Working with adults has also been interesting. By respecting their right to choose not to engage in an activity, some people have become so withdrawn from contact that it has become a habit. During a training workshop for day-centre staff, I took the hand of one young man to help him use a page and there was a sharp intake of breath from his assistant: 'Oh he's tactile defensive, we always do it for him.' He did withdraw his hand immediately afterwards but had not actively resisted that touch. In fact I was able to help him use every page of the following four stories and by the end of the session, his hand was still up by his ear but relaxed and ready to move down. He was enjoying being involved and so was receptive to the stories, the language and the fun.

Contexts of learning

Although originally devised for children and adults with PIMD, multi-sensory storytelling is an inclusive resource for listeners who have a range of different needs. These include: young children with mild learning difficulties (MLD); children on the autistic spectrum; those with attention deficit hyperactivity disorder (ADHD); children and older people with severe learning difficulties (SLD); young children who have visual impairment or no sight, or are both hearing and vision impaired, babies and toddlers with additional needs and 3 to 6-year-olds who are just not used to sitting still. This makes it ideal for a family or care home, a mainstream inclusive nursery, the special school classroom, library story times and adult services for people with profound and severe intellectual disabilities.

Issues to consider

To retain the attention of everyone in a group of children or adults with PMLD, seven listeners is the ideal size but for a group with ASD can work well with up to ten, so it depends very much on the abilities and nature of the group. Sometimes a large group will arrive at an event such as a library storytelling or a festival and then each page is delivered to a smaller number of listeners so that everyone is physically involved in turn and as often as possible whilst hearing the storyline throughout. In all situations it is the storyteller's vocal energy, enthusiasm and empathy with the storyline that is the key to sustaining the whole group's interest and interaction. In a public setting it is wise to seat the group with their backs to a wall or a corner so that if anybody runs they run towards the storyteller! For a single listener the words and the action on each page can be repeated two or three times.

Cultural factors

Multi-sensory stories are an ideal way to celebrate cultural diversity. With storylines which reflect the life of different communities, have culturally appropriate artefacts and storyboards in their languages as well as English, words, traditions, festivals, rituals and ceremonies, pastimes, natural resources and architecture can all be represented, shared and enjoyed. In English-speaking countries multi-sensory story-packs have also been used extensively with young children who have English as a second language. Initially they do not need to understand the story in order to take part, but gradually the short sentences help them to learn words and phrases.

Try it yourself

Top tips

- Familiarise yourself thoroughly with the page cards and storyline before you start and take time to arrange the listeners and support staff/carers
- Say the sentences exactly as they are written, so that the phrase of sound remains consistent
- Be energetic in the delivery so that the listeners are caught up in your enthusiasm.

Where to go

Training and a training DVD are available from Bag Books, and many libraries across the UK have received training and stock story-packs (www.bagbooks.org). The organisation PAMIS, in Scotland, is also a veteran of multi-sensory storytelling. To make a start, however, borrow a story-pack from a library, learn and practise it at home and then persuade a friend or family member to let you take their hand and try it out with them.

Bag Books: www.bagbooks.org.

PAMIS: https://pamis.org.uk.

References

Ayres, J. A. (1982). *Sensory integration and the child*. Torrance, CA: Western Psychological Services.

Charman, T., Baron-Cohen, S., Swettenham, J., Baird, G., Cox, A. & Drew, A. (2001). Testing joint attention, imitation and play as infancy precursors to language and theory of mind. *Cognitive Development*, 15(4), 481–485.

Fenwick, M. (2005). Multi-sensory sensitive stories. *Eye Contact: RNIB*, 42, 12–14.

Fenwick, M. (2007). Sensitive stories. *Insight: RNIB*, 10, 30–32.

Fuller C. (1990) *Tactile stories: A do-it-yourself manual*. London: Bag Books.

Fuller C. (1991). *Tactile stories: Training DVD*. London: Bag Books.

Grove, N. (2005) *Ways into literature*. London: David Fulton.

Hogg, J. (2004) *Bag Books Annual Review*. London: Bag Books.

Preece, D. & Zhao, Y. (2014) *An evaluation of Bag Books multi-sensory stories*. London: Bag Books.

Tallal, P. (2004) Improving language and literacy is a matter of time. *Neuroscience*, 5, 721–728.

Watson, M., Lambe, L. & Hogg, J. (2002). *Real lives: Real stories*. Dundee: PAMIS.

Webb, E. (1992) *Literature in education: Encounter and experience*. London: Falmer Press.

Young, H. B., Fenwick, M., Lambe, L. & Hogg, J. (2011) Multi-sensory storytelling as an aid to assisting people with profound intellectual disabilities to cope with sensitive issues: A multiple research methods analysis of engagement and outcomes. *European Journal of Special Needs Education*, 26, 127–142.

Chapter 14

Storytelling with nurturing touch

The Story Massage Programme

Mary Atkinson

Background

This chapter explores how the Story Massage Programme combines the fun and creativity of storytelling with the benefits of positive, nurturing touch.

Action songs and rhymes such as 'Round and Round the Garden' have been handed down through generations. Many of us remember the fun and connection of writing names or drawing pictures to tell a story on friends' backs. This natural and intuitive combination of telling stories through words and touch links my joint careers as a writer and massage therapist.

History

In 2007, I met Sandra Hooper, a teacher and therapist, and now my co-founder of the programme, and we explored the creative and therapeutic possibilities of massage stories. I was able to put the idea into practice whilst volunteering in Japan with a small charity supporting children and adults suffering trauma in the aftermath of the tsunami. The response was overwhelmingly positive with reports of a sense of peace, comfort and connection that had been lacking since the tsunami. They asked for the massage stories to be repeated with increasing levels of pleasure, relaxation, engagement and communication.

So, the question became clear in our minds. How could the benefits of massage stories be shared in a way that could be fully inclusive of all ages and abilities? The answer is the structured approach of the programme with ten simple strokes, given through clothes, that offers flexibility to bring a story to life in a meaningful way for every individual.

The Story Massage Programme

From the perspective of the programme, story is the context within which the narrative ebbs and flows. Story is any sequence of words, with a start and finish, which are relevant for the individual and enjoyed as an interactive experience. Story can be any genre of prose, poetry, rhyme or song with the words being shared through speech, singing or chanting. Narrative is the application of strokes to enhance the storyline and match the rhythm, volume, tone, pace and pauses of the storyteller's voice.

The ten strokes have a self-explanatory name such as The Wave or The Claw and an accompanying symbol as a visual cue. They are shared with sensitivity and empathy on any

DOI: 10.4324/9781003159087-14

part of the body that is accessible and acceptable for the individual. The strokes have been carefully devised to offer a choice of depth of pressure and sensory responses such as soothing or energising plus a range of descriptive movements to illustrate a variety of objects, actions and emotions in a story. Even if language cannot be heard or understood, the strokes convey the meaning of the story.

At this point, it would be helpful to have a more concrete idea of the experience of a massage story and maybe try it for yourself. Here is an example of *Incy Wincy Spider* adapted using three of the ten strokes.

Incy Wincy Spider

Strokes – Name and Symbol	Actions	Words
 The Sprinkle	With both hands working at the same time, tap the pads of your fingers in an upwards direction.	Incy Wincy Spider Climbed up the waterspout.
 The Fan	With both hands working at the same time, stroke your hands in a downward direction gently 'fanning' out.	Down came the rain And washed the spider out.
 The Circle	With one hand resting on an appropriate part of the body, use the other hand to make large, circular movement.	Out came the sunshine And dried up all the rain.
 The Sprinkle	As above for The Sprinkle.	So Incy Wincy Spider Climbed up the spout again.

Figure 14.1 Story Massage example

Theories

Central to the Story Massage Programme is a quality of touch that is described by Hewett (2007) as meaningful interpersonal touch. Regular, nurturing touch from an early age offers security and bonding and is vital to a child's early growth and development (McClure, 2000). Positive touch contributes to emotional, psychological and physical well-being (Barnes & Hewett, 2015). There is limited research into specific benefits of touch for children with special needs, however studies conducted at the Touch Research Institute in Miami show that massage therapy can improve the mood and behaviour of students with ADHD (Khilnani et al., 2003) and increase attentiveness in autistic children (Escalona et al., 2001).

Nurturing touch activates the parasympathetic nervous system and brings the body back into a state of calm and relaxation. The 'feel-good' hormone, oxytocin, is released into the bloodstream, and acts as an antidote to the stress hormone, adrenalin, which triggers the 'fight or flight' response in the body. Oxytocin helps lower blood pressure and heart rate, increases tolerance to pain, promotes learning and is the key component in the body's system for calm and connection (Moberg, 2011). Furthermore, it is released into the bodies of those giving as well as receiving touch which helps explain the sense of relaxation and focus during Story Massage sessions.

The link between touch and emotional wellbeing was highlighted by the lack of touch experienced by people isolating or living alone during the COVID-19 pandemic. People described experiencing 'touch hunger' or 'skin hunger', the biological need for touch, a longing to touch or be touched in a social way, alongside insomnia, depression and anxiety (Kale, 2020). These findings are supported by studies conducted before the pandemic exploring the detrimental effects of touch deprivation on infants. These include developmental delay (Field, 1998) and higher risks of sensory processing problems (Cascio, Moore & McGlone, 2018). And we can never forget the devastating 'failure to thrive' of neglected children in Romanian orphanages (Glasper, 2020). As Barnes (2020) describes so succinctly: 'All children need to know that touch is natural, necessary and part of what makes us human' (Barnes, 2020: 20).

Yet so many children and adults in special education are missing opportunities for safe, nurturing touch. Pupils with PMLD are less likely to receive the quantity of normal touch experience enjoyed by their peers in natural interactions in daily life (Barnes & Hewett, 2015). In addition, fears and confusion surrounding inappropriate touch and 'age-appropriateness', combined with lack of awareness of the vital importance of touch, can lead to limited or non-existent meaningful touch for many individuals (Hewett, 2007).

Some children and young adults may be sensitive to touch due to sensory processing difficulties which can further impede sharing the benefits of touch. The theory of Sensory Integration, also known as Sensory Processing, explains the way in which the brain receives and processes sensory information to enable us to function in everyday life (Bundy & Lane, 2020). For individuals with sensory integration difficulties, touch can be processed and experienced in different ways and give rise to behaviours including touch defensiveness or a craving for firm touch.

Sensory processing needs are met by careful choice and application of strokes with a deeper or more gentle pressure or by omitting some strokes completely and concentrating on others. Many children and young adults are now able to tolerate touch in a way they could not previously enjoy as they are able to explore and communicate their preferences within the structure of the programme. Some individuals may choose The Squeeze (a deep squeezing action) and The Claw (raking action with pads of fingers) while others prefer more soothing strokes such as The Calm (hands rest on body with no movement) or T Wave (wave-like, zig-zag action). Some enjoy them all!

Principles

These theories led us to develop the principles that underpin the Story Massage Programme:

- *Respectful touch.* Seeking consent to touch in a way that can be communicated effectively, responding to feedback and showing appreciation are integral to the programme. This helps teach appropriate touch, increase body awareness, self-respect and respect for others. Learners distinguish between touch that feels safe and touch that feels unsafe. They learn to give a confident 'no' to unwanted touch.
- If individuals do not want to be touched then no touch is given. They are encouraged to take part in massage stories in another way. They listen to the words, watch others and, if they have the ability, do the strokes in the air, on their own bodies or on a teddy. Those who are sensitive to touch may prefer to start by giving rather than receiving the strokes.
- *Accessibility.* Massage stories can be shared at anytime, anywhere. No clothes are removed, no oil is used and no extra resources are needed. Sessions can be an interaction between an adult and child or peer massage. They can take place in private settings or in groups, as large as school assemblies, and can be spontaneous or planned. This accessibility means the programme is widely shared within special education not only in mainstream and special schools, but also in therapy centres, hospitals, hospices and community arts, music and drama initiatives. And it brings a shared closeness and delight in stories when enjoyed with parents, carers and siblings at home.
- *Repetition and simplicity.* The simplicity of the names, symbols and actions of the ten strokes offers opportunities for individuals to enjoy the same massage stories repeated by a variety of people at school and at home. When working with pupils with PMLD, Lacey (2009) believes that activities are not repeated enough. She advocates concentrating on a few sensory experiences and repeating them many times for learning to take place. In line with the theory of enactive memory (Brouillet, 2020), repetition of words of the story combined with strokes can lay down memories like a series of movement illustrations in the body. This repetition leads to familiarity, increased engagement and the development of anticipation skills.
- *Enjoyment.* Above all, sharing massage stories is a fun and interactive experience for everyone involved.

Work in practice

I will now outline a scheduled session in a classroom with pupils aged 6–10 in a special school. There are 11 pupils, all with PMLD, and 6 members of staff, including the teacher. This model can be adapted and transferred to other settings.

Before the session

The programme is most effective if both massage story and working environment are prepared in advance.

The massage story is often based on a curriculum topic such as food, emotions or colours. Stories are also created to share a news item or personalised for special occasions or preparation for transitions. Today's massage story is *Animals in the Jungle* created by a staff member trained in the programme.

The strokes are chosen to 'illustrate' the words of the story. In *Animals in the Jungle*, The Walk (walking action with alternate hands) is used to represent the lion prowling through the jungle, while The Sprinkle (tapping action with fingers) illustrates the elephant washing itself. The words and matching strokes, with alternate ideas for strokes to meet individual preferences, are prepared either as paper document, PowerPoint or pre-recorded follow-along video.

The room is prepared to create an environment that is calm and as uncluttered as possible. Lights may be dimmed, and gentle music played. Time is taken to find a position, whether lying down, standing or sitting, that is comfortable for all adults and pupils with a good view of the lead adult and/or screen. Pupils indicate where they would like the strokes to be shared. Some like to have their thighs massaged, for example, others their chest or abdomen, another may hold out their hand or foot.

In most classes, some pupils need to wait their turn. Various strategies, such as holding a sensory prop or watching a PowerPoint, can make this less stressful.

During the session

The session begins by seeking consent to touch. This is in the format most appropriate for the individual. It may be verbal or non-verbal using a picture card or interpreting body language. The lead adult reads aloud, sings or chants the words of the story and demonstrates the strokes or plays a pre-recorded version. Everyone follows the lead adult and carefully co-ordinates the strokes with the spoken words to create a meaningful experience.

An integral part of the session is interpreting verbal and non-verbal feedback and adjusting pressure, changing the movement, altering the position or even stopping altogether. This brings the benefits of a personalised interaction within the social aspect of a group session.

The whole class feels connected. The room goes quiet as pupils focus on the experience, listening to the words, showing anticipation, sometimes vocalising and joining in a repeated phrase. Pupils show their pleasure in different ways. Some still from repetitive movements showing their concentration. Others smile, laugh or vocalise. A pupil who is congenitally blind leads the adult's hand under hers indicating the pressure she desires.

Pupils are asked if they would like the massage story repeated. This is greeted with enthusiastic vocalising and signing. The session ends by the giver thanking the recipient of the massage. Everyone is invited to evaluate the session, communicating their favourite strokes and levels of enjoyment.

Outcomes: what we look for

In 2016 we introduced Best Practice and Centre of Excellence Awards. Among the winners to date are 87 education and health professionals working in special education. Assessment strategies include observation, photographs, video clips, staff feedback forms and assessment sheets. Documentation and data show the main benefits are increased levels of:

- Communication
- Social interaction and positive relationships
- Anticipation
- Tolerance to touch
- Eye contact
- Enjoyment
- Relaxation
- Concentration and focus.

These outcomes are recorded as a massage story created by a class teacher at a special school as a way of presenting the benefits of the programme at a staff meeting.

> First it was noisy and rushed.
> Now it is calm and hushed.
> Before the children just couldn't wait.
> Now they're learning to anticipate.
> The PowerPoint reinforces every word
> Of the story they've just felt and heard.
> The pictures may be focal
> But even the quietest children become quite vocal.
> They express their preferences, wanting 'more'
> Tolerating more touch than they ever did before.
> For Green Class, Story Massage has been a positive tool
> That would benefit many children in the whole school.

The story of Josh

Josh, 10, has autism and sensory processing issues. He was highly sensitive to touch and not able to tolerate a hug from his mother. Josh's physiotherapist began including massage stories into their sessions. They worked together to find a story that Josh would engage with, finally writing one about Josh's dog. Josh experienced all ten strokes first, discovering that he actually enjoyed the sensation of The Circle and The Wave on his feet when accompanied by the words of the story. Massage stories are now part of Josh's bedtime routine and he is even starting to join in peer massage sessions at school. He asks his mother for a massage story when he needs reassurance and calming.

The story of Katy

Katy, 19, has myotonic dystrophy and attends a college for adult learners with disabilities. Katy was struggling to meet targets, including 'to be able to request desired activities'. When her lecturer introduced the Story Massage Programme, Katy became animated and began asking for repetition of the story of *Cinderella* whenever possible at college or home. She continues to be so engaged with the story that she is able to remember the words and often re-tells the story by signing. Katy's self-esteem has been boosted by sharing her skills in class, a big step for her.

Contexts of learning

Issues to consider

An essential element is safe, nurturing, positive touch and lead practitioners should follow all relevant safeguarding policies and procedures and adhere to any health and safety risk assessments. When introducing the programme, it is helpful to run one-off taster sessions for staff members and parents/carers to allay any doubts and answer questions. It is advised that lead practitioners are trained in the programme. Independent practitioners should be trained and covered by insurance.

Trusting, interpersonal relationships are at the core of the programme, and adults need to be competent and confident to share the massage story with a child or young adult. There is research to show that touch can communicate distinct emotions (Hertenstein et al., 2006). As Pistorius (2011) experienced whilst in a coma, touch can convey impatience and anxiety as well as kindness and caring. Adults are encouraged to recognise that they need to be in the right emotional state to apply the strokes with respect and sensitivity.

Cultural factors

The programme has the flexibility to respect cultural practice and religious beliefs. This may include areas of the body where the strokes can be respectfully given. Gender concerns around different sexes massaging each other should also be considered. These issues can be discussed on an individual basis, so everyone feels safe within the activity.

Massage stories are created to provide reflection on ways in which people from different cultures mark special occasions such as Eid, Hanukka or Easter and also promote awareness around events such as Black History Month.

Try it yourself

The creativity, imagination and passion of Story Massage Programme practitioners worldwide has expanded its reach far beyond our hopes and dreams. We welcome your ideas for taking the concept along new avenues to transform the lives of children and adults in special education.

Top tips

- Check all the regular updates and blogs on our social media channels and follow along with videos on You Tube and Vimeo channels.
- Practise on a cushion, pet or colleague to build familiarity and confidence. Be playful and have fun!

Where to go

For further information about the Story Massage Programme, self-study online training course, follow-along videos, book and resources, please visit: https://storymassage.co.uk.

Once upon a touch ... story massage for children (Atkinson & Hooper, 2016) is a good introduction to the programme with instructions for the ten strokes and over 25 massage stories.

Acknowledgements

The development of the programme has been a joint venture with Sandra Hooper, and it has been a privilege to share our passion with equal measures of dedication, intuition and humour. This chapter may not have seen the light of day without the encouragement and input of Julia Barnes, Sensory Manager at Ravenscliffe High School in Halifax, whose extensive practical and theoretical knowledge of the importance of human touch within special education is widely recognised and valued. And thank you to Heather North for sharing her classroom massage story and being a Story Massage Programme ambassador.

References

Atkinson, M. (2017). *Healing touch for children*. Victoria, BC: Albert Bridge Books.

Atkinson, M. & Hooper, S. (2016). *Once upon a touch … story massage for children*. London: Singing Dragon.

Barnes, J. (2020). Riding the emotional Corona-coaster and its effects on the touchscape of the classroom. *PMLD Link*, 32(3),18–20.

Barnes, J. & Hewett, D. (2015). Physical contact experiences within the curriculum. In P. Lacey, R. Ashdown, P.Jones, H.Lawson & M. Pipe (Eds), *The Routledge companion to severe, profound and multiple learning difficulties* (pp. 182–191). Abingdon: Routledge.

Brouillet, D. (2020). Enactive memory. *Frontiers of Psychology*, 11, 114. Available at: https://www.frontiersin.org/article/10.3389/fpsyg.2020.00114.

Bundy, A. C. & Lane, J. S. (2019) *Sensory integration: Theory and practice* (3rd ed.). Philadelphia, PA: F.A. Davis.

Cascio, C., Moore, D. & McGlone, F. (2018). Social touch and human development. *Development Cognitive Neuroscience*, 35, 5–11.

Escalona A., Field T., Singer-Strunck R., Cullen C. & Hartshorn, K. (2001). Brief report: Improvements in the behavior of children with autism following massage therapy. *Journal of Autism and Developmental Disorders*, 31(5), 513–516.

Field, T. (1998). Massage therapy effects. *American Psychologist*, 53(12), 1270.

Glasper, E. A. (2020). Romania's forgotten children: Sensory deprivation revisited. *Comprehensive Child and Adolescent Nursing*, 43(2), 81–87.

Hertenstein, M. J., Keltner, D., App, B., Bulleit, B. A. & Jaskolka, A. R. (2006). Touch communicates distinct emotions. *Emotion*, 6(3), 528–533.

Hewett, D. (2007). Do touch: Physical contact and people who have severe, profound and multiple learning difficulties. *Support for Learning*, 22(3), 116–123.

Kale, S. (2020). Skin hunger helps explain your desperate longing for human touch. *WIRED*. Available at: https://www.wired.co.uk/article/skin-hunger-coronavirus-human-touch (Accessed 28.5.21).

Khilnani, S., Field, T., Hernandez-Reif, M. & Schanberg, S. (2003). Massage therapy improves mood and behaviour of students with Attention-Deficit/Hyperactivity disorder. *Adolescence*, 38(152), 623–638.

Lacey, P. (2009). Developing the thinking of learners with PMLD. *PMLD Link*, 21(2), 15–19.

McClure, V. (2000). *Infant massage: A handbook for loving parents* (3rd ed). New York: Bantam Books.

Moberg, K. U. (2011). *The oxytocin factor*. London: Printer & Martin Ltd.

Pistorius, M. (2011). *Ghost boy*. London: Simon & Schuster UK Ltd.

Tiffany, F. (1998). Touch therapy effects on development. *International Journal of Behavioral Development*, 22(4), 779–797.

Chapter 15

Rich inclusion through sensory stories

Stories from science

Joanna Grace

Background

The Sensory Story Project creates stories that people can self-resource at home. These stories provide experiencers with a rich range of sensory experiences and connect them with ambitious narratives, whether factual or fictional. The aim is to have everyone feel interested and included in the story – the tellers as much as those experiencing the story.

History

The seeds of the project were sown when I first encountered sensory stories in the late 1990s–2000s. The power of these deceptively simple narratives to engage people with complex disabilities enthralled me. I realised that whilst the people with profound disabilities I was sharing stories with were caught up in the narrative adventure, often those around them (e.g. peers, support staff) were not. I began trying to create stories that would capture everyone's interest. The work began in earnest as a Kickstarter project with the aim of creating five sensory stories. I underpinned it with a thorough exploration of published research in this field and through open, frank conversations with parents of people with profound disabilities.

Theories

The work of Grove and Park (1996, 2001; Park, 2004; Grove et al., 2015), proved to me that complex narratives could be tackled within a sensory landscape and Promoting A More Inclusive Society (PAMIS) (Young et al., 2011) further inspired my desire to create ambitious narratives. Research into storytelling practice guided me as I considered how best to advise people on sharing the stories (Bag Books, 2016; Grove et al., 2015; Lacey, 2006; PAMIS, 2010; Taylor, 2006; Ten Brug et al., 2012; Young & Lambe, 2011).

It was important to me that people with profound disabilities who accessed the experience through the senses were respected as equals to the people who accessed it through language. In my later work (Grace, 2017) I came to use the terms "Sensory Beings" and "Linguistic Beings" to denote these two groups, defining each in terms of their capabilities with neither viewed as less than the other. These were originally purely working terms, denoting a recognition that there is a difference between those who have access to language, and those who do not, and a desire to articulate that difference in a way that was not hierarchical.

DOI: 10.4324/9781003159087-15

Sensory Beings are people whose primary experience of the world, and meaning within it, is sensory. The term refers to people otherwise classed as having profound and multiple learning disabilities; people with later stage dementia who no longer access language and some autistic people who do not use language and for whom the sensory world holds particular sway. *Linguistic Beings* are people who use language to represent experience and frame meaning.

These terms seem to have caught on, perhaps indicating a shift in perspective with regards to disability, a desire in people to not define by deficit, but to celebrate difference. However, there are of course some problems with categorisation. Linguistic Beings are also Sensory Beings. When our brain acquires language it changes the structuring within it, altering the way we lay down and retrieve memories. Without being able to look into the brains of autistic people not using language, or people with later stage dementia who have lost it, who are we to say whether that structuring is in place?

In essence words are units of meaning that we exchange with one another. We can express meaning in lots of other ways. If I pick a rose and I want to convey the meaning of that experience to someone else, I can say "I picked a rose," I could mime the picking of the rose, I could offer the scent of the rose and the sensation of the thorns against my finger. We could argue which expresses the meaning of my experience the best, but I think we would all agree that meaning can be expressed through sensory units (dance and music offering other examples). As someone who uses language to organise my mind I understand certain events in a certain way that way is relevant to me. But, were I to be someone who did not use language to experience and frame meaning, I would still have an understanding of events, it would just be a different form. For me, as a Linguistic Being my memory of the rose event can be writ into my mind as a narrative event. I can think "I picked a rose". But for a Sensory Being that memory might exist in the mind but be encountered in other ways, for example perhaps when they pass someone wearing a rose-scented perfume they alert to that scent in a way that they would not have done prior to the experience of picking the rose. It is not a memory they can go back and recall as I can with my memory, but there is an embodied memory there (Menary, 2008) waiting to be re-encountered. Likewise the memory could be expressed in action, perhaps the first time they encountered a rose they did not know about the thorns and reached boldly to grab it, and then the next time they encounter a rose they reach but with more caution. The impression of that experience remains, without language. It is different, but not lesser.

There is, clearly, value for all of us in connecting with the sensory world. For Sensory Beings the value in a clearly sensorially articulated story is the opportunity to connect with experience and to comprehend what is going on. Of course the whole world is sensory, but if you experience that world through a brain complicated by epilepsy and reliant on sensory systems that do not necessarily function at a speed compatible with that world then often it can be a confusing soup of experience. However if I pick things from that world, to display to you clearly, sequentially, then you can connect with it, be in it, be in the story, and truly be and understand. But there are also manifold benefits for Linguistic Beings, in truly engaging with the sensations of that narrative as they unfold. I write during the pandemic, a time that threatens mental as well as physical health. Connecting with what you touch, when you touch it, what you smell, when you smell it, performing a tiny piece of mindfulness can be a powerful way to support mental health for us all. In our busy anxious minds, when cognition is absorbed with worrying about the future or chewing over the past, if we can bring ourselves out of our heads and into our bodies and realise our presence in the here and now, it can be wonderfully therapeutic. If a Linguistic Being sinks themselves into the sharing of a sensory story not only does that improve the experience for the Sensory Being they are with, it has a nurturing effect on their own mental health. As I create narratives I try to think of the relevance of what they contain to both Sensory Beings and Linguistic Beings. So, for example, in *The Birth of a Star* it is important to me that the words are scientifically accurate, and it is equally important to me that the sensations are accurate in terms of their relevance to what they describe. Stars are formed from clouds of hydrogen gas, particle physicists would recognise the dispersal of the particles in the hydrogen clouds as being similar to the dispersal of particles in the confetti cloud that I use to represent this moment of the star's birth in a sensory communication.

Principles

- *There is no such thing as a non-communicating person*: "A person's ability to communicate is not dependent on their being able to master certain skills, it is dependent on our ability to listen and communicate responsively" (Doukas et al., 2017). Sensory story sharing is a communicative act, the words of the story form part of that communication and the sensations hold equal weight. A story, or a conversation, is not definitively word-based, but involves sharing meaning in whatever form. Recognising that communication is about meaning, not words, can be liberating for families (Murphy, 2017).
- *Rich inclusion*: Striving for inclusion is not something we do *for* people with disabilities, it is something we do for *all* people, regardless of ability, disability or neurodivergence (Grace & Salfield, 2017). Rich inclusion is a term I inadvertently coined (Grace, 2015a) when trying to explain how, when sharing stories with people with complex disabilities, it is as important to include yourself in that experience as it is them. A boring story is unlikely to be inclusive! Sensory stories can be boring if they lack a compelling narrative or if the sensory experiences accompanying them are mundane or inaccessible.
- *Simple stories require complex understanding*: It is easy to think "Oh it is only ten sentences" but actually creating a whole story with a limited amount of text is a tricky business. People often think adapting an existing story will be easier than making up their own, but then you're faced with identifying the essence of that story, maintaining all its features whilst cutting down. You will recognise this insight across other fields of knowledge: the people who understand something really, really well are the ones who can explain it clearly. The people who haven't got such a strong grasp end up waffling. To write a good sensory story you need a really clear vision of what that story will be, and how it will feel. Then you set it down in pure form. It is a process of distillation.

Work in practice

I ensure the resources for that story are readily available, along with the time and space needed to give the story the best chance of engaging and including everyone. Practically this means allocating sufficient time and hanging a Do Not Disturb sign on the door.

When sharing the story I read a section, and then share the sensory experience that goes with it, allowing time for experiencer/s to fully engage and process each sensation. I will repeat a story many times in order to allow people to orientate themselves and engage. I expect to see a person's responsiveness to a story gradually increase session by session – when it begins to wane I know it's time to introduce a new story (see also Grace & Silva, 2017).

Stories from science

Why try to use demanding and challenging scientific concepts as the basis for stories for Sensory Beings? Surely this is just tokenistic? Or pretentious? Or unrealistic? How can such an audience possibly be expected to understand these ideas …?

I think of myself reading Stephen Hawking's (1988) *A Brief History of Time* and clinging onto the tentative threads of understanding. I can almost, but not quite, understand the fantastic science it describes … so perhaps science is not for me?

Is the rule that if we cannot understand then we should not experience and learn?

That cannot be the rule. And if it is not the rule, then what is science to the person who does not understand?

Here I am, a carbon-based life form made of star dust. I am a part of all of this. The cloud of gas at the start of *The Birth of a Star* story is a part of my story. No, I do not understand how, but does that mean I shouldn't be allowed to touch the wonder?

We all crane our necks upwards at a dark night sky. By bringing *The Birth of a Star* to people with profound and multiple learning disabilities we invite them to do the same. And by creating narratives that stimulate our intellectual curiosities we invite the readers of that story to embed themselves deeper in the story sharing experience, thus enriching it for everyone.

I could write a story about a handful of confetti thrown up at a wedding, or a bowl of cereal spilled on the floor (both examples of particle dispersion) and give it to a teacher to read, and they might read it, and doubtless if they were a good teacher they would put feeling into their words as they read. But unless that story grabs them, asks their brain to peer at the confetti and look for something in it, then they won't truly be in that story with that person. Sensory Beings exist in the moment – lacking the cognitive capacity to imagine a future, or to lay down memories. They live in the here and now, and unless we occupy that same space we are not truly with them. A story that holds onto both the reader and the experiencer is, in my opinion, the most inclusive sort of story, and that's why I tackle ambitious narratives like the formation of stars in stellar nurseries.

And, quite frankly, why not? *The Bear Hunt* (Rosen & Oxenbury, 1989) is a wonderful, ready-made, sensory story. But we can't stay on a bear hunt forever.

The birth of a star

I often ask people about the sensory landscape of their lives, I find if I just rely on myself to think of sensations I come up with the same things over and over again, but if I ask a boat builder, a mechanic, a nurse, a physicist, what is the weirdest sensation in their job, or the most wonderful, then I get rich new pickings for my sensory adventures. *The Birth of a Star* tells with scientific accuracy how stars are formed in stellar nurseries. It was written in conjunction with physicists at the Max Planck Institute. The significance they accorded to sensation was a revelation. As they explained to me just how fundamental sensing becomes as they seek to push forth the boundaries of knowledge. These particle physicists told me how they have to watch for patterns in particle dispersion and that despite huge leaps in computer modelling, there is still nothing better at the job than the human eye. They must watch the dispersal of particles in their experiments just as experiencers of *The Birth of a Star* watch the dispersal of the particles in the confetti cloud.

Outcomes and evidence: what to look for

The story of a class "Voyage to Arghan"

Voyage to Arghan is a science fiction tale in which a girl has to voyage to a far-away planet with seven coloured suns to hunt for rare feathers. The class had been sharing the story for a term, using a separate room and scaling up my simple resources to an almost theatrical level. All the students knew that when they entered that room they were getting on a sensory space ship and blasting off into space. The teacher played a recording of NASA's launch sequence: *TEN, NINE, EIGHT* … whilst she and her teaching assistants jiggled the handles of everyone's wheelchairs to create the vibrations of a rocket launching and it was much enjoyed by the class. However on my visit they were a pair of hands down. In the video[1] you can see three students and one teaching assistant, who does her best to interact with two students. The student at the front of the shot has no one to "launch" her. You can see her look around expectantly, and then, marvellously, when she realizes there is no one there, she takes the decision to jiggle herself and begins stamping on her footplate to create the vibrations through her chair. It is as if to say "Everyone else is going to space and I do not want to be left behind!" This engagement and involvement in the story was made possible by the teacher's clear consistent sharing of the story, and it was utterly thrilling to see!

Sensory Beings have much to teach us, and can become consultants in the field to develop new stories and new ideas for developing resources and policies.

Contexts of learning

The stories are used in special schools, adult-care settings and by families around the globe, mainly in English-speaking countries, although teams in Italy, Portugal and Albania use the stories in state-run institutions for people with learning disabilities.

Issues to consider

Knowledge of the person you are working with is critical – as far as is possible understand their language and sensory skills, and be informed by these as you work. For example, if you know someone has poor tunnel vision you might present a visual stimulus more to the side of their head than right in front of them.

Another crucial issue is not to add extra language – sensory stories are intended to be sparse, crisp and clear like a good Haiku.[2] For people who find language a comfort there is a huge temptation to provide ongoing description. This can detract from the experience of the sensation, gives the impression that language is crucial and that sensation alone is not good enough. By holding back on language we give respect to sensation and its inherent communicative value.

Try it yourself

If you are looking to create a non-fiction sensory story choose a topic you know a lot about, or approach specialists in the field, who are often curious and keen to support. To get the story right you need to be able to distil the information to its essence, and doing that requires a high level of understanding of the topic. Remember, topics do not have to be from the frontiers of science. Narratives we might overlook because we know them so well hold enormous interest for people who haven't encountered them yet. What about the life cycle of a frog, or the water cycle, or a day in the life of your pet? I often start out by sketching out all potential sensory options in a diagram, to use as a guide. Otherwise it is all too easy to end up with a story entirely resourced from one or two senses.

Top tips

- Be consistent – aim to share the words and the sensations within a sensory story in the same way each time you tell it.
- 2.Take your time – allow time for the language to be processed, allow time for the sensations to be absorbed. It is possible to get through a sensory story very quickly, but taking time and allowing time leads to a richer experience for everyone.
- 3.Be prepared – being organised, checking that resources are there, that batteries are working and all those little logistical things is hugely important in ensuring a smooth sharing of a sensory story (Grace, 2015b).

Where to go

Visit www.thesensoryprojects.co.uk where you can find the sensory stories a free basic guide; various summary leaflets on aspects of sensory story sharing, and online training courses.

Acknowledgements

Setting up *The Sensory Story Project* was very much a case of "standing on the shoulders of giants" (Isaac Newton). In addition to my own creative practice I founded the project on the work of so many other fantastic sensory story tellers and researchers who have explored the lives of people with profound and multiple learning disabilities. Most notable to me were: Loretta Lambe, Annet ten Brug, Chantal Vlaskamp, Jenny Young, Chris Fuller, Nicola Grove, Keith Park, Penny Lacey and Flo Longhorn.

The project would not have been possible without the generous funding of 129 Kickstarter Backers to whom I am forever grateful.

Notes

1 For a direct link to this clip please visit: http://bitly.ws/b4Ut.
2 Japanese tradition of three-line poems with set syllable count.

References

Bag Books (2016). *How Bag Books help people with learning difficulties.* Available at: www.bagbooks.org/about-us/how-bag-books-helps-people-with-learning-disabilities (Accessed 1.5.21).

Doukas, T., Fergusson, A., Fullerton, M. & Grace, J. (2017). The core and essential service standards for supporting people with profound and multiple learning disabilities. Available at: www.thesensoryprojects.co.uk/PMLD-service-standards (Accessed 1.5.21).

Grace, J. (2015a). *Rich inclusion.* Available at: https://www.youtube.com/watch?v=XxsneaZAxXY (Accessed 1.5.21).

Grace, J. (2015b). *Sensory stories for children and teens with special educational needs: A practical guide.* London: JKP.

Grace, J. (2017). *Sensory-being for sensory beings: Creating entrancing sensory experiences.* London and New York: Routledge.

Grace, J. & Salfield, C. (2017). *Inclusion – for pity's sake?* TEDx Talk, Truro. Available at: https://www.youtube.com/watch?v=_PbWFcVcaWQ (Accessed 21.8.20).

Grace, J. & Silva, A. (2017). Refining the guidance for sensory storytelling with individuals with PMLD: A move towards improved research and practice. *PMLD Link*, 29(3), Issue 88, 11–15.

Grove, N., Harwood, J., Henderson, E., Park, K. & Bird, R. (2015). Literature and stories in the lives of learners with SLD/PMLD. In P. Lacey, R. Ashdown, P. Jones, H. Lawson & M. Pipe (Eds), *The Routledge companion to severe, profound and multiple learning difficulties* (pp. 258–270). London: Routledge,

Grove, N. & Park, K. (1996). *Odyssey now.* London: JKP.

Grove, N. & Park, K. (2001). *Social cognition through drama and literature for people with learning disabilities: Macbeth in mind.* London: Jessica Kingsley.

Hawking, S. (1998). *A brief history of time.* New York: Bantam Books.

Lacey, P. (2006). Inclusive literacy. *PMLD Link*, 18(3), Issue 55, 11–13.

Menary, R. (2008). Embodied narratives. *Journal of Consciousness Studies*, 15(6), 63–84.

Murphy, E. (2017). *Communicating without words. Little Mama Murphy.* Available at: www.littlemamamurphy.co.uk/2017/05/communicating-without-words.html (Accessed 1.5.21).

PAMIS. (2010). *Multi-sensory stories research.* Available at: www.pamis.org.uk/_page.php?id=24.

Park, K. (2004). Interactive storytelling: From the Book of Genesis. *British Journal of Special Education*, 31, 16–23.

Rosen, M. & Oxenbury, H. (1989). *We're going on a bear hunt.* London: Walker Books.

Taylor, J. (2006). Using multisensory stories to develop literacy skills and to teach sensitive topics. *PMLD Link*, 18(3), Issue 55, 14–16.

Ten Brug, A., van der Putten, A., Penne, A., Maes, B. & Vlaskamp, C. (2012). Multisensory storytelling for persons with profound intellectual and multiple disabilities: An analysis of the development content and application in practice. *Journal of Applied Research in Intellectual Disabilities*, 25, 350–359.

Young, H., Fenwick, M., Lambe, L. & Hogg, J. (2011). Multisensory storytelling as an aid to assisting people with profound intellectual disabilities to cope with sensitive issues: A multiple research methods analysis of engagement and outcomes. *European Journal of Special Needs Education*, 26 (2), 127–142.

Young, H. & Lambe, L. (2011). Multisensory storytelling for people with profound and multiple learning disabilities. *PMLD Link* 23(1), Issue 68, 29–31.

Chapter 16

Describing and evaluating the storytelling experience

A conceptual framework

Tuula Pulli

This chapter describes an approach to multisensory storytelling developed in Finland with children and adults with severe disabilities, using a model which emphasises aesthetic, social and cognitive aspects of a drama-based interaction that goes beyond speech and provides novel ways to cope with the limits of human capacity.

Background

Traditional narratives such as epics, legends, fairy tales, poems and songs tell us who we are and how we cope with the social and the natural world. Their images and archaic characters arise from an eternal shared past and future. This property belongs to everyone. It can and should be accessible to everyone, and explored irrespective of physical or mental skills. The best stories succeed in moving us because they are based on the origin of human mind and body, beyond all formal languages (Grove, 2005; Peter, 1994, 1995, 1996; Ricoeur, 1991; Turner, 1982, 1995). Multisensory and co-experienced storytelling with a rich range of artistic experiences refreshes our minds and enhances shared attention to a common interest for children and adults who have difficulties in perception, social life, cognition and speech. It provides not only an access to culture but also a way of implementing community-based rehabilitation (Grove & Park, 1996, 2001; Maes et al., 2007; Mitchell & van der Gaag, 2002; Peter, 2003; Pulli, 2010).

Work in practice

Traditional narratives can be told with severely disabled persons in various ways. There are three main approaches, which can also be combined:

- *Performance*: One or more storytellers perform a story using rich body language (such as voice variations, space and rhythm). Additional multisensory items (such as fire, music, dance, choir, sound effect, blowing air or smell) or a few objects (such as food, mask on face, clothes or blanket) may be also used. The aim is to intensify the feeling of presence by providing concrete clues that convey the worlds which exist behind the story themes and metaphors we are using.
- *Co-creating*: The storyteller acts as a 'conductor' to organise participation by the audience, providing material for them to use. For example, to make fire they may wave sparklers or colourful silk scarves. In exploring characters they may wear cloaks, hats or make sounds. They may remain seated or, voluntarily yet guided, move across the room or step on stage for a short while. The conductor or the performers' group is in charge of the action.

DOI: 10.4324/9781003159087-16

- *Adapted process drama*: The group tells the story together and explores chosen themes. They follow freely the pre-text made by the conductor(s), who also takes responsibility for conveying the gist of the plot and prompting the group to perform episodes. Participants can reflect spontaneously on what they have been told, what is happening or will happen, why it happens or what else might happen. They may act as a choir or take on roles. Support workers can be grouped or paired with the persons with disabilities – sharing participation and roles with them. When co-creating interaction in episodes seems to flow, the conductor(s) reduces their guidance. They remain responsible, however, for story clarity and dramatic tension, and group dynamics and psychic safety. To ensure they work ethically, they use various conventions in drama education (e.g. O'Toole, 1992, 1996).

All approaches are enriched by artwork such as music, colour and movement, which may be created together or found. In *Odyssey Now*, projections of images from relevant art galleries are used as illustrations (Grove & Park, 1996; see also Carroll, 2000).

Sharing an experience: staff members cross between worlds

More capable people support the less capable ones but they simultaneously experience the event as participants. For the staff too, a fictive, magical and substitute world offers a haven to throw oneself into. Research document accounts by support workers describe having found novel ways of interaction that do not take place in daily routines. They also report having noticed positive, unused capacity, which hides behind challenging or withdrawing behaviour (Dobson et al., 2002; Maguire, 2003; Pulli, 2010). A lived experience endures, and enriches everyone (Conroy, 2009; van Manen, 1990). While experiencing the magic together we emerge as members of the group. For many, belonging to a group or a performance is more important than communication, as Ferguson (1994) says: "We sit in the boat of Odysseus and float on a stormy ancient sea [*we wave; the wheelchairs surrounded by dark blue silk on our skin*]. Suddenly we get wet [*because someone sprays us with water*]. Fellows, take the rope!"

An intensified shared story moment brings us emotionally close and makes us sensitive to each other. This breaks down the barriers between ability and disability, and points to equality. In a story world we can look from a distance but still explore things close up and through our bodies. Thus we may justify Heidegger's (1927) observation that as a being everyone is anyone.

Theories, principles and planning

Grove (2005) has developed a framework that allows teachers and therapists to explore and analyse the responses of pupils to rich imaginative experiences in ways that help them plan and evaluate their sessions. The motivation for this was in fact the remarks of a sceptical bureaucrat in the government-run curriculum authority, who poured scorn on Grove's hesitant suggestion that assessments should be designed to take into account responses such as the spontaneous, fleeting but magical eye contact made by a very autistic teenager during an episode of *Macbeth* (Grove & Park, 2001). The ideas for the framework came from the world of arts education (Ross, 1978; Webb, 1992), special education (Brown, 1996) and cultural theory (Geertz, 1973). The dimensions considered are: *engagement* (using Brown's model, which moves from *encounter* – being present – to active *involvement), feeling* (empathy and affect), *cognitive* (thinking and language) and *aesthetic* (creativity, social impact, formal properties). Figure 16.1 provides a schematic outline of the approach (for full details see Grove, 2005). Fornefeld (see Chapter 12) and McCaffrey (see Chapter 4) have also developed multidimensional frameworks that take account of creativity, emotional responses and aesthetic properties.

The framework devised in the course of my own research on storytelling by adapted process drama with severely disabled and speechless adults (Pulli, 2010) drew on some of these ideas. The conceptual framework is based on the links between special education, drama and art education, speech and language therapy and critical education philosophy. These four disciplines are approached by phenomenology and hermeneutics, focusing embodied knowledge (see Dillon, 1991; Kolb, 1984; Merleau-Ponty, 1970, 2002; van Manen, 1990). Content analysis has demonstrated that those disciplines and approaches share the ethics of concern for otherness, communality, equality, empowerment, alternative ways of viewing, creativity, knowledge in action and experiential learning. Similar ideology can be found in the literature of devised and applied drama (e.g. Baldwin, 2008; Hellier-Ticono, 2005; Nicholson, 2005a, 2005b). I explored the conceptual model in analysing the responses of 18 disabled participants and 16 staff members (12 videotaped sessions, each 60–90 minutes, time range 6 months). The framework was useful in describing, understanding and evaluating the emergence of themes and other rehabilitative items, and what was happening during and after sessions.

There are three dimensions in the model shown in Figure 16.1: *aesthetic* (beauty/lived experience), *social* (sharing/partnership) and *cognitive* (comprehension/understanding).

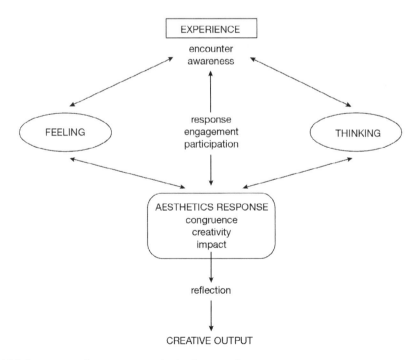

Figure 16.1 Response to literature: an evaluative framework

Table 16.1 A framework for developing narrative skills through multisensory storytelling

| | Dimensions | | |
	Aesthetic	Social	Cognitive
Art education			
Why?	Art *itself*, as a *value*	Art as a shared *process*	Art as a means of *experimental learning*
Dimensions in storytelling	*Beauty*	*Partnership*	*Comprehension*
What?	Performance form: space, rhythm, tension Sensation Appraisal Flow	Membership Equality Co-creating	Forming images Seeking insight Meaning-making Symbol function
The experience of storytelling	*Lived experience*	*Involvement*	*Understanding*
How?	Apprehension Embodied knowledge Feeling	Inner/outer activity Mutual respect Turn-taking	Wondering Viewing in other ways

- *Beauty* refers to responding to the artistic form by sensation, appraisal and feelings evoked by the story – a lived experience arises in an immediate and unconscious apprehension which stays in the memory of embodied knowledge.
- *Partnership* refers to involvement and sharing which arise in the process of living the story through together, as an equal member of the group – audience and actors are all participants.
- *Comprehension* refers to learning about the world by forming images and meanings, and by exploring different options – it arises in wondering what and why something is told in the story and how it connects to real life (see Carroll, 2000; Nicholson, 2005a, 2005b).

Guidelines for implementing and evaluating multisensory storytelling

The aesthetic dimension: use the principle of beauty to design story presentations in order to create lived experience

Some principles of the following guidelines are common in applied drama (e.g. Baldwin, 2008; Hellier-Ticono, 2005; Nicholson, 2005a, 2005b). They have long been a focus in early interaction methods (e.g. Coupe & Goldbart, 1978; Nind & Hewett, 1994).

Frame a session with a plain structure – like a picture frame, which separates the image from the background, unobtrusively. Use 'initial hooks': everyday materials in new settings, such as snow or the smell of a horse in a living room. Use opening and closing rituals. Make transitions slowly. Wait – repeat – ritualise – surprise – rest – reflect, over and over again. Increase tension gradually but decrease it quickly and early.

Create impressions of shifting in space and time (use a mask, a light, an odd sound, a frozen movement, a sound effect). Provide aesthetic experiences by distinction and contrasts (such as noise before silence, light before darkness) but do not exaggerate stimulation (see Grove & Park (1996) on concepts of foregrounding and backgrounding in multisensory environments).

While liberating oneself from the past and the future, you and the participants may achieve full presence and flow.

Assess and evaluate the lived experience noticing how the participants:

- **Focus on a story**: Pause in expectation, use their senses, seem to be present
- **Move through an imaginative world**: Play seriously, leave routine behaviours behind, accept dramatic tension
- **Throw themselves into**: Follow and/or play 'make-believe', step into a pretend world knowing that it is not real.

The social dimension: to create a shared feeling of 'us', a community, make it clear that partnership arises only in respect and love

Support everyone to feel that they are equal and unique. Respect individual territories and allow voluntary participation. Everyone – the staff included – has the right to determine the degree to which they join in. Never force, correct or instruct: 'Do it this way'. Repeat and ritualise: 'we all do this', enticing them to join a magic circle of shared beliefs and meanings.

For co-creating, suppress your own ideas when you become aware of an idea or initiative made by a participant. If a passive person demonstrates any activity (voice, gesture, etc.) which could be interpreted as carrying a meaning in the actual episode, respond to it positively. Encourage others to reinforce it as well.

Help the participants to feel how the characters feel and understand what they want. In our voyage, it is not only the captain who faces a challenge, we all do. Structure the story so that people at all levels of ability are enabled to take part. In early interaction skills, the goal of joint attention may be sufficient – to focus on the same target (light, sound, etc.) with the partner or group. In Grove and Park's *Macbeth* resource (Grove & Park, 2001), which is structured to promote social cognition, joint attention is the foundation of all of the activities.

Within the social dimension, evaluate how the participants:

- *Become empowered*: Influence the action, sense of being important to others; for example by sitting in the middle, calling out
- *Show membership*: Aim for a common goal, seek and get help, seem to feel empathy
- *Interact with each other*: Reflect, initiate, respond, take turns, cooperate; for example joining in clapping, giving a rope to a fallen sailor.

The cognitive dimension: to develop comprehension, let people learn by wondering and by doing

Provide problems with options and new horizons, but also things that they already know and can do. Choose one, two or three themes and make them visible; clarify but do not explain. If you are using a process drama approach, stick to the plot but allow for changes and breaks, and make the participants feel that with mutual respect almost anything is allowed to happen.

Use real objects, pictures, gestures, signs and any other forms of communication to substitute for and support speech. However, do not stick to any particular language form and do not expect all the participants to understand the plot. Each creates their own meanings: one person may try to establish causes and effects, another may recognise familiar objects, a third may think about a character's feelings or goals. Simplify archetypes (well-known characters such as Cinderella or the witch) by marking them with one item (e.g. bare foot, wooden spoon) and characteristic behaviour (e.g. sweeping the floor, witchy laugh). Do not use theatre spectacle but a miniature stage. Symbols and meanings come up in a story without the same chaos of time and space that they have in everyday life.

Create anticipation by using intensified attention. For instance, a trumpet sound is heard but nothing else happens – yet. One person may learn to expect the sound to be repeated. Another may learn to expect a king's appearance. Another may even try to guess the king's thoughts. Let these different levels shift and intertwine. In storytelling, as in real life, we manage quite well by guessing – using love, respect and good will.

Within the cognitive dimension evaluate how the participants:

- *Form mental images*. Assign meanings to objects and actions; learn marks or symbols referring to something that is not necessarily present.
- *Wonder*. Contemplation through looking for a long time, smiling, repeated touching; seek connections and explanations – asking 'what/to whom/why does this happen'
- *Try to find new points of view*. Seek new solutions, encounter different persons and gain insight into them.

Why the crown of a king in a story is attractive: three ways of answering the question

Baroque music is playing and a golden crown is slowly passed around a circle. All sit calmly, waiting for their turn to hold the crown to play the role of king. Then something surprising takes place. While wearing the crown an autistic youngster who normally finds it hard to sit still waves his hand, first imitating his caregiver. He then continues on his own to act like a king. He looks at the audience and raises his hands like a king to greet the people, and interacts with them non-verbally. He then sits down calmly and takes a deep breath. How could this happen, when he does not seem to consciously know what a crown, king or power means?

- An *aesthetic* explanation lies with sensation, apprehension and emotion. A shiny, distinctive object, combined with aristocratic music, stimulated him to accept the offered gesture.
- A *social* explanation relies on the desire to get attention and acceptance from the group. They shared a common goal. He noticed that the others wanted to have the crown, and so did he. He desired to be part of a shared and empowering experience.
- According to a *cognitive* explanation he had an inner clue that the crown may possess a meaning, is something more than an interesting object. Without knowing history he realised that a crown may change not only a person's looks but also their image. He explored this idea – the idea of a symbolic function – by curiosity leading to knowledge. He seemed to have the capacity to learn to read and use symbols, perhaps also for learning a language. He may also have memories of this behaviour from television, books or theatre – the important thing is that he is drawing on these memories and using them appropriately.

Summary

Persons with special needs have the right to learn about the cultural heritage of stories that give rise to questions about life and ourselves – that move everybody. The best stories do it in concrete and abstract ways simultaneously, and these can be combined in hands-on work.

Thus classic literature can provide basic experiences performed with aesthetic sensation (*beauty*), with respect and love (*partnership*) and with clarity of meaning (*understanding*). These three dimensions form an evaluation model for multisensory storytelling in education and community-based rehabilitation. Stories can be performed by storyteller(s), co-created with an audience or told by adapting process drama with all the people who are present. In all approaches, the participants' embodied knowledge interfaces with symbolic interpretations in a story – for the *equal* and the *eternal* to emerge.

Resources

- www.art-stream.org (creates artistic opportunities for individuals in communities traditionally underserved by the arts)
- www.avoin.jyu.fi/draamakasvatus (a Finnish centre delivering drama education at Jyväskylä University)
- www.idea-org.net (International Drama/Theatre and Education Association)
- www.fideafinland.fi (Finnish Drama/Theatre Education Association)

Acknowledgements

Thanks to Nicola Grove, who was one of the four supervisors in the research. She found the framework internationally interesting and adaptive. Her products and enthusiasm influenced the text. *Odyssey Now*, especially should be kept alive — it is an eternal book of archetypes and a storytelling manual beyond cultures.

References

Baldwin, P. (2008). *The primary drama handbook*. Thousand Oaks, CA: Sage.

Brown, E. (1996). *Religious education for all*. London: David Fulton.

Carroll, N. (Ed.) (2000). *Theories of art today*. Madison, WI: University of Wisconsin Press.

Conroy, C. (2009). Disability: Creative tensions between drama, theatre and disability arts. *Research in Drama Education: The Journal of Applied Theatre and Performance*, 14(*1*), 1–14.

Coupe, J. & Goldbart, J. (1978). *Communication before speech*. London: Croom Helm.

Dillon, M. C. (1991). Merleau-Ponty and postmodernity. Foreword in M. C. Dillon (Ed.), *Merleau-Ponty vivant* (pp. ix–xxxv). New York: State University of New York Press.

Dobson, S., Upadhyana, S. & Stanley, B. (2002). Using an interdisciplinary approach to training to develop the quality of communication with adults with profound learning disabilities. *International Journal of Language and Communication Disorders*, 37, 41–57.

Ferguson, D. (1994). Is communication really the point? Some thoughts on interventions on membership. *Mental Retardation*, 32, 7–18.

Geertz, C. (1973). *The interpretation of cultures: Selected essays* (pp. 3–30). New York: Basic Books.

Grove, N. (2005). *Ways into literature: Stories, plays and poems for pupils with SEN*. London: David Fulton.

Grove, N. & Park, K. (1996). *Odyssey now*. London: Jessica Kingsley.

Grove, N. & Park, K. (2001). *Social cognition through drama and literature for people with learning disabilities: Macbeth in mind*. London: Jessica Kingsley.

Heidegger, M. (1927). *Sein und Zeit*. Tübingen: Max Niemeyer Verlag.

Hellier-Ticono, R. (2005). Becoming-in-the-world-with-others: Inter-act theatre workshop. *Research in Drama Education*, 10(2), 159–173.

Kolb, D. (1984). *Experiential learning: Experience as a source of learning and development.* Englewood Cliffs, NJ: Prentice Hall.

Maes, B., Lambrechts, G., Hostyn, I. & Petry, K. (2007). Quality-enhancing interventions for people with profound intellectual and multiple disabilities: A review of the empirical research literature. *Journal of Intellectual and Developmental Disability*, 32(3), 163–178.

Maguire, N. (2003). Group counseling for people with mild to moderate mental retardation and developmental disabilities: An interactive-behavioral model and a single session. Video review, ed. by V. Brabender. *International Journal of Group Psychotherapy*, 53(1), 125–128.

Merleau-Ponty, M. (1970) [Trans. 1963]. *In praise of philosophy and other essays.* Evanston, IL: Northwestern University Press.

Merleau-Ponty, M. (2002) [Trans. 1962, rev. 1981]. *Phenomenology of perception.* London: Routledge & Kegan.

Mitchell, J. R. & van der Gaag, A. (2002). Through the eye of the cyclops: Evaluating the multi-sensory intervention programme for people with complex disabilities. *British Journal of Learning Disabilities*, 30, 159–165.

Nicholson, H. (2005a). *Applied drama: The gift of theatre.* New York: Palgrave.

Nicholson, H. (2005b). On ethics. *Research in Drama Education*, 10(2), 119–125.

Nind, M. & Hewett, D. (1994). *Access to communication: Developing the basis of communication with people with severe learning difficulties through intensive interaction.* London: David Fulton.

O'Toole, J. (1992). *The process of drama: Negotiating art and meaning.* London and New York: Routledge.

O'Toole, J. (1996). Towards a poetics of drama research. In P. Taylor (Ed.), *Researching drama and arts education: Paradigm and possibilities* (pp. 147–155). London: Falmer Press.

Peter, M. (1994). *Drama for all.* London: David Fulton.

Peter, M. (1995). *Making drama special: Developing drama practice to meet special educational needs.* London: David Fulton.

Peter, M. (1996). *Art for all.* London: David Fulton.

Peter, M. (2003). Drama, narrative and early learning. *British Journal of Special Education* 30, 21–27.

Pulli, T. (2010). *Totta ja unta [The real and the illusory]. Drama as a means of community-based rehabilitation and experience for persons with severe learning and speech disabilities.* Doctoral dissertation in special education, Studies in Education, Psychology and Social Research, Jyväskylä University.

Ricoeur, P. (1991). Life in quest of narrative. In D. Wood (Ed.), *On Paul Ricoeur: Narrative and interpretation* (pp. 20–33). London: Routledge.

Ross, M. (1978). *The creative arts.* London: Heinemann Education.

Turner, F. (1995). *The culture of hope: A new birth of classical spirit.* New York: Free Press.

Turner, V. (1982). *From ritual to theatre: The human seriousness of play.* New York: Performing Arts Journal Publications.

van Manen, M. (1990). *Researching lived experience: Human science for an action sensitive pedagogy.* New York: State University of New York.

Webb, E. (1992). *Literature in education. Encounter and experience.* London: Palmer Press.

Chapter 17

Sensitive stories

Tackling challenges for people with profound intellectual disabilities through multi-sensory storytelling

Loretto Lambe, Jenny Miller and Maureen Phillip

Foreword

The late Loretto Lambe, founder of PAMIS, Promoting a More Inclusive Society, a charity based in Scotland that solely supports children, young people and adults with profound intellectual and multiple disabilities (PIMD) and their families to lead healthy, inclusive and valued lives, was passionate about the lifelong learning for people with PIMD. She spent several decades building on the work of Chris Fuller to provide a model to support those with PIMD to understand and learn about sensitive topics that presented issues and further exacerbated their exclusion from aspects of life. She led the research within PAMIS that developed the Multi-sensory Sensitive Stories but that has also been the basis for our ongoing commitment to inclusion and lifelong learning using a range of multi-sensory stories and approaches.

The content of the original chapter in the previous edition of this book, written by Loretto and Professor James Hogg, remains relevant and an important contribution to this area of work. Across the world Loretto's pioneering work has been acknowledged and her vision for more extensive research has been realised as can be seen within this book and the updated references cited here.

Background

History

The development of multi-sensory storytelling took as its starting point the expressed need in the late 1990s of family carers, teachers and other professionals for the development of a holistic context for an enjoyable and meaningful activity with developmental significance for people with profound intellectual and multiple disabilities (PIMD).

PAMIS responded by developing the work of Chris Fuller at Bag Books (Fuller, 1990, 1999; and see Chapter 13) through the creation of individualised, personal stories. Fifty-four personal story boxes were created, each based on a real-life event in someone's life. Each story had three identified learning targets built into it (Watson, Lambe & Hogg, 2002). These are still the most borrowed items in the PAMIS library. By individualisation we mean not only a narrative of personal significance but also a choice of materials that are appropriate and personal in terms of age, sensory characteristics and relevant interactions.

Subsequently these stories evolved to provide a means for parents and teachers to engage individuals with PIMD with topics that presented difficulties for them with respect, for

DOI: 10.4324/9781003159087-17

example, to sexual development, transitions or health interventions (Fenwick, 2005, 2007; Young et al., 2010; Lambe et al., 2014)

The approach is particularly aimed at children and adults who have PIMD; that is, they have complex health needs, sensory impairments and great difficulty in communicating, in addition to intellectual disabilities (Hogg, Juhlberg & Lambe, 2007; Nakken & Vlaskamp, 2002).

The starting point is the development of a narrative relevant specifically, but not necessarily exclusively, to a given individual. This begins with the identification of events and experiences of importance to the person, as reported and developed by those most familiar with him or her, typically a parent and/or professional.

This narrative consists of a set of events, typically real-world experiences, linked causally and/or temporally in a connected sequence. We view storytelling as the sequence of communicative acts conveying the narrative through interactive, multi-sensory presentation. It is important that each of these interactions are seen as part of the whole and related to the overall meaning.

Theories

The theoretical basis of multi-sensory storytelling is grounded in an understanding of the nature of PIMD and their impact on development, including:

- *Communicative difficulties* resulting in the failure of other individuals to respond contingently and consistently to communicative approaches. Consequently there is in a breakdown of interaction, which may be abbreviated and inconsistent (Grove et al., 1999).

    The activity of storytelling provides a single context with a joint focus in which the storyteller and individual with PIMD may interact. Careful structuring of the story within a defined timeframe permits the storyteller to pace contingent responses and, where necessary, intervene to facilitate interaction with the material.
- *Sensory impairments*: Impairment of vision and hearing are highly prevalent (Evenhuis et al., 2001; Soorya et al., 2018), restricting what may be experienced in the natural environment.
- *Personhood*: In people with PIMD, personhood is viewed as the outcome of social interaction and the meaning of individuals to each other (Hogg, 2011; Kittay, 2011), including the acknowledgement of the value of their lives. At the core of the creation of these presentations of multi-sensory stories is the acknowledgment of the individual as a person with unique interests and concerns. In the telling of the story, the personhood of that individual is the focus of joint attention without other distractions.
- *Learning*: It is now widely accepted that individuals with PIMD have the capacity to learn, given appropriate interventions, though the conditions under which learning does occur are often not available (Hogg & Sebba, 1986a, 1986b). The use of multi-sensory stimuli not only increases retention of information but also develops motivation to learn (Matos et al., 2015). Clear learning outcomes are intrinsic, and applied through repeated sessions that ensure consistent practice and feedback. Learning takes place most effectively when a person is enjoying an activity and motivated to engage in it (Miller, 2003; Matos et al., 2015; Winther Hansen, Erlandsson & Leufstadius, 2021; Keilhofner, 2009). Hence we need to be aware of frequent changes of mood and motivation in people with PIMD (Ross & Oliver, 2003; Adams & Jahoda, 2019).

Multi-sensory storytelling is inherently enjoyable for both listener and storyteller, meaning that engagement, critical for learning, is intrinsic. However, such enjoyment can be an end in itself and use of the stories as a pure leisure activity is of course entirely legitimate.

Principles

The guiding principles cover the creation of the story, its production as a physical entity and the way in which it is told.

All stories are personal to the intended listener. Each story is developed through colla- boration between caregivers and practitioners. Where relevant, specialists are consulted: for example, a community dentist, a learning disability epilepsy nurse or a community nurse specialising in sexual health. Each draft of the narrative is reviewed and developed by the team, who also choose sensory stimuli and trial their use with the individual.

Work in practice

The story book

The book cover is a cardboard box containing the pages of the story with the sensory objects, and the storyline written on a single laminated sheet. The box is easy to transport when the story is lent to a family or school. It also gives a clear indication to the person with PIMD that the story is about to be told, emphasised by a visual and tactile stimulus on the 'spine' of the box.

There are between six and eight laminated A3 board pages in a story, which is designed to last about 3 minutes, following research findings (Ten Brug et al., 2016). The sensory stimuli are attached to each board, which is neutral in colour to promote maximum perceptual acuity, typically there is one object per page. The objects are personal to the listener, appropriate to their age and stage of development and convey the key concept of an episode. Attaching objects keeps them on the right page, and reduces any risk of swallowing or throwing.

One or two short sentences for each page are written on a matt laminated story card. The words relate directly to the stimulus, are age appropriate and comprehensible. Infection control procedures should be in place before and after use of the story.

The space

If indoors, find a suitable quiet room or therapeutic space – calm, uncluttered, warm, safe, perhaps using a particular smell to build recognition of the setting. If possible, provide a space to which people can retreat if they feel overstimulated or overwhelmed, which allows them to hear the story and interact as they wish. Outdoor spaces and story walks are also appropriate and fun.

Internal space

Our lives are a series of events, some of which are formed into storylines that shape our identity. The story space is a safe space that can support the exploration of these events and the associated emotions. Often, it's difficult to make time and space for the exploration of

Figure 17.1 The components of a PAMIS multi-sensory story

the emotions we may experience during life events and there is no more precious gift than to give someone the time and presence to listen to their story.

Telling the story

Ensure consistency of telling, without deviation or improvisation, by following the guidance on the reverse of the storyline card.

- Present the page accessibly and within the person's field of vision and reach.
- Use voice expressively, with varied intonation, pitch and volume to convey atmosphere and meaning.
- Speak slowly, and use pauses, to support processing of the information.
- Allow time for exploration.
- Repeat the story over a period of time. Between 5 and 10 readings appear to be effective for the development of engagement and anticipation (Watson et al., 2002; Young et al., 2011; Ten Brug et al., 2016).

Outcomes and evidence: what we look for

We recommend assessing the mood, physical wellbeing and environmental considerations which may cause engagement with the story to fluctuate. Ten Brug and her colleagues suggest building in evaluation time for the sessions, asking the following questions:

- Are the stimuli still adequate or could we think of better ones?
- Is the reading time sufficient for the listener to engage in the story?
- Is the sentence length and language used appropriate or does this cause the listener to lose focus?
- Does the listener have the time and opportunity to manipulate the stimuli?

Multi-sensory storytelling has been extensively evaluated, using multi-method research techniques. Behavioural analysis of videoed sessions – typically of the first storytelling session, a middle session and the final session – (cf. Brewer & Hunter, 2006; Watson et al., 2002; Young et al., 2011). These computerised recordings allowed us to look at a range of representations; for example, graphing the relationship in time between page presentation and withdrawal, key behaviours related to engagement with the story and storyteller and learning objectives. Figure 17.2, for example, shows (A) an increase in both looking at and touching the stimulus objects, and (B) the simultaneous reduction in visual social engagement with the storyteller.

Parents and professionals were interviewed at the end of the project about their experience of multi-sensory storytelling and how effective it had been in enabling their son or

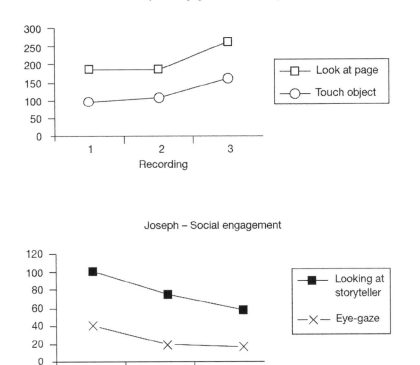

Figure 17.2 An example of data derived from the computerised analysis

daughter to cope with the sensitive issue (Young et al., 2011). Further research has explored: staff interactive style, consistency and meaningfulness to carers (Maes & Petry, 2006; Penne & Maes, 2011; Preece & Zhao, 2015; Ten Brug et al., 2012, 2016; Vlaskamp et al., 2011).

In the 'Real Lives: Real Stories' project learning targets were linked to individual educational programmes, and included a goal suggested by the parent. Teachers reported that the stories fitted well into the curriculum and that pupils and their classmates enjoyed repeated readings of the story. Parents reported that the stories gave them another enjoyable activity to do that provided a means of helping their children understand concepts and situations.

The story of Craig

Craig was 14 years old with PIMD, and quadriplegia. He was about to become an uncle and his mother wanted to develop a story about the new baby. His learning targets from school were to understand 'big' and 'small' and to reach out to explore objects. When the baby was born, Craig had his picture taken holding her and was able to give her a present. The school reported that from their perspective his learning targets had been met. This particular story is still very popular, with everyone.

The story of Lee

Lee was an 11-year-old with PIMD and autistic spectrum disorders. *Lee Goes to the Dentist* was designed to reduce his anxiety, challenging behaviour and teeth-clenching. The significant pages depicted the dentist using three different instruments: a mirror, a toothbrush and a tooth polisher, occurring one after the other and used to encourage Lee to open his mouth for the instruments.

Analysis demonstrated that Lee's engagement developed over the sessions, with an increase in touching the dental equipment and opening his mouth. Lee's mother reported that situational anxiety had reduced, as did his challenging behaviour during storytelling; Lee associated the stimuli in the story with the instruments used at the dentist and he remained engaged with the story. For the first time, Lee allowed his mother to read the story to him at home, which had not been accepted with standard storybooks. Lee's teacher reported that he was focused during the story and used the objects more appropriately across sessions of storytelling.

Contexts of learning

Although the stories developed in the PAMIS 'Real Lives: Real Stories' project were created for specific individuals, the intention was that they could be enjoyed by others with PIMD. In practice this certainly proved to be the case, with a high and steady flow of requests for loans throughout Scotland. Full details, with illustrations of the material, are presented in Lambe and Hogg (2011).

PAMIS have continued to use this methodology developed in 'Real Lives: Real Stories' and have supported a wider range of sensitive topics including one of the most challenging areas of PIMD, bereavement. PAMIS have developed individual stories that have not only supported the bereaved person with PIMD but also family carers (Young, Garrard & Lambe, 2014). This has included working with a family carer in palliative care who wanted her grandson prepared for her death in a sensitive and appropriate way. This beautiful resource took many months to prepare working at the pace of both the grandmother and the grandson but has had benefit for both.

During the COVID 19 pandemic, it became clear that people with PIMD were suffering a new kind of trauma; isolation, loneliness, lack of routine and services, lack of physical contact all negatively impacted on individuals. PAMIS developed a multi-sensory resource using storytelling, art, music and drama to promote exploration of these feelings. Information about *The Imagination Toolkit* is available on the PAMIS website.

Issues to consider

In the development of your own sensitive stories note that the information gathering process may stir emotions or forgotten memories for the carer. Be prepared to take the time necessary to complete this in a sensitive and appropriate way. This will be particularly relevant in the development of sensitive stories about bereavement or loss (Young, 2017). PAMIS have specific resources to develop these personal sensitive stories (Young et al., 2014).

The lack of standardised measures to identify motor and sensory impairment in this group emphasises the role of family carers and known practitioners in creating the sensory profile (Wessels & van der Putten, 2017; Soorya et al., 2018) and selecting stimuli to be used. Impairments are addressed either by increased emphasis on the senses that are available or through accentuating the intensity of stimuli in the impaired modality. However, caution and discussion are needed to safeguard against any adverse reactions to stimuli, and to be aware of the emotional impact of a stimulus, a memory and the story.

Try it yourself

Top tips

- Prepare thoroughly in collaboration with the person with PIMD, family members and relevant professionals.
- Try out the materials and stimuli and then fine-tune them. Practise telling the story.
- Seek out additional information such as a sensory profile and where possible a functional visual assessment.
- Be alert to emotional trigger factors in the story; discuss thoroughly with the team.

Where to go

- For further information, resources, training and templates for multi-sensory sensitive stories see: www.pamis.org.uk.
- Phillip, M. (2021). *PAMIS Creative Arts*. PAMIS. Available from: https://pamis.org.uk/creative-arts (Accessed 7.5.21).
- For sensory profile support, training and information see: www.motorvatetherapies.co.uk (Accessed 28.5.21).

References

Adams, T. & Jahoda, A. (2019). Listening to mothers: Experiences of mental health support and insights into adapting therapy for people with severe or profound intellectual disabilities. *International Journal of Developmental Disabilities*, 65, 135–142.

Brewer, J. & Hunter, A. (2006). *Foundations of multimethod research: Synthesizing styles*. London: Sage.

Evenhuis, H., Theunissen, M., Denkers, I., Versschuure, H. & Kemme, H. (2001). Prevalence of visual and hearing impairment in a Dutch institutionalized population with intellectual disability. *Journal of Intellectual Disability Research*, 45, 457–464.

Fenwick, M. (2005). Multi-sensory sensitive stories. *Eye Contact: RNIB*, 42, 12–14.

Fenwick, M. (2007). Sensitive stories. *Insight: RNIB*, 10, 30–32.

Fuller, C. (1990). *Tactile stories: A do-it-yourself guide to making 6 tactile books*. London: Bag Books.

Fuller, C. (1999). Bag Books tactile stories. *The SLD Experience*, 23, 20–21.

Grove, N., Bunning, K., Porter, J. & Ollson, C. (1999). See what I mean: Interpreting the meaning of communication by people with severe and profound intellectual disabilities. *Journal of Applied Research in Intellectual Disability*, 12, 190–203.

Hogg, J. (2011). *What is the nature of people with profound intellectual and multiple disabilities? Philosophy and Research*. Paper presented at the First International Association for the Scientific Study of Intellectual Disability Asia-Pacific Regional Round Table on Profound Intellectual and Multiple Disabilities, Kyoto, Japan, 22 October 2011.

Hogg, J., Juhlberg, K. & Lambe, L. (2007). Policy, service pathways and mortality: A 10-year longitudinal study of people with profound intellectual and multiple disabilities. *Journal of Intellectual Disability Research*, 51, 366–376.

Hogg, J. & Sebba, J. (1986a). *Profound retardation and multiple impairments: Volume 1: Development and learning*. London: Croom Helm.

Hogg, J. & Sebba, J. (1986b). *Profound retardation and multiple impairments: Volume 2: Education and therapy*. London: Croom Helm.

Kielhofner, G. (2008). *Model of human occupation: Theory and application*. Baltimore, MD: Lippincott, Williams & Wilkins.

Kittay, E. F. (2011). Forever small: The strange case of Ashley X. *Hypatia*, 26, 610–631.

Lambe, L., Fenwick, M., Young, H., & Hogg, J. (2014). The use of a personalised multi-sensory sensitive story to prepare a young man with profound intellectual disabilities and autism for oral health care: A case study. *Journal of Disability and Oral Health*, 15(4), 154–158.

Lambe, L. & Hogg, J. (2011). Multi-sensory storytelling: PAMIS' practice, experience and research findings. In B. Fornefeld (Ed.), *Multi-sensory storytelling: An idea gets through* (pp. 15–40). Berlin: Lit Verlag Dr. W. Hopf.

Maes, B. & Petry, K. (2006). Engagement and pleasure of children with profound multiple disabilities in interaction with adults during multi-sensory activities. *Journal of Applied Research in Intellectual Disabilities*, 19, 265.

Matos, A., Rocha, T., Cabral, L. & Bessa, M. (2015). Multi-sensory storytelling to support learning for people with intellectual disability: an exploratory didactic study. *Procedia Computer Science*, 67, 12–18.

Miller, J. (2003). Personal needs and independence. In P. Lacey & C. Ouvry (Eds), *People with profound and multiple learning disabilities: A collaborative approach to meeting their needs* (pp. 39–48). London: David Fulton.

Nakken, H. & Vlaskamp, C. (2002). Joining forces: Supporting individuals with profound multiple learning disabilities. *Tizard Learning Disability Review*, 7, 10–15.

Penne, A. & Maes, B. (2011). Multi-sensory storytelling: Current research results. In B. Fornefeld (Ed.), *Multi-sensory storytelling: An idea gets through* (pp. 63–91). Berlin: Lit Verlag Dr. W. Hopf.

Penne, A., Ten Brug, A., Munde, V., van der Putten, A., Vlaskamp, C. & Maes, B. (2012). Staff interactive style during multi-sensory storytelling with persons with profound intellectual and multiple disabilities. *Journal of Intellectual Disability Research*, 56, 167–178.

Preece, David & Zhao, Yu. (2015). Multi-sensory storytelling: A tool for teaching or an intervention technique? *British Journal of Special Education*, 42, 429–443.

Ross, E. & Oliver, C. (2003). Preliminary analysis of the psychometric properties of the Mood, Interest & Pleasure Questionnaire (MIPQ) for adults with severe and profound learning disabilities. *British Journal of Clinical Psychology*, 42, 81–93.

Soorya, L., Leon, J., Trelles, M. P. & Thurm, A. (2018). Framework for assessing individuals with rare genetic disorders associated with profound intellectual and multiple disabilities (PIMD): The example of Phelan McDermid Syndrome. *The Clinical Neuropsychologist*, 32(7), 1226–1255.

Ten Brug, A., van der Putten, A., Penne, A., Maes, B. & Vlaskamp, C. (2012). Multi-sensory storytelling for persons with profound intellectual and multiple disabilities: An analysis of the development, content and application in practice. *Journal of Applied Research in Intellectual Disabilities*, 25, 350–359.

Ten Brug, A., van der Putten, A., Penne, A., Maes, B. & Vlaskamp, C. (2016). Making a difference? A comparison between multi-sensory and regular storytelling for persons with profound intellectual and multiple disabilities. *Journal of Intellectual Disability Research*, 60(11), 1043–1053.

Vlaskamp, C., Ten Brug, A. & van der Putten, A. (2011). Multi-sensory storytelling in the Netherlands. In B. Fornefeld (Ed.), *Multi-sensory storytelling: An idea gets through* (pp. 107–122). Berlin: Lit Verlag Dr. W. Hopf.

Watson, M., Lambe, L. & Hogg, J. (2002). *Real lives: Real stories*. Dundee: PAMIS.

Wessels, M. D. & van der Putten, A. J. (2017) Assessment in people with PIMD: Pilot study into the usability and content validity of the Inventory of the Personal Profile and Support. *Cogent Psychology*, 4(1), 1–10.

Winther Hansen, B., Erlandsson, L.-K. & Leufstadius, C. (2021). A concept analysis of creative activities as intervention in occupational therapy. *Scandinavian Journal of Occupational Therapy*, 28(1), 63–77.

Young, H. B., Fenwick, M., Lambe, L. & Hogg, J. (2011). Multi-sensory storytelling as an aid to assisting people with profound intellectual disabilities to cope with sensitive issues: A multiple research methods analysis of engagement and outcomes. *European Journal of Special Needs Education*, 26, 127–142.

Young, H. B., Lambe, L., Fenwick, M. & Hogg, J. (2010). Using multi-sensory storytelling with people with PIMD. *Journal of Applied Research in Intellectual Disabilities*, 23, 497.

Young, H., Garrard, B. & Lambe, L. (2014). *Supporting bereaved people with profound PMLDs and their parents and carers*. Dundee: PAMIS.

Young, H. (2017). Overcoming barriers to grief: Supporting bereaved people with profound intellectual and multiple disabilities. *International Journal of Developmental Disabilities*, 63, 131–137.

Chapter 18

Social Stories™

Carol Gray

Background

In an advertising campaign a few years ago, Starbucks encouraged us to 'Share your Story'; preferably, we assume, over a cup of coffee! Marketing genius. People universally recognise, respect and respond to 'story' across country and culture. According to a research summary published in *Scientific American Mind*, we are 'wired' and naturally influenced by story, with links to our evolutionary history, as well as our social and emotional development, formation of beliefs and attitudes and decision-making (Hsu, 2008). Story is the common thread of human culture and communication that, regardless of topic or purpose, supports us as we interpret, learn, share and organise our experiences.

It is unsurprising then, that when I introduced Social Stories™ as an instructional tool for use with children, adolescents and adults with autism spectrum disorders (ASD), parents and professionals immediately recognised an idea that 'just might work'. Just as 'story' plays an important role in human development and helps Starbucks persuade us to buy a cup of coffee, it also structures our efforts to teach social concepts and skills to those in our care. As we will explore in this chapter, Social Stories harness the positive potential of 'story' to support the social and emotional learning of individuals with ASD.

It could be said that Social Stories are patient and unassuming narratives of life on Earth. Each one shares accurate information with the audience, most frequently a child, adolescent or adult with ASD. As parents and/or professionals, you and I are the 'authors' who tailor the story to meet the needs of the audience. Each Social Story describes a situation, skill or concept according to procedures and a writing format defined by ten criteria. Addressing infinite topics, the criteria ensure an overall easy-going story quality, and a format, 'voice' and content that is descriptive and meaningful, and physically, socially and emotionally safe for the audience.

Principles

Social Stories are based on two signature principles. The first is a prerequisite acknowledgement that the *social impairment in autism is shared*. The definition of 'social' requires more than one person, rendering any 'social impairment' the responsibility of all who engage in a given interaction. The social challenge is equally rooted in mistakes on both sides of the social equation. Individuals with ASD are often unaware of the perspective of others and unable to interpret social context as fluently as their typical peers. This results in statements and behaviours that frequently take others, who regard the situation differently,

DOI: 10.4324/9781003159087-18

by surprise. Parents, professionals, friends and family members may mistakenly attribute negative intent ('it's rude', 'impolite', 'offensive') to responses that seem quite logical to the person with ASD.

Closely related to the first principle, the second is to *abandon all assumptions*. Authors work from a non-judgemental vantage point as they research, write and implement each story. Concepts and terminology like 'inappropriate' have no value or purpose in the art and science of Social Story development. These terms reflect a social arrogance: 'my perception is the only right perception' that can derail even the very best of intentions. It is not surprising, then, that 'inappropriate' is one of seven forbidden terms that never appear in a Social Story.

These two principles form the foundation of all Social Stories. We gather information with a mind that is a 'clean slate', one that is minus judgement or preconception. The assumption-free vantage point is reflected in the selection of a Social Story topic, as well as its format, 'voice', text and illustration and implementation. The recognition of a shared social challenge and a willingness to abandon assumptions that work so well for us most of the time are the start-to-finish guiding principles of every Social Story.

History

I developed Social Stories early in 1991, while working as consultant to students with ASD at Jenison Public Schools, in Jenison, Michigan. I was working with one of my secondary students, Eric. Eric continually interrupted in class. Regardless of what his instructors said, Eric had a response. For years I had tried to teach Eric to raise his hand and wait for a turn to talk. Despite Eric's sincere and frequent promises to stop interrupting, his interrupting continued unabated. For all of our efforts, Eric had never – not once – independently raised his hand in class.

An all-school assembly marked a major turning point. The speaker walked onto the auditorium stage and said, 'I'm going to talk to you today about change.' Eric interrupted the assembly with an immediate response. The following day, I called Eric down to my office to review a videotape of the assembly. We took notes on a large display tablet as we compared our perceptions of what had occurred. Eric said there were two people in the assembly: Eric and the speaker. Suddenly Eric's 'interrupting' made sense to me. Eric was doing what I had taught him to do as a young child; if someone talks to you ... answer. From Eric's perspective, he was being attentive and responding to each of his teachers.

After Eric had shared his description of the assembly it was my turn. Without discrediting Eric's ideas, I indicated that I saw about 500 students. In the course of comparing our notes, Eric said he wanted to stop interrupting. He began to create a 'to do' list. To my surprise, it was a list of all of the behaviours I had been trying to teach him. Upon his return to class, Eric's 'interrupting' was immediately replaced with a raised hand. Eric's success generalised to his other classes.

For years Eric had confidently told me that he would try to stop interrupting. I mistakenly assumed he knew what that *meant*. Despite my knowledge of Eric's social impairment, somewhere I was harbouring a mistaken attitude that Eric and I have the same set of social equipment. At the same time, I had underestimated his potential. Previous to the assembly conversation, if someone had asked me if Eric had the ability to apply an accurate description of an event to his own behaviour, I would have said no. Within a week of my conversation with Eric, I promised myself to abandon all assumptions when working on behalf of people with ASD.

Along with my instructional assistants, I began writing stories for students to share information that they may be missing. Success with one story led to writing another … and another … and another. A few stories were unsuccessful. Curious about those stories that had 'worked', we discovered that they all had a positive and supportive tone. We worked to identify and describe their shared characteristics (Gray & Garand, 1993). The article presented a research-based rationale and suggested the first guidelines for writing Social Stories.

The original guidelines have since been revised (Gray, 2004, 2010), updated, reorganised and expanded to emphasise safety and include the processes for the research, development and implementation of each Social Story (Gray, 2010). Referred to as Social Stories 10.1 (Gray, 2010) they are the most recent description of what is – and what is not – a Social Story.

Work in practice: developing a Social Story

Initially, it may seem difficult to identify a Social Story that is 'typical' or representative. After all, most Social Stories are individually tailored to a child, adolescent or adult with a specific constellation of learning characteristics, interests and preferences. In addition, many story topics are untraditional, reflecting what may be singular perceptions, interpretations and conclusions of the audience. Despite these unique factors, each Social Story has the characteristic patient and positive tone (similar to the very first Social Stories) that renders it a suitable representative of the rest. In this section, I will briefly summarise the ten criteria that ensure Social Story quality.

The first two criteria get each new Social Story off to a good start. Authors begin with a goal to meaningfully and safely share accurate information with the audience (1st criterion: The Goal). A Social Story is often written in response to a challenging situation, to teach a new concept or skill or to praise a current skill or achievement. Information is gathered from a variety of sources to help an author identify a specific topic (2nd criterion: Two-Part Discovery), and to set the stage for writing and illustration.

Most of the criteria structure story content and define the characteristics of the document. Consistent with sound story structure, each Social Story has a title, introduction and conclusion (3rd criterion: Three Parts and a Title). Information is meaningfully presented, with detailed consideration of the ability and learning profile of the audience (4th criterion: FOURmat). Additionally, audience interests are often included to make a story fun, interesting to review and potentially easier to recall and apply (9th criterion: Nine Makes it Mine).

The 5th criterion (Five Factors Impact Voice and Vocabulary) ensures the characteristic patient and positive tone of every Social Story. To maintain a non-judgemental tone, second-person statements never appear in a Social Story. Authors use first and/or third-person perspective sentences exclusively (1st factor). Information is presented positively (2nd factor). To support relevant connections between past, present and future, authors frequently include descriptions of related past experiences or possible future outcomes (3rd factor), often answering topical 'wh' questions in the process (6th criterion: Six Questions Guide Story Development). An individual with ASD may interpret statements literally. For this reason, vocabulary in a Social Story is carefully selected for accuracy (5th factor), and can be interpreted literally without changing the intended meaning of text and illustration (4th factor).

There are seven types of sentence in a Social Story (7th criterion: Seven Sentence Types). Descriptive sentences are required. Often called the heart of a Social Story, descriptive sentences factually describe the story context and main ideas. The other sentence types are optional and are used to describe the thoughts and feelings of others (perspective sentences); identify possible responses of the audience or those on his or her team (three sentences that coach); reinforce meaning of surrounding statements (affirmative sentences); or build interest and support comprehension (partial sentences).

To understand the role of the 8th criterion (A Gr-eight Formula), think back to the history of Social Stories and my conversation with Eric. Eric helped me to appreciate that he may not always be privy to the seemingly intuitive social information that guides most of us through each day. Providing accurate information helped Eric understand the rationale behind the behaviours that I was teaching him. For this reason, every Social Story describes more than directs. The 8th criterion defines the relationship between all of the sentence types to maximise description and minimise direction. It is central to the unassuming and respectful signature quality of every Social Story.

The 10th criterion structures the implementation of a Social Story (Ten Guides to Editing and Implementation). This equips authors with the information they need to edit, introduce and review a story, as well as check for comprehension and build related concepts and skills over time. It is the final checkpoint in the Social Story process, one that ensures that the positive patience of the document is reflected in the processes that surround it from start to finish.

The story of Andrew

Andrew is 9 years old and diagnosed with autism. His parents have an opportunity to go on a three-week church choir tour of Germany. If they decide to go, it will mean that Andrew and his three sisters, Jennifer, Angela and Monica, will be staying with a series of church families. Considering the challenges that Andrew encounters with new situations, his parents decide to decline the invitation. The promise of a comprehensive Social Story reverses their decision. The story will provide Andrew with a one-page description of each day during his parents' absence.

Information is carefully gathered. Andrew's parents provide details regarding their schedule and that of their children. This information is merged with knowledge of Andrew's need for predictability and routine, and his cognitive strengths, reading abilities and illustration preferences.

The 21-page story is housed in a three-ring notebook that provides Andrew with a day-by-day description of his schedule, and that of his parents. The first page describes the events on the day of the tour departure, including visiting the airport and returning home with his first host family. The final page describes visiting the airport, picking up Mom and Dad and returning home. To create a reassuring predictability, despite the different host families, each page in the body of the story shares a similar text and fill-in-the-blank format. For example, each page is titled, 'Andrew's Day on _____ (date)', followed by the same opening paragraph, sequencing (Andrew's day is described first, then that of his parents on the same day) and concluding statement. In advance of their departure, Andrew's parents interview each host family to complete the fill-in-the-blank statements. Each family is advised to select activities that are not likely to change or be cancelled to complete their page of the story:

Andrew's Day on _____. (date)

My name is Andrew. On this day _____ will take care of me. Most of the time we will be at _____ house. Jennifer, Angela and Monica will be there, too.

We will eat and sleep on this day. We will also do other things. We may

_____

_____

_____.

My mom and dad are in Germany on this day. They are singing for the people in Germany.

In _____ days, Mom and Dad will return. On that day, Mom, Dad, Jennifer, Angela and Monica and I will return home.

Each page of the story includes a diary that Andrew may use to describe his day. Space is provided for photos or drawings. This makes Andrew an author of his own 'story'. At the close of the tour, Andrew will use his completed diary to tell his parents about his experiences during their absence.

To help Andrew keep track of the days remaining until his parents return, a simple calendar with 21 boxes is developed with a photo of each host family pasted on their corresponding date. At the conclusion of each day, after getting ready for bed and completing his diary page, Andrew places an 'X' through the day's box. Then he counts the remaining days. This number is inserted into the final paragraph of Andrew's story for the day; for example: 'In 8 days, Mom and Dad will return.'

Andrew's parents completed their tour, and Andrew completed his tour of host families with confidence. The story is credited with much of Andrew's success, as measured by Andrew's diary, the glowing reports from each host family and the relief of Andrew's mother, in particular.

Outcomes and evidence: what we look for

Social Stories are evaluated on two fronts. First, in practice, it is informal observation (like that of Andrew's parents) or basic data collection that often determines if a Social Story has 'worked'. For example, a mother writes a Social Story for her son, Zachary, about taking a bath. After one review of the story, Zachary's bath time tantrums disappear. Or a social worker develops a story for Angie, who never uses toilets outside her home. In the week following the introduction of the story, Angie uses the toilet at school ten times. Results like these earned initial credibility for Social Stories in the early 1990s, and have resulted in the enthusiastic affection of many parents, professionals and individuals with ASD that continues to this day

This grassroots acceptance of Social Stories preceded the second evaluation front of formal research. Social Stories have challenged scientific study (e.g. Reynhout & Carter, 2006). In practice, Social Stories are highly individualised, making them most suitable for case studies (Moore, 2004; O'Conner, 2009; Rowe, 1999). Case studies, however, provide little information about the value of Social Stories on a larger scale. In addition, Social Stories are frequently used in homes, classrooms, clinics and communities, where it is difficult to isolate variables that may impact results. Despite these challenges, and their relatively short history, Social Stories are regarded as an evidence-based practice. In a major study to identify evidence-based practices and instructional interventions in the education of individuals with ASD, the National Autism Center (2009) listed 'story-based intervention packages' (with Social Stories identified as the most well known) as one of 11 established treatments for children on the autism spectrum, and Reynhout and Carter (2006) suggested that this was an intervention which was simple to implement and full of promise

Contexts of learning

Social Stories are likely to be most effective with students on the autism spectrum between the ages of 6 and 14 years (National Autism Center, 2009: 50). Since their inception, it has been theorised that children with an early ability to read or interest in letters and numbers may be excellent Social Story candidates. However, I have on occasion developed simplified, straightforward, brief, home-based Social Stories (or elements of) for very young, preverbal children, with informally declared successes by their parents. Because they are stories with a supportive tone, it is suspected that Social Stories may be helpful for individuals with other learning challenges, or those without impairments. Research continues to help us to understand and more effectively harness the positive potential of Social Stories.

Cultural issues

As mentioned earlier, the goal of every Social Story is to share relevant social information. However, what may be relevant, valued and/or appropriate as a social skill in one culture may be undesirable in the next (see Meng, 2008). Cultures differ in the importance placed on the various and detailed aspects of many social traits, like independence and conformity. Additionally, even within a given culture, what is allowed or 'OK' in one family may not be acceptable practice in the home next door. To achieve the Social Story goal of sharing relevant information, the first step is to carefully gather information from a wide variety of sources. This always includes an individual's parents or caregivers. The required assumption-free vantage point supports not only the possible differences in social perception between audience and author, but cultural differences as well. It builds respect for cultural, social and familial norms (both expected and unforeseen) between author, audience and all others impacted by the story, into each story's foundation.

Try it yourself

We have learned a lot about Social Stories in their first 20 years as an instructional tool. Here are three important points:

Top tips

- Focus on process to achieve the best product. The processes used to develop and implement Social Stories are as important as the document itself. Take time to learn them, and use them consistently.
- Join others in protecting the integrity of Social Stories. We will be ever-increasing the availability of accurate information about Social Stories in the coming years. Stay continually curious about what is new with the approach. We look forward to hearing from you.

Where to go

Seek accurate information about the approach. The grassroots popularity of Social Stories has unfortunately given rise to a host of inaccurate and misleading websites. Start with reliable and accurate information, always available at www.thegraycenter.org and also at www.CarolGra ySocialStories.com. Worldwide training opportunities are always listed there. In addition, look for the Social Stories logo on training brochures and published materials, and seek workshops conducted by Team Social Stories and/or Social Story Satellite Schools and Services members.

References

Gray, C. (2004). Social Stories 10.0: The new defining criteria and guidelines. *Jenison Autism Journal*, 15, 2–21.

Gray, C. (2010). Social Stories tutorials. In *The new Social Story book: Revised and expanded 10th anniversary edition* (pp. xxv–lxxi). Arlington, TX: Future Horizons.

Gray, C. & Garand, J. D. (1993). Social Stories: Improving responses of students with autism with accurate social information. *Focus on Autistic Behavior*, 8, 1–10.

Hsu, J. (2008). The secrets of storytelling: Why we love a good yarn. *Scientific American Mind Online*, 18 September. Available at: www.sciam.com/article.cfm?id=the-secrets-of-storytelling.

Meng, Hongdang (2008). Social script theory and cross-cultural communication. *Intercultural Communication Studies XVII*, 1, 132–138.

Moore, P. S. (2004). The use of social stories in a psychology service for children with learning disabilities: A case study of a sleep problem. *British Journal of Learning Disabilities*, 32, 133–138.

National Autism Center (2009). *National standards report: The National Standards Project – addressing the need for evidence-based guidelines for autism spectrum disorders*. Available at: www.nationala utismcenter.org/pdf/NAC%20Standards%20Report.pdf.

O'Conner, E. (2009). The use of social story DVDs to reduce anxiety levels: A case study of a child with autism and learning disabilities. *Support for Learning*, 24(3), 133–136.

Reynhout, G. & Carter, M. (2006). Social Stories™ for children with disabilities. *Journal of Autism and Developmental Disorders*, 36, 445–469.

Rowe, C. (1999). Do social stories benefit children diagnosed with autism in mainstream primary schools? *British Journal of Special Education*, 26, 12–14.

Chapter 19

Storysharing®

Personal narratives for identity and community

Nicola Grove and Jane Harwood

Background

Storysharing® is an approach based on the ways we tell stories in everyday life. We define *narrative* as the broad skill of recalling and structuring an event – such as a factual account of the day, a scientific report, an evidence statement. A *story* is told about a specific event, to maximise its meaning and significance. We want to make sense of our experiences, affirm who we are, imaginatively relive the event and to have fun – and we need empathetic listeners! Storysharing® is distinguished by a collaborative approach: we tell stories *with* others, as well as *to* others, and is grounded in a social theory of narrative.

History

Storysharing® came from the experience of running a storytelling group in a special school with a group of teenagers with moderate and severe intellectual disabilities. I started with the intention of teaching children to retell a personal story individually. We would create an event (memorably, breaking an egg when trying to bake a cake) and then structure recall by immediately working in pairs, using prompt questions: 'Where were we? What happened? Who did it?' etc. Unfortunately, even with the help of picture cards, the children found it impossible to remember the story themselves. They could get one or two things right, but the task was too challenging. They also lacked the confidence to tell the story independently. In retrospect this was because they were all functioning below the age levels at which children are able to cope with these demands. Through trial and error we started telling the story as a group, so that the youngsters could join in as and when they wanted, linking events with the simple '*and then*' rather than more complex constructions. This was successful, I think, because all pressure was removed and the model was continuously available – children started by imitating, but increased spontaneous contributions over time. Further development came through work in day centres, homes and schools with individuals with profound intellectual disabilities.

Theories

Oral, conversational telling is very different from stories written on a page. The space is intimate – people lean in to each other. There is a definite rhythm – tellers and listeners perform a kind of co-ordinated dance that involves both voice (spoken words, sounds, exclamations) and movement, as the speaker gesticulates, and listeners mirror, shifting body position. If two people are reminiscing, there will be interruptions, switching, confirmations, challenges. The

DOI: 10.4324/9781003159087-19

structure of the story is felt in the bones as the speaker uses pause, speed, pitch and intonation to build anticipation, reach a climax and wind down.

This rhythmic cycle of emotional tension and release in stories is characteristic of the earliest exchanges with babies (Fogel, 1992; Trevarthen, 2005). Infants gain a huge amount of practice in how to build up and resolve a tiny story.[1] Development of narrative is a *socially co-constructed* process (Labov & Waletzky, 1976; McCabe & Peterson, 1991; Peterson & McCabe, 1983; Peterson, Jesso & McCabe, 1999). Vygotsky's term 'scaffolding' (1978) describes how adults provide structure which they gradually withdraw as the child becomes competent. At first the child contributes maybe one piece of information – it is adults who build the story (Scollon, 1979; Miller & Sperry, 1988), allowing children to experience what it is to be a competent and confident narrator. The child touches her head and whimpers, and the adult responds with a mini tale: 'Oh no, did you hit your head? On the table? Oh, poor baby. Naughty table!' The next stage comes when the child is able to signal a specific topic and pull it into the conversation. From birth, babies seem to be sensitive to the difference between new and old information (Roder et al., 2000). Around their first birthday, children can attract attention to what is new and surprising – they will look and point whilst reacting and looking at the adult. This ability to attend simultaneously to an event and to another person is a critical stage in cognitive and linguistic development (Baker & Greenfield, 1988; Benigni et al., 1979). It is the beginning of true storytelling (Ellis, 2007).

Children appear to remember more detail of events if parents have engaged them in supportive, elaborated telling rather than focusing purely on *what, who, where, why* (Bauer, 2007; Reese, 2013). Active, co-narrating listeners positively affect the way stories are told (Bavelas, Coates & Johnson, 2000). Other important sources are Norrick (2000), who documented adult conversational stories; 'small stories' research (Bamberg & Georgakopoulou, 2008) and Hymes (1981), whose work amongst First Nation peoples led him to emphasise the role of poetic structures in oral narrative speech.

Principles

Key principles similar to other interactive programmes (Forster & Iacono, 2014; Mosley & Tew, 1999; Nind & Hewett, 2006), include respect, attunement, responsivity and valuing of all forms of communication. The principles and theory of sharing narratives are:

- Stories are built around events that stand out as different enough to deserve our attention; they are 'reportable' (Labov & Waletzky, 1976). Grey (2002) found that the earliest autobiographical memories in young children are built around atypical events.
- The event generates emotional reactions (e.g. excitement, fear, bewilderment), motivating us to share the memory.
- Meaning and understanding accrue as we tell the story, giving narrative shape to the experience.
- The rhythm and musicality of telling are as important as the content.
- Stories are told together, scaffolded by more experienced partners.
- Questions are minimised to avoid the telling becoming an interview.
- The audience must actively listen and respond.
- Stories are repeated over and over again. This gives plenty of opportunity for it to become practised and internalised. The story may change over time but the core will always have the same elements and becomes relatively scripted.

- Care is taken not to overuse props, pictures and whiteboards, as these distract from the intimate dynamic of the telling space.

Work in practice

Storysharing® can happen anywhere at any time, and once you are familiar with the techniques, you can immediately scaffold a story during the day. Dedicated group sessions can be up to an hour, including breaks, depending on numbers and attention levels; a typical structure is described below:

- *Create the space*: A circle small enough for everyone to be heard and for a dynamic rhythm of telling and listening to build up, but not so close as to overpower
- *Who is here today?* A song or ritual to build awareness of each other
- *Who's got a story? What's happened?* Stories of the week, recorded by families or staff – we used a colourful postbox in one setting
- *Remind how to listen*: Active listening involves joining in by saying something like 'Oh no!', 'Wow!', 'Really?', by mirroring gestures of the teller and by echoing key words (listeners can use the communication aid as well as tellers).
- *Tell the story*: The individual (maybe more than one) is encouraged with adult and peer support to join in telling. The structure of the dialogue involves:

  - The invitation to listen: 'Guess what happened to Laura and Imram yesterday'
  - Sentence prompts
  - Encouragement to the audience to listen actively and empathetically
  - Closure or resolution, usually provided by the supporting adult.

In the following example, Laura and Imram are pupils. A basket of apples and a sticking plaster are props.

ADULT: We were in the ...LAURA AND IMRAM: Garden.
ADULT: Garden, yeah, and Laura was collecting the ap ...
LAURA: Apples
ADULT: The apples, when suddenly Imram yelled, didn't you, you went ...
IMRAM: Ow!
ADULT: And Laura dropped *all* her apples, didn't you, they all fell, they all fell ...
LAURA: Down.
ADULT: And we rushed over to Imram and he was clutching his ... (cues Imram by pointing to his knee)
IMRAM: Ow! (rubs knee)
LAURA: Knee.
ADULT: Because he'd tripped over a big branch and his knee was ...
IMRAM: Bleeding.
ADULT: And Imram was so brave, he was amazing. It's OK now, though isn't it? Show everyone your knee Imram.

Everyone looks, and responds with 'Wow!', 'Oh no!', 'Really brave'.

This story is likely to cue other memories of accidents (a fruitful source of anecdotes). So we ask if anything similar has happened to anyone else. There are many ways of developing the story:

- A permanent record, with a picture, object or scrap; for example, the bloodstained tissue, a photo of the apple, a piece of bark from the branch and accompanying words. This is *not* a full literary exercise, though a book or multimedia presentation can be created later (McCormack, 2020).
- A drama, where children take turns to be Imram, Laura and the teacher, following Paley's (1991) inspirational guidelines.[2]

The session ends with another song or ritual, thanking the tellers for their stories.

Outcomes and evidence: what we look for

Storysharing® in schools has been independently evaluated (Bunning et. al., 2013, Bunning, Gooch & Johnson, 2017; Peacey, 2010). In residential and day-care settings, Storysharing® was part of a Mencap national programme to develop participation in decision-making (Involve Me[3]). In Somerset, a three-year project ran in eight homes, involving over 70 adults and 100 staff (Harwood, 2010). It is important to note that we look equally at the skills of story sharers and their interactive partners, and we also consider the development of a narrative culture in the relevant setting.

In summary, the findings show that over an average ten-week period:

- Participation levels, expressive communication narrative skills, listening and peer interactions increase
- Staff become more confident as supporters, and use a wider range of strategies
- As the archive of stories builds up, a real sense of community identity and friendship develops.

Assessment

For verbal individuals, narrative strengths and needs are profiled in six dimensions: *structural* (memory and sequencing for events); *feeling* (range of verbal and non-verbal emotions); *social* (getting and maintaining attention); *linguistic* (vocabulary, sentence construction); *poetic* (rhythm, narrative devices and figures of speech) and *active listening* (Grove, 2014). We also record the type of story and the balance between narrator contributions. The profile is applicable to fictional and imaginative as well as personal storytelling, and is culturally adaptable and dynamic (see Gutierrez-Clellen & Quinn, 1993). Any existing communication assessments can also be applied.

For preverbal individuals, levels of engagement levels are documented, using Brown's original framework (1996):[4]

Encounter	*Learner is present but shows no apparent awareness*
Awareness	Some awareness of interactions
Response	Some differentiated responses
Engagement	Consistent attention and response
Participation	Begins to take turns, anticipate and respond, with prompting
Involvement	Spontaneously and actively joins in

For interactive partners, we assess their proficiency in seven key skills of storysharing, including responsivity, elicitation strategies and use of resources. Narrative culture is demonstrated through visible evidence of stories and storytelling in the environment and in organisational structures.

The story of Ricky

Ricky and Susie took part in an inclusive story sharing project between a special and a mainstream school.

Ricky was an active 10-year-old with difficulties understanding, listening and relating to others. At first restless and rather disengaged, once he became familiar with the structure he was an enthusiastic storyteller, and began adding information that made his stories very enjoyable. He also learned to respond actively to the stories of others. The final observations about Ricky were:

> He can remember the sequence of events, and use his voice and face to show lots of feeling. He loves the punchline: ' Oh no, the doughnuts!' and adds a little coda of his own: 'One yummy doughnut – and I ate it!"

He also connected with his mainstream partner – Ricky had felt sick on a sea crossing, and his friend said his sister had felt the same. Such tiny links are the building blocks of empathy. By the end of the project, Ricky was able to articulate feelings explicitly, saying to another child: 'You must be really sad that your guinea pig died.'

The story of Susie

Susie was a non-verbal 7-year-old with severe intellectual difficulties who also found it very hard to sit still and listen. Her mother was a wonderful support, making her stories each week in a picture book that she co-told with props and a Big Mack.[5] Over time, she started to enjoy looking at the book, watching and listening as others responded to her experiences. She began to be a real group member, handing props to others when asked, and keeping very focused on her own story. Finally, she began to actively respond to the stories of others – when her partner told us about her visit to Diggerland, Susie leaned forward and looked at her. She smiled when she heard an 'Oh no!' response on the Big Mack, and she joined in with jigging up and down to represent how the digger moved.

Contexts of learning

The approach is designed to be maximally inclusive. Because it involves no pressure to communicate and lots of modelling, it can also be used with individuals who struggle with a second language or who have social and emotional difficulties.

Sharing personal experiences supports not only language and emotional development, but self advocacy and recovery from trauma (Cohen, Meek & Lieberman, 2010; Davis, 2002; Goldstein et al., 2015) – vitally important in times of crisis. During the pandemic, teachers and therapists successfully ran sessions online. Storysharing® has been used in reviews by young people to advocate for themselves; and in school councils to problem solve (Grove &

Chalmers, 2014). For adults, the process can lead to political empowerment. For example, adults with severe and profound disabilities co-told their stories to their Member of Parliament, persuading him to lobby against the planned removal of mobility benefit from disabled people in state-run homes.

Issues to consider

It is important to set aside enough time to share stories properly, so news time on a Monday morning is not ideal! In school, small plenary sessions, English and personal social education or citizenship lessons offer good opportunities for Storysharing®. In social care settings, we ran weekly sessions, but best of all is to regularly share the day's/week's events together.

With individuals on the autistic spectrum, telling personal stories presents challenges because, by definition, these involve an unpredictable or new event, associated with emotions, and requiring social interaction. With this group, and those who are anxious or overactive, we tend to downplay the unpredictable bits of the story and emphasise the ritualised calming elements. We start with what is known and feels comfortable, and gradually build up the story. We let them join in gradually, perhaps making brief contributions from the back of the room. This helps them to process and integrate complex feelings raised by unexpected and emotional events. For a similar graduated approach, see Peter and Sherratt-Smith (2001).

For those with complex health needs and a limited attention span, it is important to keep the story very short and give them a role that plays to their strengths. We have found that even if this person can contribute very little, the session often increases the awareness of others that here is a friend with a story, not just someone who sits passively in the room.

It can be hard for families to gather stories, with all the other demands of life. Valence School in Kent combined home–school books with a Big Mack, giving just enough information for the parent to get the gist of the story but leaving the punchline with the child. A parent support worker at Oakleigh School ran groups with culturally diverse families using picture prompt cards and souvenirs of events (Barton, 2012).

It is important to recognise that co-tellers influence each other. A story can change over time in how it is told and how closely it adheres to the original event (you know this yourself of course!). In relaxed conversations, there is leeway for creative divergence. However, in situations where accurate memory for facts is critical (e.g. legal contexts, interviews), the support person should supply only small facilitative neutral prompts.

Cultural factors

Personal storytelling is very culturally specific. We know, for example, that Japanese, African American and Hispanic cultures tell anecdotes in ways that may differ from the expectations of white Western-educated teachers (Gutierrez-Clellen & Quinn, 1993; McCabe & Bliss, 2003). The collaborative approach we describe here may not be seen as appropriate in some cultures. So it is really important to work with families to find out how and when they tell these little stories, what if any cultural constraints there are and whether there are specific conventions they might use. Actually, this means that there are exciting opportunities to learn from the families and to involve them in the work you are doing.

Try it yourself

Top tips

- Spot the good stories as they happen in real life: capture them in your story butterfly net!
- Support and prompt, minimise diet questions.
- Have a Big Mack ready and waiting! But don't overload with props.

Where to go

Resources, films and further information can be found at: https://storysharing.org.uk.

Training is at three levels: Introductory; Practitioner; Tutor. It is provided online and through consultancy.

Grove, N. (2014). *The big book of Storysharing: A handbook for personal storytelling with children and young people who have severe communication difficulties*. Abingdon: Speechmark.

Acknowledgements

The trademark for Storysharing® is owned by the charity Openstorytellers (https://www.openstorytellers.org.uk) whose support is gratefully acknowledged, along with our funders: The Big Lottery; Somerset Partnership Board; Esmée Fairbairn Foundation; Paul Hamlyn Foundation and the Rayne Foundation. Flo Hopwood and Katrina Arab, Three Ways School, have provided invaluable support for the development of Storysharing®.

Notes

1 An audio podcast of a lecture by Professor Trevarthen in 2009 demonstrates this very clearly: www.iriss.org.uk/resources/why-attachment-matters-sharing-meaning-colwyn-trevarthen [retrieved 16th March 2012].
2 Gussin Paley describes how she encouraged children to share a memory, which was turned into drama by the protagonist directing others. NG used this with May, who had hated her injection: May told NG to play her, whilst she took on the role of the nurse delivering the injection, with classmates taking other roles such as Mum.
3 http://openstorytellers.org.uk/pages/what_we_do.html.
4 Now developed into a statutory Engagement Model https://www.gov.uk/government/publications/the-engagement-model.
5 Big Mack available from AbleNet: www.ablenetinc.com.

References

Baker, N. & Greenfield, P. (1988). The development of new and old information in young children's early language. *Language Sciences*, 10, 3–34.

Bamberg, M. and Georgakopoulou, A. (2008). Small stories as a new perspective in narrative and identity analysis. *Text & Talk – An Interdisciplinary Journal of Language, Discourse Communication Studies*, 28, 377–396.

Barton, R. (2012). For the journey. *SEN Magazine*, 60. Available at: https://senmagazine.co.uk/p ersonal-stories1259.

Bauer, P. (2007). *Remembering the times of our lives: Memory in infancy and beyond*. Mahwah, NJ: LEA.

Bavelas, J., Coates, L. & Johnson, T. (2000). Listeners as co-narrators. *Journal of Personality and Social Psychology*, 79(6), 941–952.

Benigni, L., Bretherton, I., Camaioni, L. & Volterra, V. (1979). *The emergence of symbols: Communication and cognition in infancy*. New York: Academic Press.

Brown, E. (1996). *Religious education for all*. London: David Fulton.

Bunning, K., Gooch, L. & Johnson, M. (2017). Developing the personal narratives of children with complex communication needs associated with intellectual disabilities: What is the potential of Storysharing®? *Journal of Applied Research in Intellectual Disabilities*, 30, 743–756.

Bunning, K., Smith, C., Kennedy, P. & Greenham, C. (2013). Examination of the communication interface between students with severe to profound and multiple intellectual disability and educational staff during structured teaching sessions. *Journal of Intellectual Disability Research*, 57, 39–52.

Cohen, H., Meek, K. & Lieberman, M. (2010). Memory & resilience. *Journal of Human Behavior in the Social Environment*, 20(4), 525–541.

Davis, J. (Ed.). (2002). *Stories of change: Narratives and social movements*. Albany, NY: State University New York Press.

Ellis, L. (2007). The narrative matrix and wordless narrations: A research note. *Augmentative & Alternative Communication*, 23, 113–125.

Fogel, A. (1992). Movement and communication in human infancy: The social dynamics of development. *Human Movement Science*, 11(4), 387–423.

Forster, S. & Iacono, T. (2014), Affect attunement with adults with PIMD. *Journal of Intellectual Disabilities Research*, 58, 1105–1120.

Goldstein, B., Taufen Wessels , A., Lejano , R. &Butler, W. (2015). Narrating resilience: Transforming urban systems through collaborative storytelling. *Urban Studies*, 52(7), 1285–1303.

Grey, A. (2002). Children's earliest memories: A narrative study. *Australian Journal of Early Childhood*, 27(4), 1–5.

Grove, N. & Chalmers, S. (2014). Come on feel the noise! or, who will stack the chairs?: A year in the life of a special school council. *Special Children*, 217, 18–19.

Gutierrez-Clellen, V. & Quinn, R. (1993). Assessing narratives of children from diverse cultural/linguistic groups. *Language, Speech and Hearing Services in Schools*, 24, 2–9.

Harwood, J. (2010). Storysharing in Somerset 2008–2011: Final report. Available at: https://storysha ring.org.uk/wp-content/uploads/2021/05/STORY SHARING-IN-SOMERSET-2008-2011-FINAL-REPORT.pdf (Accessed 27.5.21).

Hymes, D. (1981). *'In vain I tried to tell you': Essays in native ethnopoetics*. Philadelphia, PA: University of Pennsylvania.

Labov, W. & Waletzky, J. (1976). Narrative analysis: Oral versions of personal experience. In J. Helm (Ed.), *Essays on the verbal and visual arts* (pp. 12–44). Seattle, WA: University of Washington Press.

McCabe, A. & Bliss, L. (2003). *Patterns of narrative discourse: A multicultural lifespan approach*. Boston: Pearson Education.

McCabe, A. & Peterson, C. (Eds). (1991). *Developing narrative structure*. Hillsdale, NJ: LEA.

McCormack, N. (2020). A trip to the caves: Making life story work inclusive and accessible. In M. Nind & I. Strnadová (eds.). *Belonging for people with profound and multiple disabilities: pushing the boundaries of inclusion* (pp. 98–112). London: Routledge.

Miller, P. & Sperry, L. (1988). Early talk about the past: The origins of conversational stories of personal experience. *Journal of Child Language*, 15, 293–315.

Mosley, J. & Tew, M. (1999). *Quality circle time in the secondary school: A handbook of good practice*. London: David Fulton.

Nind, M. & Hewett, D. (2006). *Access to communication* (2nd ed.). London: David Fulton.

Norrick, N. (2000). *Conversational narrative in everyday talk*. Amsterdam: John Benjamins.

Paley, V. G. (1991). *The boy who would be a helicopter: Use of storytelling in the classroom*. Cambridge, MA: Harvard University Press.

Peacey, L. (2010). *A storytelling project in two sets of co-located mainstream and special schools in country and city: Findings from an action research project*. London: SENJIT Institute of Education.

Peter, M. & Sherratt-Smith, D. (2001). *Developing drama and play for children with autistic spectrum disorders*. London: David Fulton.

Peterson, C., Jesso, B. & McCabe, A. (1999). Encouraging narratives in preschoolers: An intervention study. *Journal of Child Language*, 26, 49–67.

Peterson, C. & McCabe, A. (1983). *Developmental psycholinguistics: Three ways of looking at a child's narrative*. New York: Plenum Press.

Reese, E. (2013). *Tell me a story: Sharing stories to enrich your child's world*. Oxford: Oxford University Press.

Roder, B., Bushnall, E. & Sackerville, A. (2000). Infants' preferences for familiarity and novelty during the course of visual processing. *Infancy*, 1(4), 491–507.

Scollon, R. (1979). A real early stage: An unzipped condensation of a dissertation on child language. In E. Ochs & B. Schieffelin (Eds), *Developmental pragmatics* (pp. 215–228). New York: Academic Press.

Trevarthen, C. (2005). First things first: Infants make good use of the sympathetic rhythm of imitation, without reason or language. *Journal of Child Psychotherapy*, 31, 91–113.

Vygotsky, L. (1978). *Mind in society*. Cambridge, MA: Harvard University Press.

Chapter 20

Personal storytelling with deafblind individuals

Gunnar Vege and Anne Nafstad

Background

This chapter describes the process of co-creating stories with persons with congenital deafblindness (CDB) and those who share their lives. CDB is rare, resulting from a combination of severe visual and hearing impairments, onset within the first year, before the development of basic communication relations (Nafstad & Rødbroe, 2015). Causes can be genetic, virus infections or prematurity, and co-occurrence of other conditions is frequent.

For these individuals, the world consists of experiences of touch and movement felt with and on the body. For sighted, hearing partners, it's hard to understand how this world feels or what it "looks" like. Asymmetry builds up, as each partner uses and understands different clues to what is happening. There is no shared culture, and, as a result, thoughts, feelings and needs can easily be misinterpreted. To change this situation, the interactive partner must take responsibility for establishing mutual, shared understandings. Narrative provides a fundamental structure for organising this process (Hanning-Zwannenberg et al., 2015). Stories grab and maintain interest, cultivate imagination, make events understandable and add vitality, content and comfort to life. We define *narrative*, as "the unfolding of events through time as told from a particular perspective of time, persons and situations", within which a *story* centres on "a departure from the expected canonical happening, requiring reflection and explanation" (Nelson, 1996: 189). Once the narrative structure of an event has been shared in the here-and-now, it is available to be re-constructed as a co-authored story, building a store of memories that amount to a shared culture.

History

Originally, education for persons with CDB focused on *training* communication skills. The late 1990s saw a shift from a monologic to a dialogical perspective (Linell, 2009) which suggested new possibilities for the development of an authentic language and the expression of thoughts within a dialogical space. In our centres, we developed and began to use a framework for recalling and co-creating memories of meaningful events.

Theories and principles

To meet the challenge of working with people with such complex needs, clear theoretical foundations are essential (Nafstad & Daelman, 2017). The framework described here

DOI: 10.4324/9781003159087-20

combines the concepts of *dialogical co-presence* and *narrative meaning-making* through *embodied language*. We begin by considering the nature of *perception* for a person with CDB.

Perception

Sighted, hearing people immediately gain a multi-dimensional complete image of the world, but those with CDB risk having very fragmented experiences. They are dependent on their proximal senses (touch, movement, smell and taste). However, touch provides only partial information, and perceptual guidance is needed (Gregersen, 2020). This helps the person to build up mental images, through exploratory use of refined touch patterns that function like central vision. A person may use her toes or fingertips, perhaps with the tip of the tongue and the lips, the tip of the nose in combination with smell and taste. Other body parts – her own, or a companion's – such as the forehead, cheeks, chest or back, can be used as perceptual *background* for building up a distinctive perceptual *figure*. Different body parts fulfil different compensatory functions: the hands become the eyes, ears and voice of the deafblind person – she can switch from watching to listening, to thinking, to sharing attention (Miles, 1998). Over time, she weaves a mental image through recycled attempts, connecting these small, fragmented touch impressions into a holistic pattern (Nafstad & Rødbroe, 2015; Costain, Souriau & Daelman, 2019). She must be not only awake, but active and motivated to engage cognitively in registering and connecting the impressions.

Dialogical co-presence

Vege (2009) defines co-presence as a state of intense mental, bodily and emotional awareness of the other person, being engaged emotionally and psychologically. This offers the person with CDB perceptible signs of attentiveness, through expressions that affect the partner/companion emotionally. Markova (2016: 186) emphasises that this co-presence is not about being present in the same physical space, but about dialogical co-presence. Linell (2009) distinguishes *dialogue* (an overt exchange of utterances) from *dialogicality* — the capacity of making sense through interactions. Dialogicality and narrativity can motivate the person with CDB to let her perception be guided by a companion into a world beyond immediate reach. Emotional co-presence is the motivational source, and the trick is to build this into the communicative flow, as if we were dancing the tango. The challenge is how to do it!

Embodied language

The authentic language of persons with CDB is embodied, gestural and dialogically negotiated (Nafstad & Rødbroe, 2015; Souriau, 2015) as exemplified in documentary video sequences (Vege, Nafstad & Bjartvik, 2007). Lack of distal senses impacts on semantic memory, but memory can be activated through *bodily emotional traces (BETs):* salient bodily sensations (movements) and associated feelings connected with an experience (Daelman et al., 2004; Janssen & Rødbroe, 2008; Vege, 2009). The natural law is that:-*impressions leave memory traces that emerge as expressions*. This leads to the creation of meaning with narrative.

  The companion must communicate athletically, knowing that every pattern in directed motion, posture and change in muscular tension should be readable by the other person through touch. If we are floppy, vague and noisy in our bodily way of being and touching, we will be unreadable to the other. And that is not all. We need to offer her access to a perceptual field with an event structure that can also be perceived. This requires strict sequential and spatial choreography of the targeted scenario.

The dynamic structure of narrative experience

Nelson (1996) describes narrative as a macro-structure consisting of a sequence of smaller micro-structures, sharing the same dynamic pattern. The recycled pattern amounts to a sequence characterised by a gradual building up of tension which triggers curiosity, induces excitement and sharpens attention. A classic example is found in fairytales where the micro-structure is recycled three times, building up more and more tension in the macrostructure towards a climax followed by an unexpected twist of fate that releases tension (see Chapter 1). In our planning, we need to have this dynamic pattern in mind. Provided there are no elements disturbing perception of the pattern, we can give access to *flow*, a precondition for triggering motivation and cognitive engagement (Gibson et al., 2020).

The narrative event must make an impression, and this requires arousal. Arousal is generated by variations of tension and release which Stern (2010: 92) describes as the flesh of the narrative. To generate sympathetic experience, the companion must also be involved. The sympathetic experience of tension directs our attention to the ongoing events which then stick in our memory. The event experience becomes a biographical story when a person can access all the impressions that connect to create the flow of the narrative dynamic structure. The flow will be fragmented if the companion drops out of the continuous hand-over-hand contact to do something else, or if part of the ongoing event is not accessible. A cup will emerge "from nowhere", a fishing line is pulled up intangibly. The narrative then lacks coherence and dynamic flow, and will be impossible to understand and recall.

Work in practice

The process is illustrated through the story of Ingerid and Gunnar's venture to the fjord. The original video-recordings (Vege et al, 2007) have been identified as clearly demonstrating dialogicality and embodiment (Souriau, Rødbroe & Janssen, 2008; Markova, 2016; Linell 2017). To make the practice explicit and shareable, we describe it here as it was planned and performed by Gunnar.

Ingerid was a playful, curious, trustful and communicative young woman. However, like many other persons with multiple disabilities she had relatively limited access to interactional experiences. She initiated very little outside daily routines. Ingerid helped us understand the importance of co-authoring stories about her life, building on experiences with an emotional dynamic structure founded on coherent bodily-tactile impressions. We learned that we could re-enact past events by referring collaboratively to particular *places* on the body, felt as experiential peaks in the event, and to *the manner* in which these peaks were felt. These memory traces were charged with an *emotional* contour.

In the following example, Gunnar planned a joint trip. Just bringing Ingerid along would not do. Access to a shareable social context had to be carefully planned to include an unforeseen event that would create narrative tension. Here, Gunnar had "planted" some crabs at the end of a fishing line hanging from the fjord pier in a bucket.

Work proceeded in two stages: 1. The event itself, 2. Co-authoring the story.

I The event

In planning, we must strip down all the potential sense impressions to the embodied components that are essential to an event structure perceptible to the person. Because they had been to the pier several times before, the event was meaningful to Ingerid. She expects (as before) to get into a boat. However, this time Gunnar invites her to kneel down and find the fishing line. Tension is introduced through this novel component, sharpening the senses and attention and charging us with emotional preparedness. To progress this as a sympathetic experience of variations in tension, Gunnar focuses on the transition from the expected to the unexpected event, marked in hand-over-hand tactile sign language "BOAT-THERE (points)-NO-NOT BOAT-NOW-DOWN HERE" (points), followed by support for her to kneel. They then accompany each other in an experiential wave of increasing tension towards the peak of feeling the crab move up the lower arm from its original source in her palm.

Crabs are unpredictable creatures that we feel hesitant about touching! The progress of the damp creature up Ingerid's arm leaves memory traces that can be re-created later in co-authoring the story. So Gunnar painstakingly and slowly builds up tension, impression after impression, narrative component after narrative component, increasing the intensity in his voice, his vibrating touch-to-touch contact, the airflow in his breathing, recycling these over and over again with small variations. Again and again, the crab drops into Ingerid's palm and crawls up towards her elbow where it is either caught or falls to the ground. During these recyclings the source of the dynamic tension is the companion's manner of participation. The rising tension and increasingly rapid rhythmical vibrating small motion patterns in the companion's hands and fingers, sensed by light hand touch, map on to the embodied sense of rising expectation of what is to come next. Additionally, Gunnar scaffolds the crab's escape route up the arm by his touch, enabling Ingerid to feel and trust that his attention is aligned with the crab's motion path on her arm.

Creating dialogical space

It is important not to get so lost in the activity that we suppress emergence of the dialogical space where thoughts and feelings are expressed and shared. Gunnar takes care to give Ingerid her own subjective space to think and reflect on what is happening. One way of doing this is to stop the flow of events and ask what happened just now, what she felt. He asks her "WHAT-WHAT-WHAT FELT-YOU-THERE?" using tactile signing and synchronous speech with a clear narrative contour – where the peak maps on to the raised tone of a question. He uses his voice, not in any expectation that she will hear, but because vocal tone helps him emphasise the same vitality in his signing. He points by touch to the place where she just felt an impression, adding a supportive touch on her own body, triggering her to form a mental image from this trace. This happens several times, allowing her to co-create both meaning and language. She has the option to hesitate, turn her attention inward towards herself and reflect on her own subjective experience of the previous moment (Nafstad, 2015; Markova, 2016).

Thus co-presence enables both partners to share the script of the narrative event, which becomes part of the implicitly shared social world. A story co-authored on this basis will help Ingerid define her own perspective and position in relation to that of the other, and to the world of WE/US/ of shared belonging.

2 Co-authoring the story

The following day, Gunnar and Ingerid were together, recalling a different event. ("Orange in the Rucksack"). Suddenly, in the middle of re-enacting it, Ingerid hesitated. Gunnar recognised that she wanted to shift from listening position (light hand listening touch over speaker's signing/talking hand) into the reciprocal speaker position. With a big smile on her face (she is totally blind, the smile must be authentic) she uttered in creative iconic/deictic referential gesture "UP-ARM-THIS MANNER!"

How and why did this spontaneous shift take place? Shared elements in events (here, *rucksack, plate, knife* and *orange*) enable a conceptual blend in memory. Applying Ask Larsen's mental space model (2006) we assume the key memory that led to the new unexpected co-referential mental space was the crab moving up her arm. In this moment, Ingerid herself transforms the narrative from a challenging on-the-edge-of-endurance here-and-now event into a powerful story where she constructs herself as hero in her own life, meeting the challenge and overcoming barely endurable tension to become equal to her companion, daring to let a crab crawl up her arm, just as she had felt Gunnar do himself. It was her victory – but within a shared-accomplishment, like climbers reaching the top of a hard route together. Ingerid went on to elaborate more of the story, with Gunnar allowing her space to initiate, every re-iteration allowing her to envision herself for a moment as the person she was yesterday. Her concept of self (I), of the Other and of WE/US becomes firmer and more robust, enlarged through the dimension of time, of *me-in-the-past* being the same as *me-in-the-present*.

Contexts of learning

Issues to consider

Impressions can easily be too fresh to properly digest, unless you mark them with a pause to recycle and communicate them immediately during the experience itself. As the impressions are totally fresh the companion can remember them very precisely so that her own gestural expressive forms blend with her BETs and become recognisable and understandable to her. The companion also then has precise fresh memories of what he presumes to be her experiential perspective – both can then start to symbolically co-create a shared narrative world.

It can be challenging for the companion to maintain enough intensity to sustain the participation of the person with CDB. If tension is felt as too high, her attention will decrease. The intensity needs to come from heightening small changes in degrees of emotional charge, just as parents do when communicating with infants. Co-presence is not mystical, it is just takes a level of concentration and involvement in the other that is not common in ordinary conversations when we have more shared language to rely on.

Outcomes and evidence: what we look for

Successful co-presence is evidenced in the transformation of shared narrative to co-authored story, where perspectives are exchanged dialogically. We also found that this transformation generated *language*, enabling Ingerid to live in a shared social world and be liberated from the negative and lonely tension of always living in the present. That smile of Ingerid, we choose to think, is a smile of freedom. Over the years, Ingerid's authentic language has expanded through transforming narratives into stories. The most important theme, with the biggest potential for meaning making, seems to be resilience – how she is someone who can endure and overcome tension. We have seen similar narrative developmental paths in other persons with CDB (Hanning-Zwannenberg et al., 2015). With *interactive partners* we are looking for co-presence and competency as revealed through attentiveness, perspective taking, intention sharing and the ability to build narrative tension and release.

Try it yourself

This chapter has of necessity provided only a brief introduction to the highly complex and skilled but enormously rewarding task of remembering events with people who have severe sensory impairments. If you are working with people who have CDB, specific training is absolutely essential.

Our guidance is also relevant to many persons with developmental disabilities, including those with functional vision and hearing, but difficulties with perception and the ability to sustain attention through the distal senses, impacting on semantic memory.

Thus these resources can be cultivated whenever access to a sharable linguistic practice is weak or distorted.

Top tips

- Rehearse your narrative with a partner who does *not* have disabilities (but could be blindfolded) to practise and adapt as necessary.
- Switch on your "inner camera". "Record" exactly what is happening, so you can know in depth how the person receives, responds and initiates through sensation and movement, both spontaneously and with support.
- Repeat the story many times so that the person can increase their participation.

Then introduce novelty – create tension which can activate the person mentally, motivating them to act and communicate.

Resources

- If you can see it, you can support it – A book on tactile language. Nordic Welfare Center. NVC, https://nordicwelfare.org/wp-content/uploads/2019/06/If-you-can-see-it-you-can-support-it-a-book-on-tactile-language.pdf.
- Tactile Communication Network http://tcn.deafblindinternational.org.
- Tactile Reciprocal Interactions and BETs https://library.tsbvi.edu/Play/13204.
- Texas School for the Blind and Visually Impaired https://www.tsbvi.edu.
- Rose, S. (2021) A framework for learners developing bodily-tactile communication and tactile sign language skills Version 1.1. https://steverosetherapy.co.uk/tactile-framework.

Acknowledgements

We would like to thank everyone who contributed to the TRACES documentary video project – colleagues and leaders from Signo and Skådalen/Statped and Briskeby HLFs school and resource centre, especially Reidun Frantzen Bjartvik and Rolf Svendsen. ~~Special~~ Deep appreciation is due to Ingerid and her family from whom we learned so much.

References

Ask Larsen, F. (2006). Mental space theory and introduction to the 6 spacer. *Communication Network Update Series (CNUS) No 7*. Available at: https://nordicwelfare.org/wp-content/uploads/2017/10/CNUS_07.pdf (Accessed 21.6.21).

Costain, K., Souriau, J. & Daelman, M. (2019). Embodied cognition and language appropriation: Recycling with difference by a child with congenital deafblindness and multiple disability. *Journal of Deafblind Studies on Communication, 5, 4–34.*

Daelman, M., Janssen, M., Ask Larsen, F., Nafstad, A., Rødbroe, I. & Souriau, J. (2004). Congenitally deafblind persons and the emergence of social and communicative interaction. *Communication Network Updates Series No. 2.* Available at: https://nordicwelfare.org/en/publikationer/congenitally-deafblind-persons-and-the-emergence-of-social-and-communicative-interaction (Accessed 18.6.21).

Gibson, J. et al. (2020). *Climbing the wall: Assessment of cognition through video analysis.* Nordic Welfare Center. Available at: https://issuu.com/nordicwelfare/docs/revealinghiddenpotentials_webb (Accessed 18.6.21).

Gregersen, A. (2020). Are we getting to all that matters? The need for perceptual guidance. *Journal of Deafblind Studies on Communication, 6, 46–60.*

Hanning-Zwannenberg, A., Rødbroe, I., Nafstad, A. & Souriau, J. (2015). Narrative based conversations with children who are congenitally deaf-blind. *Journal of Deaf Blind Studies on Communication, 1, 40–53.*

Janssen, M. & Rødbroe, I. (2007). *Communication and congenital deafblindness: II. Contact and social interaction.* The Netherlands: VCDBF and Viataal, St. Michielsgestel.

Linell, P. (2009). *Rethinking language, mind and world dialogically.* INC: Information Age Publishing.

Linell, P. (2017). Dialogue and the birth of the individual mind. *Journal of Deafblind Studies on Communication, 3, 59–79.*

Markova, I. (2006). On "The Inner Alter" in dialogue. *International Journal of Dialogical Science, 1,* 125–147.

Markova, I. (2016). *The dialogical mind: Common sense and ethics.* Cambridge: Cambridge University Press.

Miles, B. (1998). *Talking the language of the hands to the hands.* DB-LINK, The National Information Clearinghouse on Children who are Deafblind, Monmouth, OR. Available at: www.dblink.org.

Nafstad, A. (2015). Communication as cure. Communicative agency in persons with congenital deafblindness. *Journal of Deaf Blind Studies on Communication, 1, 23–39.*

Nafstad, A. & Daelman, M. (2017). Excursions into the richness of human communication: Theory and practice during and before the International Master Programme on Congenital Deafblindness, *Journal of Deaf Blind Studies on Communication, 3, 4–27.*

Nafstad, A. & Rødbroe, I. (2015). *Communicative relations.* Available at: https://www.statped.no/globalassets/laringsressurs/dokumenter/02-bokhefte/communicative-relations-uk.pdf (Accessed 18.6.21).

Nelson, K. (1966). *Language in cognitive development: The emergence of the mediated mind.* Cambridge: Cambridge University Press.

Souriau, J. (2015) Blended spaces and deixis in communicative activities involving persons with congenital deafblindness. *Journal of Deaf Blind Studies on Communication*, 1, 5–22.

Souriau, J., Rødbroe, I. & Janssen, M. (2008). Emergence of gestures based on shared experiences. In J. Souriau, I. Rødbroe & M. Janssen (Eds), *Communication and congenital deafblindness: Meaning Making*, Booklet III. The Netherlands: VCDBF and Viataal, St. Michielsgestel.

Stern, D. (2010) *Forms of vitality: Exploring dynamic experience in psychology, the arts, psychotherapy and development*. Oxford: Oxford University Press.

Vege, G. (2009). *Co-presence is a gift – Co-presence as a prerequisite for a sustained and shared here and now*. MSc. thesis, Educational Sciences, University of Groningen.

Vege, G., Nafstad, A. & Bjartvik, R. (2007). TRACES, DVD and booklet. Oslo: Andebu Døvblindesenter, Andebu Kompetanse- og Skolesenter and Skådalen Recourse Center. The commented sequences are available as DVD in J. Souriau, I. Rødbroe & M. Janssen (Eds), *Communication and congenital deafblindness: Meaning Making.*, Booklet III. The Netherlands: VCDBF and Viataal, St. Michielsgestel.

Chapter 21

Personal storytelling for children who use augmentative and alternative communication

Annalu Waller and Rolf Black

Background

Personal storytelling is a social activity vital to our day-to-day interactions. We tell others what we did, what we liked or did not like, how we laughed or cried. Telling stories involves turn-taking, naturally drifting from one story to the next with no knowing where you will end up. This makes it particularly challenging for aided communication, where utterances must be prepared in advance.

Cheepen (1988) calls this type of talk 'interactional' conversation. She categorises conversation as: transactional, phatic communication and free narrative. Transactional, goal-driven interactions communicate needs and wants, and the sharing of information (Bowden & Beukelman, 1988). Phatic communication is used for social relationships and etiquette – the 'glue' that keeps conversations going. Social closeness achieved through the exchange and discussion of personal experiences, however, is best communicated through free narrative – or 'story'.

The term 'augmentative and alternative communication' (AAC) denotes strategies and systems that support the communication of individuals with little or no functional speech. People who use AAC tend to have a physical impairment and may have additional sensory and/or intellectual disabilities. 'Aided' AAC systems range from *low-tech*, such as symbol or word boards, to electronic devices such as single-switch voice recorders and *high-tech* voice output communication aids (VOCAs) with specialised software for spoken and written communication (Beukelman & Light, 2005). Individuals also use 'Unaided' communication, including vocalisations, facial expressions and gestures or manual signs.

At Dundee University we have been investigating how the pragmatic design of AAC technology can enable non-speaking individuals to engage in interactive conversation since the 1970s. This has ranged from early research into word prediction systems to providing access to conversational phrases, sentences and narrative (Waller, 2019).

We know that relating and sharing personal experiences is a complex skill that develops in early childhood, facilitated through scaffolding and successful experiential learning (Bruner, 1975). AAC devices support transactional communication well (Waller, 2006, 2019). They can be used for active participation in story retelling, through stored phrases or sentences, but are not designed to support free narrative, making it difficult to scaffold personal storytelling with children who depend on AAC.

It is essential to support both *fictional* and *personal* storytelling through AAC. Unfortunately, in many cases it is only *fictional* storytelling that attracts attention in the classroom,

DOI: 10.4324/9781003159087-21

within the context of literacy teaching. In this chapter we briefly discuss fictional storytelling. We then describe ways of supporting *personal* storytelling, using examples from the How was School today ...? research project.[1]

AAC and story genres

Fictional storytelling

Practitioners have developed innovative ways to involve children who use AAC in fictional storytelling. These range from enabling children to choose what story they want to read at an early age, to supporting children to create their own stories. Light, Binger and Kelford Smith (1994) observed that parents of children with severe disabilities were more likely to choose different books to read to them, whereas non-disabled toddlers chose their favourite stories over and over again. The Tango[TM] device[2] included phrases to prompt choice of stories; for example: 'Ask me if I want a funny story or a scary story.'

Story vocabulary can be stored on devices to allow children to participate in group storytelling; for example, a single word like 'boo!' on a single-switch device; key words such as 'bear' and 'Goldilocks'; phrases and sentences that allow interjections or links such as 'and then'.

Story writing is also supported within the classroom, using templates and appropriate written vocabularies, with and without symbol support.[3] Learners are able to generate and tell simple stories by completing different parts of the templates.

Engaging in fictional storytelling is comparatively straightforward; it is the sharing of personal experience which poses the greater challenge for children who use AAC.

Personal storytelling

Most children who use AAC access words and phrases by looking at and choosing pictures or words (a graphic interface). To find a word or sentence, the child needs to know the target item *and* remember where it is on the 'page'. Three main strategies help children locate a phrase or sentence: sequences of icon keys for a set number of core words (e.g. the Unity® system may use 'apple' + '2nd layer verb' to say 'eat'[4]); dynamic screens where the items are stored under a hierarchy of topic and activity screens (e.g. 'pets', 'places', 'days of the week' or 'chat' 'questions'[5]) and visual scene displays (items are accessed by pressing hotspots on a picture/photograph). Whichever, the child has to know not only the words they want to access, but where these are stored.

Some children do become skilled AAC users, but typically their communication output is limited to one or two-word utterances. Aided communication is characterised by the child responding to closed questions from a speaking partner. Successful storytelling is usually dependent on the conversation partner knowing the context of the story so that appropriate questions can be asked. A storytelling exchange which relies on information in a school-home diary might go:

MUM: I hear you went to the zoo?
CHILD: (Might indicate 'yes' non-verbally)
MUM: And you saw a ...?
CHILD: Penguin.

(The parent may need to support the child to navigate through the hierarchy of pages on the AAC device)

If the word 'penguin' was not on the device, the child might answer 'animal', prompting the parent to request descriptive information: 'What colour animal?' and 'Where does it live?'

As an alternative, school staff might store a structured story in the AAC device. Storytelling using this approach might result in:

MUM: I hear you've a story to tell. (Having read the home–school diary)
CHILD: My class went to the zoo today. We saw the penguins, the lion and the ostrich.
  (Parent may need to support child to navigate through hierarchy of pages to the 'story' page for today)

Theories and principles

The Vygotsky principles of the 'more knowledgeable other' and the 'zone of proximal development' underpin the importance of providing children who use aided communication with opportunities to engage in successful storytelling. The role of communication partners in providing the scaffolding and modelling the use of aided AAC is crucial if the child is to develop the skills needed to share personal experience.

Another key working principle is that of 'total communication': the recognition that communication is naturally multimodal and that all forms used by the child are to be valued.

Work in practice

The storytelling research projects at Dundee University[6] are developing systems and strategies to allow children to share their experiences in conversational environments. Here we focus on the use of multi-message voice recording switches, such as the Step-by-Step[7] device, and high-tech symbol-based AAC devices based on touch-screen tablet computers.

Our aims are to:

- Enable children to relate their own experiences, including feelings and views
- Promote interactive conversation in which all partners collaborate in the storytelling
- Support multimodal communication, including vocalisations and non-verbal communication
- Support children to communicate the meaning the story has for them – through providing ways of signalling feelings.

In order to achieve these aims, four stages must be completed:

1 **Story identification:** The experience must be identified.
2 **Story preparation:** The story vocabulary (content words and/or stored stories) must be stored in the device.
3 **Story retrieval:** The child needs to know what vocabulary is stored, and where.
4 **Story narration:** The child needs to tell the story interactively.

Story identification

What is a good story? An experience is worth telling if it has some meaning for the child (Grove, 2014; Labov & Waletzky, 1967). In natural conversations, stories emerge spontaneously. In the case of AAC, experiences with the potential to be a story must first be identified.

This task lies mainly with the person supporting the child at the time, where possible with their involvement. This can be immediately after the experience or before transitions (change points).

After the experience

Photographs of important events, taken at the time, can be used as prompts. A diary next to the child can be used to jot down interesting incidents. Both methods aid recall when preparing the AAC device and/or prompting/scaffolding during subsequent narration.

Before transitions

Transitions provide powerful opportunities to share stories. In addition to the main transition of the day, going home, many happen during the school day, for example when a child returns to class after therapy or play. The aim is to empower the child to tell parents, siblings, fellow pupils and staff about what they have been doing.

Setting time aside with children before the transition, to review the day or recent activity is important to allow them to own their stories. Reviewing the day can be tricky if more than one staff member has been involved. Possible story events can be identified by: reviewing the child's timetable (did anything out of the ordinary happen?); messages or diary entries; using photographs taken during the day.

Story preparation

Having identified potential stories the next step is to prepare them for the AAC device. This can involve new voice recordings, inputting story texts or helping the child access existing or new vocabulary. For a successful interaction, the child needs to know how to access their story utterances before they tell the story.

When recording or storing new phrases, it is important to segment the story into separate utterances to ensure interactive telling – monologues make it difficult for a communication partner to interact with the child.

Voice recordings

When preparing a device with new messages we employ the following strategies:

- Record all messages in the first person, as if the child were speaking.
- Record short messages with the minimum of information.
- Do not give all the information away in one message – build up the suspense.
- It is not always appropriate to include information the child can communicate without the AAC device (e.g. emotions), although this may be required to provide children with the experience of *evaluation* – reflections about the event (Labov & Waletzky, 1967).

- 'Empty' messages at the beginning and end of a story can be useful. By recording a few seconds of silence for the first message we can avoid an unintended story start if the child hits the switch by accident. Silence or a definite story ending for the last message avoids a mistaken: 'Is that all?' question from a partner.
- If the device can store several stories (e.g. a high-tech device or multi-message recorder with different channels or levels) it is possible to retain favourite stories for longer-term use, but beware of time-restricted phrases like 'today'.
- 'Attention grabbers' such as 'hey!' can help the child find listeners. For example, on some multi-message recorders a message can be repeated until a special button is pressed by the communication partner; on high-tech devices the child can repeatedly use a phrase.
- With high-tech devices, consider the child's physical abilities when deciding whether to store a story under one button (similar to a Step-by-Step), or several. Some children can be physically too exhausted after school to fully operate the devices and it may be preferable to use simpler means to access the story.

Remember the main aim of personal storytelling. This is not about giving a factual *report*, but enabling children to share and reflect on their experiences in a way that is entertaining for both themselves and the listener.

High-tech devices

For high-tech devices, story templates can be helpful. These provide a layout for story messages, comments, access to related and older stories and utterances that support interactivity (e.g. asking the listener about their experiences). We have developed a story template for symbol-based dynamic screen devices (Black et al., 2012; Black et al., 2010; Todman, Elder & Alm, 1995). This consists of four rows of five buttons in each row (see Figure 21.1 for a worked example).

Story retrieval

Stories emerge in social interaction. Hence the user must have ready access to the stories to tell them whenever the opportunity arises. This presents a challenge for several reasons:

Table 21.1 Story template

Row 1:	*Operational functions (e.g. 'Close window')*
Row 2:	Story messages, beginning with a time reference (e.g. 'This was on Tuesday, 19 December')
Row 3:	Perspective shift questions, allowing the storyteller to ask questions (e.g. 'Do you know Jenny?')
Row 4:	Evaluation expressing emotions and judgement statements (e.g. 'That was good', 'I was scared') (see Labov & Waletzky, 1967)

- Multi-message devices usually only have capacity to save up to three stories at any one time – stories are recorded over each other and then deleted.
- The child needs to have ready access to the device. If you have to take the Step-by-Step out of the bag before you can tell the story, the moment is gone. Instead, place the device so it is ready to use at all times (e.g. on a lap tray) or use devices that can easily be carried around by children who can walk.
- If a device can store several stories, make sure the most appropriate story is readily available.
- High-tech devices usually have one story button/page reserved for the story of the day. This should be available on the home page so the child (or support person) does not have to search for it.
- If multiple stories are stored the user needs to be able to find them. Difficulty of retrieval increases with the number of stories stored. Make sure to use easily remembered filenames/codes/dynamic displays.

It is imperative that children have the opportunity to both collect and retain their favourite stories. Telling and retelling stories is an essential part of language development. The only way to keep stories using current multi-message devices is to transcribe the recordings before stories are over-recorded, a strategy employed by the Bridge School in San Francisco (Hamilton, 2010). In order to support more effective multi-message storytelling, we are developing a mobile phone multi-message application that allows for the recording of many stories (Tintarev et al., 2014). In the meantime, important stories may need to be re-recorded to allow learners to access them.

Retaining stories is simpler on high-tech AAC devices, where a story page can have several buttons relating to different stories (e.g. *The Horseriding Competition* or *My 10th Birthday with the Magician*). Each one links to the appropriate page based on a template. However, the child still has to remember where the story is stored; current devices make it very difficult for users to find stories by keywords (e.g. inputting 'magician' or 'horseriding').

Story narration

Narrating a story is an interactive process. By storing stories in short segments the user is able to step through the story, inviting comments and questions from the conversational partner. Here is an example from a story about being snowed in at school.

CALENDAR: This was in December 2010.
SNOW: We had so much snow. The school was really struggling.
BUS: There was even so much snow that the buses would come to pick us up!
CAMP: I and some of my friends had to stay at the school overnight!
PIZZA: The teachers drove to ASDA to get medicine and a pizza.

This story page was created to support the telling of the snow story. The second row is used for the story utterances. The question-mark buttons allow the narrator to ask about the partner's respective experiences: 'Did you have much snow?', 'Were you ever stuck somewhere?' The bottom row is reserved for generic evaluations, such as positive/negative phrases: 'It was great', 'It was awful' and story-specific evaluations: 'It was a bit scary'. The

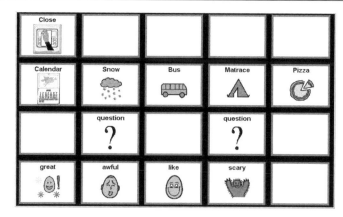

Figure 21.1 A story page on a symbol-based dynamic screen device

child is also able to add evaluations to the story – these are not built into the messages, but can be used to reflect the child's emotional response to the event as the story unfolds.

Additional buttons are provided for yes/no responses. A 'next' button was introduced to allow the telling of the story step by step.

Outcomes and evidence

Longitudinal studies, for example Waller et al. (2001), Waller & O'Mara (2003), have demonstrated how children can develop the ability to construct and share appropriate personal stories in conversation if they are supported to develop these skills through the use of appropriate tools; appropriate language to relate the story; and successful storytelling opportunities. When children are given the ability to relate past experience interactively they appear to take more control in conversations if they have access to personal stories (Black et al., 2010; Waller et al., 2001). They are better able to initiate and respond to questions, and show increased self-esteem (Waller, 2006; Waller et al., 2001) and development of storytelling skills (Waller & O'Mara, 2003).

The story of Peter

Ten-year-old Peter has athetoid cerebral palsy, with very little functional speech. He has difficulties accessing technology, using a combination of gross and fine motor movements for switch access or eye pointing with an E-Tran[8] folder. His multi-message device is mounted on the lap tray on his wheelchair.

During a therapy session, Peter and Sarah, his therapist, played a new card game, 'Pairs'. Each player uncovered pairs of pictures; Peter using eye pointing. The game was a great success. However, at the end, one single card was left – a cat was missing its partner.

Sarah encouraged Peter to tell his class about his success with a new activity. She suggested each message to Peter before recording it onto the device. The following sequence was designed to raise listener curiosity and prompt questions which would be answered by the subsequent interaction.

1 I played my new pairs game with Sarah.
2 I won the game 4–3.
3 The cat was missing.
4 Where's the cat?

Message 1 sets the scene and prompts the question 'And who won?', hence the second message. However, message 3 introduces a twist in the tale. The most interesting part of the experience was the missing card – this led to plenty of excited interaction during the game: 'Where was it? Did it get lost? Where was it hiding?' So a fourth message was added. Peter replayed these messages before returning to class. Both authors were in the session and everyone enjoyed reliving the experience as Sarah prepared Peter's story with him.

As everyone walked back to class, Peter enthusiastically pressed his switch, going through the story. When he met his teaching assistant in the corridor, the story had reached its last message: 'Where is the cat?', 'I know where the cat is!' she exclaimed as she turned around to fetch it from the classroom. A lively discussion ensued with much hilarity.

Try it yourself

Identify events which have resulted in some emotional response – laughter/ frustration/success. Record a story onto a multi-message recorder or high-tech device. Send the child to visit another class or teacher to tell their story.

Top tips

- Identify interesting stories during the day: What do speaking children talk about? What is interesting to the child?
- Practice is everything – for both the child (access the story) and the support person (recording it).
- Create opportunities (big and small) for the child to tell their story in school – weekend news on Monday morning with stories from home; returning to class from therapy, swimming, playtime, lunch.

Where to go

- For further information about the AAC research projects at the University of Dundee, Scotland, visit https://aac.dundee.ac.uk.
- For general information on AAC, visit https://www.communicationmatters.org.uk (UK) and https://isaac-online.org (international).

Notes

1 See https://aac.dundee.ac.uk/how-was-school-today (accessed 6 January 2021).
2 See https://www.spectronics.com.au/product/tango-2 (accessed 6 January 2021).
3 For examples of story templates with symbol support, see literacy materials from https://learning tools.donjohnston.com/product (accessed 6 January 2021) and https://www.widgit.com/resour ces (accessed 6 January 2021).

4 See https://www.prentrom.com/prc_advantage/unity-language-system (accessed 6 January 2021) for an example of a sequence-based retrieval system.
5 See, for example, CALLTalk by CALL Scotland, in: A. Wilson (Ed.) (2000) *AAC 2000: Practical Approaches to Augmentative and Alternative Communication*. ISBN 1 898042 17 9.
6 See https://aac.dundee.ac.uk/research (accessed 6 January 2021).
7 See https://www.ablenetinc.com/little-step-by-step-choice-with-levels (accessed 6 January 2021).
8 The E-Tran (eye-transfer) folder contains pages of communication items (symbols and pictures) accessed using an eye gaze method, see https://www.communicationmatters.org.uk/types-of-aac/e-tran-frames (accessed 23 March 2021).

References

Beukelman, D. R. & Light, J. (2005). *Augmentative and alternative communication: Supporting children and adults with complex communication needs*. Baltimore, MD: Paul H. Brookes.

Black, R., Reddington, J., Reiter, E., Tintarev, N. & Waller, A. (2010). Using NLG and sensors to support personal narrative for children with complex communication needs. *Proceedings of the NAACL HLT 2010 Workshop on Speech and Language Processing for Assistive Technologies* (pp. 1–9). Los Angeles, USA, 1–6 June. Stroudsburg, PA: The Association for Computational Linguistics.

Black, R., Waller, A, Turner, R. & Reiter, E. (2012). Supporting personal narrative for children with complex communication needs. *ACM Transactions on Computer-Human Interaction*, 19(2), Article 15.

Bowden, P. & Beukelman, D. (1988). Rate, accuracy, and message flexibility: Case studies in communication augmentation strategies. In L. Bernstein (Ed.), *The vocally impaired* (pp. 295–311). Philadelphia, PA: Grune & Sutton.

Bruner, J. (1975). From communication to language: A psychological perspective. *Cognition*, 3, 255–289.

Cheepen, C. (1988). *The predictability of informal conversation*. Oxford: Printer Publishers.

Grove, N. (2014). *The big book of storysharing*. Abingdon: Speechmark.

Hamilton, H. (2010). Read all about it! 'Home News' informs AAC System development and instruction. *Proceedings of the 14th Biennial Conference of the International Society for Augmentative and Alternative Communication*. Barcelona, 24–29 July. ISBN: 978 0 9684186 9 7.

Labov, W. & Waletzky, J. (1967). In J. Helm (Ed.), *'Narrative analysis'. Essays on the verbal and visual arts* (pp. 12–44). Seattle, WA: University of Washington Press. Reprinted in *Journal of Narrative and Life History*, 1997; 7, 3–38.

Light, J., Binger, C. & Kelford Smith, A. (1994). Story reading interactions between preschoolers who use AAC and their mothers. *Augmentative and Alternative Communication*, 10, 255–268.

Tintarev, N., Reiter, E., Black, R. & Waller, A. (2014). Natural language generation for augmentative and assistive technologies. In A. Stent & S. Bangalore (Eds), *Natural language generation in interactive systems* (pp. 252–278). Cambridge: Cambridge University Press.

Todman, J., Elder, L. & Alm, N. (1995). Evaluation of the content of computer-aided conversations. *Augmentative and Alternative Communication*, 11, 229–234.

Waller, A. (2006). Communication access to conversational narrative. *Topics in Language Disorders*, 26, 221–239.

Waller, A. (2019). Telling tales: Unlocking the potential of AAC technologies. *International Journal of Language and Communication Disorders*, 54, 159–169.

Waller, A. & O'Mara, D. (2003). Aided communication and the development of personal story telling. In S. von Tetzchner & N. Grove (Eds), *Augmentative and alternative communication: Developmental issues* (pp. 256–271). London: Whurr.

Waller, A., O'Mara, D., Tait, L., Booth, L. & Brophy-Arnott, B. (2001). Using written stories to support the use of narrative in conversational interactions: Case study. *Augmentative and Alternative Communication*, 17, 221–232.

Chapter 22

Self-created film and AAC technologies

Mascha Legel and Christopher Norrie

Background

Throughout this book, the transformative potential of storytelling in a multitude of contexts is made exquisitely clear. For us, an overriding question is: how might the enabling advantages of digital technology be harnessed to support and enrich access to shared personal narratives? In this chapter we introduce and describe the method Film as Observable Communication (FaOC), which explores how digital film – created by narrators themselves – may be used as one of the underpinning building blocks in communication and storytelling (Legel, 2012; Legel et al., 2017; Legel et al., in preparation 2021a, 2021b).

As individuals, in order to share our stories dynamically (and most efficiently), we may adopt strategies from a diverse constellation of resources, for example: spoken/written/ signed language; gestures; vocalisations; eye-pointing; facial expressions and, as described here, other visual cues such as images. Self-created film is the empowering process of documenting experienced life events, as filmed and edited by the key participant/narrator themselves (Legel, 2012). It can be used to capture detailed contextual information about an experienced event, to encapsulate a mix of those sensory elements (e.g. aural/visual) that may prove definitive. Where a disabled user experiences communicative challenges, augmentative and alternative communication (AAC) solutions – tools and/or strategies that support people with limited functional speech – can assist them in expressing their thoughts, ideas and emotions.

A strength of today's increasingly affordable, and thereby ubiquitous, digital technology is that we now have the means to support every learner in becoming their own filmmaker and storyteller. The unique, multimodal properties of film distinguish it as a practical and accessible medium for storytelling, one that goes beyond the conventional borders of language. How useful and, importantly, how much *fun* would it be to merge digital self-created film and AAC technology to support users in the sharing of their stories? Ethnographic methods or approaches have been adopted – and shown to be highly effective – in supporting the learning/teaching process of using digital film and AAC technologies, both in school and at home (Norrie et al., 2016; Norrie, 2021; Norrie et al., 2021; Legel et al., 2012; Legel et al., in preparation 2021a, 2021b).

History

In 1995, during the course of her studies in visual anthropology, Mascha Legel was inspired by the idea of handing the camera to her participants in order to get their unique points of

DOI: 10.4324/9781003159087-22

view – rather than restricting her research to only the anthropologist's perspective. Subsequently Mascha continued using this ethnographic methodology in a variety of research projects and documentaries. Since 2010, through her work as an AAC researcher at Radboud University Nijmegen, the University of Dundee and the charity Com in Beeld, Mascha has further developed this technique into a variety of teaching methods and projects in the field of AAC supporting storytelling and language development. One of these methods is the FaOC teaching method *My Film, My Story*, which was devised and refined over the duration of a five-year ethnographic research project (Legel, 2012; Legel et al., 2012; Legel et al., 2021a, 2021b). In 2018 Mascha launched the film studio Cam on Wheels, where a diverse mix of young adults – some with, and some without, disabilities – create professional film productions, based upon the novel concept of merging film and AAC to boost cooperation and communication. Since 2016, Mascha and Christopher Norrie have been collaborating – most recently leveraging the dynamic interactions of self-created film with aided communicators to build their skills in sharing personal narratives, and promote the use and impact of their AAC technologies.

Theories and principles

Two main fields of study underpinning this practice are:

- Visual anthropology (using visual methodologies)
- AAC strategies and solutions.

Visual anthropology and storytelling

In visual anthropology, photography, film and storytelling have been used to foster greater understanding among collaborators, and to collect and document knowledge during ethnographic studies (Pink, 2020; MacDougall, 2006). Photographs and film, including those created by participants, can be collected as data in ethnographic research. Captured images provide access to specific moments, locations, activities and rituals through a visual language accessible by both researchers and participants. Any lived experience takes place in a vibrant, four-dimensional context, with interacting parameters that may be documented such as a location, actors, objects, colours, smells or sounds. As social creatures, when we share our stories we attempt to provide as much sensory or contextual information as possible in order to express a vivid picture of our experiences to others. In this way we may nurture mutual understanding, potentially building lasting bonds. But to achieve this we typically need language and communication to convey the information in our heads – the story behind the picture.

AAC strategies and solutions

AAC is a term used to describe the diverse range of strategies and technologies adopted by people living with communication disabilities to support (augment) or replace (alternative) spoken communication and promote enduring independence. High tech AAC technologies such as speech generating devices (SGDs) can be very effective tools, but are often complex or otherwise challenging to operate[1] and maintain. A holistic approach towards supporting emerging aided communicators – characterised by early intervention, ethnographic methodologies and collaborative action research – has been shown to be a promising means of helping them to acquire the necessary competencies (Norrie, 2021; Norrie et al., 2021).

Teaching and learning framework

The rationale behind providing access to this potent mix of tools and resources, filmmaking and AAC is to encourage and motivate individuals with complex communication needs (CCN), young and old, to share their personal stories. Digital self-created film is fun to share. Moreover, engaging in it may also flatten the – often steep – learning curve towards gaining important AAC competencies (Light, 1989). Using this approach, communication partners already have the insights provided by a picture – facilitating easier access to a pedagogical, formative interaction. The first sketches of the story are already there, reducing barriers (Baxter et al., 2012; Hodge, 2007) between the aided communicator and their AAC technology as a means of projecting personal narratives. Capitalising on these combined strengths of film and AAC technologies, FaOC has been developed into a practical teaching method for use in an array of settings. A range of tools are used in this approach.

Teaching method: My Film, My Story

To promote the practical application of FaOC, a language teaching method – *My Film, My Story* – has been developed for children and young adults with CCN. This method can be utilised by the target group themselves, and by teachers and speech language therapists (SLTs) both in both school and at home. Cam on Wheels,[2] a film production house that

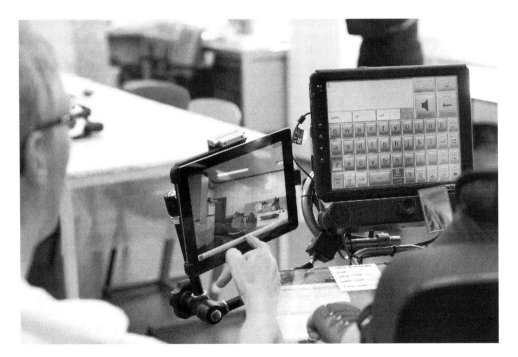

Figure 22.1 AAC tech and film

specialises in bringing together young filmmakers both with and without disabilities, uses this method daily in its audiovisual productions, and supports children, teachers, SLTs and assistive technologists (ATists) with training and (online) workshops in how to apply it.

My Film, My Story comprises the three phases listed below (Grove, 2014; Legel et al., 2021a):

1   *Story collecting*: (filming – operating the camera to capture relevant footage)
2   *Story preparation*: (post-production/editing the film with AAC using computer workstations and video editing software)
3   *Story sharing*: using the film with AAC (interactive group activities supported by self-created and highly personalised visual cues).

The TACTS framework

The TACTS (Transforming Assistive Communication Technologies Support) framework (Norrie, 2021) can act as a practical, evidence-based guide for supporting filmmaking and AAC technologies in different settings. ATists, or similarly skilled practitioners, can implement the framework to support both young people with CCN and other stakeholders (e.g. teachers, SLTs, family members) in learning to use film and AAC solutions. For the most effective support to be achieved, both home and school settings should be included in a concerted approach towards teaching and sharing stories.

An ethnographic attitude

Based on an ethnographic approach, including participant observation, we stay close to our participants to learn from them; and provide them with the opportunity to learn from us. Through observation, we can see how they view the world – and instruct them on how best to capture their own unique perspectives on film. By observing how they communicate, we can learn how we might improve their communication using their AAC device(s). By observing how they share their stories, we can teach them and their co-narrators to utilise their AAC technology and the film footage they capture most effectively. Conversely, as researchers and AAC tech developers we can learn from the participants how to improve our methods and technologies.

Work in practice in three steps

1 Story collecting and filming

With film, you can collect moments, locations, events, actions and people as visual story elements. Optimal results should reflect the perspective of the narrator themself, or with assistance. Topics, small or large, could be daily life activities, for example a school day or baking cookies.

2 Story preparation

This activity consists of film-editing and preparing other resources to share the story, for example programming appropriate vocabulary into AAC devices. The participant can edit their own film independently or with some assistance, but stays in control of choice making. Editing is selecting the scenes you want to use in story sharing, assembling a beginning, middle and end. Also adding (programming in) vocabulary, pictures, graphic symbols or screen taxonomies onto a user's SGD, for example preparing the story sharing about a visit to a farm, a child may need access to a page with words or symbols for the animals they encounter.

3 Story sharing with self-created film/AAC methods and technologies

Finally the big moment of story sharing arrives (Grove, 2014)! This exciting event will require a screen where the film may be viewed by both the narrator and their co-narrator(s); and a control interface to start, pause, rewind or fast forward the completed movie. It is essential that the narrators know that they can all control the film. A dynamic and interactive milieu (e.g. asking questions and volunteering comments on events unfolding on the screen) is what makes the storytelling sparkle. In other words, not being quiet while watching the film as in traditional movie consumption, but chatting and narrating, engaging: this is the overarching goal. By pausing the film, and selecting a certain frame of interest, participants can use the image as a visual cue to elaborate upon, and thus stimulate responsive, empowering conversational discourse. As with any interaction involving aided communicators, co-narrators or facilitators can assist in this process by encouraging a supportive environment, adopting strategies detailed within the TACTS framework such as aided language stimulation and also – within the context of informal chatting – ensuring sufficient time is given for conversational turns.

Outcomes and evidence: what we look for

The dynamic interaction between film and AAC tech creates a natural environment potentially leveraging all the captured resources. The outcome can be observed in more elaborate and extensive story sharing. Norrie concluded in his TACTS study (2021) that appropriately supported access to AAC technical tools, strategies and solutions improves daily communication and language development. Legel (2021b) concluded that the use of self-created film by the participant as one of the resources in daily storytelling improves topic development and leads to better and more rapid attainment of mutual understanding.

The story of Adam

Adam (11 years) and Colin (9 years) are two of the participants of the projects *My Film, My Story* and TACTS. Adam uses an iPad for filming by hand, or mounts his cam onto his walker. At home he uses idiosyncratic sign language to communicate with his parents, but in school nobody understands his signing, so he uses a lettercard on paper or very limited Proloquo4text on his iPad. He is a very creative and expressive boy, with an almost literary way of telling stories. Still, it remains challenging for him to give others the complete picture of an event. Adam made a film about his grandfather's shed, a man who was his best friend, but had sadly passed away. When they had to empty the house, Adam made a film to capture his memories and to tell his friends in school about the shed and his grandfather's tools. He filmed all the gear carefully, and when he came home he edited the film, including adding some of the names of the tools. Later on, in class, he showed the film and elaborated upon his story in detail with words using his lettercard and iPad. The class was impressed and touched by the film and his story.

The story of Colin

Colin, a wheelchair user, uses an SGD, augmented by gestures and vocalisations. The ATist worked closely with him and the team around him to improve understanding of how to develop his expressive communication, and tried to identify the most effective way for Colin to create his own films in tandem with his SGD. With the iPad (as a camera) mounted securely on his wheelchair, Colin filmed at home: his room, his bed and his pet rabbit. The following day at school, Colin showed his film to his classmates on a large liquid crystal display (LCD) screen, and expanded upon the story using his SGD, enabled further by his teacher who asked him questions reflecting the visual cues he had placed in his film. When the rabbit was shown, Colin made the sign for "rabbit". When he saw his favourite book on his bed, he used his SGD to find and select the picture of that book. All the classmates responded in their own way to the film, but all were enthusiastic about the rabbit running free in the living room. This was an inspiring event that would otherwise have been very challenging for Colin to describe effectively.

Contexts of learning

Home

A learner's home setting is as important as their school setting. As far as possible all potential communication partners, including family members and friends, need familiarity with the methods and technologies used by the individual aided learner to communicate and share their experiences. Supporting stories to travel seamlessly between home and school environments is essential in forging continuity and reinforcing learning. Traditional questions associated with speaking children – How was your day at school? What did you do over the weekend? – have equal validity for those with CCN, and can lead to important and enriching interactions. The teaching method *My Film, My Story* can also be used in the home setting by the narrator with CCN and communication partners such as parents, carers and siblings.

School

School is a very practical environment for learning how to use film and AAC in storytelling constructively. There, a key goal is building communication and storytelling skills to improve language development. The multidisciplinary team around the child can assist this in daily practice. Stakeholders and practitioners such as teachers, SLTs, classroom assistants – perhaps with the co-ordinating influence of an ATist – can work towards nurturing the learner at the centre of a joined-up, informed support network.

Studio Cam on Wheels

Cam on Wheels in Rotterdam (Netherlands) are currently engaged in rolling out our approach to Dundee (Scotland), and other countries, to delivering (online) FaOC education and initiating local Cam on Wheels chapters. The aim of Cam on Wheels is to work in close collaboration with local film students/institutes and filmmakers. There, students with CCN learn and work closely with their speaking peers, gathering the skills required to become filmmakers in professional productions. The Cam on Wheels crew consists of a dynamic, stimulating mix of filmmakers who use AAC to communicate, non-disabled film students, film professionals and an ATist whose role is to make AAC and assistive technology understandable and accessible for all participants.

The crew assists in film education with the FaOC teaching method *My Film, My Story* and produces professional audiovisual productions. They take a facilitating lead in the overarching production process. Film and AAC technology is merged, becoming an integral part of daily communication at Cam on Wheels during brainstorming, script development, filming, interviewing, editing, presenting and – very importantly – during everyday social interactions around the coffee table. In this way the unique perspective of the AAC user is captured and shared in Cam on Wheels productions.

Figure 22.2 Cam on Wheels in action

During the COVID-19 pandemic, Cam on Wheels innovated an international coronavirus YouTube channel to share visual stories and bring young people together, crossing borders and language challenges. This is an initiative that we plan to continue long after the coronavirus threat is overcome, in collaboration with ISAAC-LEAD (visit https://isaac-online.org/english/about-isaac/activities-and-projects/people-who-use-aac-lead).

Issues to consider

- There are no specific limitations or problems as long there is adequate access to the required resources, i.e. to film and to AAC (technology).
- Anyone can do this – some may need a little more help and assistance than others, but a priority is that the focal narrator stays in the lead!
- As true anthropological-ethnographic tools, film and AAC cross the barriers between language and culture. As in any culture, be respectful when, who and how you film – and always ask for permission to do so.
- Young adults who want to learn and use film and AAC technologies together can visit Cam on Wheels, or become part of our Cam on Wheels crew (see 'Try it yourself' section below or visit www.camonwheels.nl).

Figure 22.3 My Film, My Story

Try it yourself

Filming

- Ensure the results reflect the perspective of individual narrators faithfully, and be responsive to provide any assistance that the aided communicator requires.
- Always be conscious of what you are filming – that will make the imagery better and improve your final masterpiece!
- Take a mixture of pictures, close-up and far away (wide view). It is better to capture a close-up by moving nearer to your subject than by using your zoom function, whenever possible.
- Try filming from above (bird's eye view) ... or film from low on the ground looking up (frog's perspective). Switch between these camera positions for added interest.

Preparation

Through editing you develop a storyline by selecting scenes, but you can also just use the raw footage. It is important that the AAC support, for example the user's SGD, is updated with the necessary resources (words, symbols, sounds, etc.) linked to the film and/or the experience. This may be done with the help of an ATist, or a technically-competent friend or relative.

Sharing

Now go and share your story. Find a good audience or communication partner to share your story with. Together, the film and AAC technology should form a multimodal whole, a dynamic mix of different communication modes.

Where to go?

For FaOC education (the *My Film, My Story* teaching method) and technical advice on combining assistive and AAC technologies with film media, feel free to contact www.camonwheels.nl; www.cominbeeld.nl; www.beweginginzicht.nl/en/team/MaschaLegel;

chris@camonwheels.nl | @chrisnorrie

mascha@camonwheels.nl | @LegelMascha | @Cam_on_Wheels

Notes

1 Particularly so for individuals with physical or cognitive impairments.
2 www.camonwheels.nl.

References

Baxter, S., Enderby, P., Evans, P. & Judge, S. (2012). Barriers and facilitators to the use of high-technology augmentative and alternative communication devices: A systematic review and qualitative synthesis. *International Journal of Language & Communication Disorders*, 47(2), 115–129.

Grove, N. (2014). *The big book of Storysharing: A handbook for personal storytelling with children and young people who have severe communication difficulties.* Abingdon: Speechmark.

Hodge, S. (2007). Why is the potential of augmentative and alternative communication not being realized? Exploring the experiences of people who use communication aids. *Disability & Society*, 22(5), 457–471.

Legel, M. (2012). *Film as Observable Communication (FaOC), My Film, My Story.* Paper presented at the 15th Biennial Conference of the International Society for Augmentative and Alternative Communication, Pittsburgh, USA, 28 July–7 August.

Legel, M., Steenbergen, B., Soto, G., Grove, N., Waller, A., Norrie, C. S., Deckers, S., Spanjers, R. & van Balkom, H. (in preparation 2021a). *Film as Observable Communication (FaOC): A triple case study with the use of a PVS.*

Legel, M., Steenbergen, B., Soto, G., Grove, N., Waller, A., Norrie, C. S., Deckers, S., Spanjers, R. & van Balkom, H. (in preparation 2021b). *Sharing personal stories in AAC with Personal Video Scenes (PVS).*

Light, J. (1989). Toward a definition of communicative competence for individuals using augmentative and alternative communication systems. *Augmentative and Alternative Communication* 5(2), 137–144.

MacDougall, D. (2006). *The corporeal image: Film, ethnography and the senses.* Princeton, NJ: Princeton University Press.

Norrie, C. S. (2021). Valuing the child: A person-centred framework for assistive technologists within a special education setting. PhD thesis, University of Dundee.

Norrie, C. S., Waller, A. & Hannah, E. F. S. (2021). Establishing context: AAC device adoption and support in a special education setting. *ACM Transactions in Computer-Human Interaction*, 28(2), Article 13, April. Available at: https://doi.org/10.1145/3446205 (Accessed 27.5.21).

Norrie, C. S., Waller, A., & Potter, D. (2016). *In support of personal narrative elicitation: Identifying discrete moment of interest event cues within digital video footage.* Paper presented at Bringing Us Together: 17th Biennial Conference of the International Society for Augmentative and Alternative Communication. Available at: https://discovery.dundee.ac.uk/en/publications/supporting-personal-narrative-elicitation-identifying-discrete-mo (Accessed 27.5.21).

Pink, S. (2020). *Doing visual ethnography.* London: Sage Publications.

Chapter 23

Learning to tell

Teaching skills for community storytelling

Nicola Grove and Jem Dick

Background

This chapter describes the development of a training course in community storytelling designed for (and in collaboration with) people with learning and communication difficulties.

History

The project grew from a storytelling group which ran for a year, with nine verbal individuals. They all enjoyed the experience of telling different kinds of stories: traditional, fictional (Wizard of Oz) and personal – memories of the war and childhood exploits (Grove, 2004). Funding was then secured to take this work forward and explore the possibility of a story-telling company who could go out and run workshops, perform at festivals and events and find new ways of making familiar tales relevant and meaningful.

Together we worked out what we meant by a story – it had to have a 'sparkle' in it (Grove, 2015) something to catch and hold the attention of an audience – more than a list of what happened, when and where. So a story, in this course, is defined as a sequential account about some-thing of interest. We experimented with ways of drawing 'story', using circles, hills and journeys. And when we reflected on our storytelling skills, we always came back to the idea of the sparkle in the story – the crest of the hill, the sunburst, the climax, the unforeseen event along the route.

Theories and principles

We see storytelling as a social process, whereby the arts of narration are learned through valued participation, close observation of good models and appropriate support. The role of tutors is to scaffold (Vygotsky, 1978) the abilities of everyone in the group, to research and share the rich heritage of stories available in the oral tradition and to show by example how stories can be told together. We also adopt a collaborative approach – identifying what each person can contribute to the telling of a story, and focusing on their strengths.

Though some people proved very adept at telling individually from the start, our basic approach was team or tandem telling, where two or more people share the task. We found that this increased confidence and teamwork, improved listening skills and enabled people to jointly reflect on their skills and learning. Some of our tellers were good at recalling events but found it hard to express feelings or to vary facial expressions. Others were so verbally fluent that they found it hard to know when to stop talking! Others, who could only use a few words, were good at sign or gesture. Everyone was able to use a musical instrument or

DOI: 10.4324/9781003159087-23

show a prop at an appropriate time. As we worked together we began to find a different approach to narrating.

Our company emphasises participatory and communal storytelling, which develops an intensity of listening to the teller, an atmosphere in which a contribution told from the heart is valued for what it communicates about our common humanity. We seek to make connections between powerful archetypal traditional myths and the lived experience of day-to-day challenges and triumphs, and to illuminate the importance of the small, the unnoticed, the unorthodox for our audiences (see Grove, 2009: 15).

Our inspiration also came from a well-known tale:

> Walking down the road a boy falls into step with an old traveller making for a village. Asked how he makes a living, the traveller tells the boy to watch and listen. Arriving in the market square he makes a fire, takes a pan out of his sack, fills the pan with water and sets it to boil. Then he takes a stone from his pocket and drops it in. Intrigued, the boy – and a queue of villagers – ask what he is making. 'Stone soup,' replies the traveller. 'Best soup ever, but it just needs – let's see – an onion/a carrot/a potato ...' naming the vegetables that he sees in the villagers' baskets. Each villager donates something to the soup and, in the end, everyone shares it and pronounces it the best ever.

This story teaches us so many important truths: that a story is made by a community; that it involves a generous process of sharing; that everyone contributes; and that the inert, inanimate stone is the critical ingredient, whose role in the story is created by the tinker – or support person. We create stories together, and everyone can put in something.

The focus of the course is on oral traditional tales: myths, legends and folk tales, and on the personal experiences that these evoke. For example, in one of our first shows, *Days and Knights in the Kitchen*, we told the tale of Sir Gareth of Orkney from the Arthurian cycle. In this story, Gareth leaves home against the wishes of his mother and rides to join his brothers at Camelot. Not wanting to capitalise on family connections, he disguises himself as a poor man and is set to work in the kitchens, where he is bullied and reviled. Finally, he embarks on a quest and accompanies the scornful Linet to rescue her sister from the Red Knight, having defeated several knights in the interim.

This story had many resonances for our group: leaving home, working in kitchens, bullying and name-calling, fear of assault, as well as triumphs (the defeat of three knights likened to the hat-trick in a football match scored by one member) and romance. We interspersed the traditional tale with personal stories and took it out to conferences as workshops where others too could share their memories of successes and difficult times.

We guided people towards traditional stories because we wanted to broaden their experience and because, as storytellers, we had a firm belief in the power of these tales to help us live our lives. However, there was also space for members to choose to tell stories they knew well, from films or favourite books or TV.

Work in practice

Course structure

As described in the manual, *Learning to Tell* (Grove, 2009), four strands of storytelling are addressed each session: *story themes, story lines, story skills* and *story company*.

- *Story theme* relates to the fundamentals of storytelling: What is a story? Where do stories originate? Who are the tellers? Who owns the story? How can stories be shared? What do stories do for us? The theme functions to nourish the imagination with powerful and resonant symbols and to develop personal myth-making. Story themes are developed through telling stories and discussing their meaning (often at the beginning of the day).
- *Story lines* involve the collection and development of different kinds of story, recorded in personal portfolios and are chosen by the students themselves.
- *Story skills* involves activities to practise specific strategies for telling and listening, categorised into four domains, based on narrative development research by Labov and Waletzky (1976) and Peterson and McCabe (1983).

  - *Structural* The who? where? when? what happened? and why? aspects.
  - *Feelings* Expressed verbally and non-verbally, through facial expression, body language and gesture, and vocal intonation.
  - *Social skills* How to interact with an audience; how to listen.
  - *Language* Developing vocabulary, use of verbs and story conventions such as how to start, how to end, metaphors.

- *Story company* develops a sense of group identity and social skills through games, discussion of group rules and conventions and the use of rituals: starting and finishing, allocating responsibilities and evaluating how we are doing as a group of storytellers.

Running the group

This course runs from 10.00–15.00, once a week. Each week, a different person is in charge of running the day. Members get into small groups of three or four to share news. Story-sharing sheets with spaces for the elements of a story are helpful (see Chapter 19). Groups appoint a spokesperson, whose job is to speak last in the group, listen to the others and summarise the news briefly in key points for the plenary session, which is the official start of the day. This process was initiated early in the project because people were originally quite dependent on tutors for validation. By systematically encouraging peer support, the company became highly collegiate.

The leader draws up the list of activities, using pictures and symbols. Each member decides which activity they will run (the morning warm up, the skills session, etc.) and their photo is affixed.

Then each member decides on their personal goal, and these are noted. Each person is thus in control of their own development, and feels the autonomy that can be so lacking in other areas of their lives. Using the images along with the record of the feedback from the week before ensures that any individual goals that were not covered can be addressed in, and inform the thrust of the upcoming day's activities.

The planning meeting is followed by a fun warm-up game, led by a group member. Warm-up games developed through discussions as to what skills each game helps with. Now most of the group are able to invent new games, or adapt existing ones to enhance whatever skill is being explored on that day.

The rest of the day includes rehearsals for upcoming events, work on individual stories, story skill development, a story told by a tutor and stories told by members. The meaning of these stories is discussed in small groups. During lunch, members relax and chat informally; they may also meet with a tutor to discuss a particular issue about their progress. The day ends with feedback, where each person contributes a reflection on the experiences of the day and whether their goals have been met. Finally, we say goodbye with a gesture symbolising all the stories flying out across the world.

Outcomes and evidence: what we look for

Assessment frameworks

We originally used a system of profiling whereby people are filmed telling different types of story: a routine event (what happens when you go swimming); personal experiences; a folk or fairy tale they know well (e.g. *Cinderella*) and, finally, making up a story to go with a stimulating art postcard (e.g. Magritte's *Golconda* – tiny men raining down onto a red roof). Reviewing the film, we note whether people show any specific skills in one genre or another (the last activity is the hardest, the first the easiest) and how they express themselves – their strengths and needs in each case. This can be used as a baseline from which to measure subsequent progress. The course can also be used as the basis for developing accredited skills in storytelling, for example with organisations such as Open College Network (https://www.nocn.org.uk).

Outcomes

All 16 participants on the first *Learning to Tell* course successfully achieved entry level or level 1 national Open College Network (OCN) qualifications in inclusive storytelling. Questionnaires and interviews with staff and families showed that members were felt to have developed confidence and improved their communication skills. A key aim of the project was to reduce social isolation and increase community participation and cultural access, which was achieved by taking people to story circles and festivals, and enabling them to deliver high-status workshops and performances at conferences, in homes and in schools. All but one member of our group had scarcely left Somerset at the beginning of the project; four people now regularly travel with us to different locations in England and abroad. In-depth interviews with course members carried out by an independent researcher showed how much they had gained from the experience:

> When I first started I felt like I was … on me own a lot, but when I went to storytelling I then felt like it's being in a great big circle, to me it feels like being in a family of professional storytellers.

During the final year of the project, members of the company visited another group in Birmingham and provided two days training. Subsequently, a group was set up for 12 people. Analysis of their skills in storytelling, using a profile of structural components and a standardised narrative assessment (Renfrew, 1997) showed that narrative abilities improved between the start and finish of the course, and that, in turn, their self-esteem and ability to share experiences was enhanced (Johnson, 2009).

We also use stories to empower people and to challenge preconceptions and beliefs about disability (Kondrat & Teater, 2009; Walmsley & Johnson, 2003). Latterly the company have been tackling hidden histories.[1] Through the stories of Fanny Fust (an heiress with severe learning disabilities abducted for her fortune in the eighteenth century) and Peter the

Wild Boy (Branch et al., 2018) exhibited at the court of George II, we explore not only past and present attitudes to disabled people – prejudice, fear – but also acceptance and support.

The story of Alicia

Alicia is a young woman interested in all things macabre, especially literary sources. The group was working on the Welsh myth of the Birth of Taliesin. She told the part of the story where the witch/goddess Ceridwen gathers the ingredients to create a spell. Alicia invented all sorts of terrible ingredients and told them with great relish. She then chose to work on the story of Andrew Crosse, an early pioneer of researches into electricity, who it is believed may have been the inspiration for Mary Shelley's *Frankenstein*. She is very self-aware and has found ways of expressing herself within the *Learning to Tell* structures. Memorising chunks of story is a problem for her, so a flexible approach allows her to combine reading, picture description and dialogue within a group storytelling context (see also Grove et al., 2022).

The story of Michael

Michael was 20 years old when he started the course. He was already a very accomplished dancer and used to acting and performing on stage, but was not a confident narrator – he spoke quietly and hesitantly. Through dedicated rehearsals for performance he developed skills in manipulating a large puppet and speaking through this figure. In 'tandem' telling (with a partner), he took a strong role and his voice was clear and carrying as he narrated in role as a boy with learning difficulties looking for a job – a situation which echoed his own experience.

The story of Robin

Robin, now in his forties, is a founder member of the company who had a great interest in history and legends and was a keen artist, but only as a hobby. Robin has proved himself as one of our most accomplished tellers, and now has his own business as an artist and illustrator. This is as a result of a great deal of hard work and self-reflection, as demonstrated in his thoughtful reflections on his own progress:

> I've always had an interest in stories and I've always had dreams about stories, ones that are quite true and ones that I've heard from other people. Sometimes I've even made up stories which I think when you make up a story it's like you make up an image of a story that someone else is going to be interested in, and that story comes alive and people can feel what the story is like, they can feel the vision of what the story is about and even feel like they're in a world where these stories can come out at them and they feel really adventurous.

Contexts of learning

The course works best for students in secondary and further education who have some ability to recall their own experiences, who enjoy working in groups and who can attend and listen to stories and to the conversations of others. The course is flexible and can accommodate students with limited expressive language, but to get the most out of it they do need to be able to understand and follow a story.

Issues to consider

Sometimes stories will bring up very strong feelings; you are unlikely to know enough about personal histories to predict when this occurs. For example, the story of the *Children of Lir*[2] involves loss of home, family ties and banishment. Someone listening burst into tears and it turned out that her father had recently left the family. It's important to have processes in place that allow people to express their emotions, and systems for referring on to relevant services. We sometimes took out a session to work together with the feelings raised in the story through art, dance and music, getting the group to support each other. Generally, we have found that good stories carry within them the resolution of feelings and can bring a sense of closure (see also the chapters in this book on therapeutic approaches).

Cultural factors

Culturally, the course is adaptable. We recommend that if students from multi-ethnic cultures are attending it is really important to:

- Explore with them stories from their own cultural traditions that are significant and the meanings within that culture. This should involve meeting with people from that culture who can talk with students about the meaning and use of the stories within that community. Actively research on the Internet and make contact with key storytellers if you cannot meet people directly.
- Find out about traditional oral storytelling within that culture. For example, in Africa there is a strong tradition of call and response, and of actively engaging and discussing the morals of stories as they are told. All cultures have some specific ways of starting and finishing stories, which are useful to incorporate.
- Invite a storyteller or artist from that tradition to work with the group.
- Remember to be sensitive to particular taboos; for example, when telling stories about animals, remember which animals are sacred and which are perceived as unclean.
- Be sensitive about using sacred stories. Some storytellers feel it is inappropriate to use stories which were collected from sources without permission, such as by anthropologists in previous centuries. Raven tales from First Peoples of North America or dreamtime stories of Aboriginal Australian people are examples. An alternative view is that the stories are now out and available, and that the imperative is to tell them for a good reason and in a respectful way (Schieffelin, 2014). So find out about the origins of the story and be clear why and how you use it.

Try it yourself

It's worth running one-off workshops or taster sessions to interest people and explore the ways you want to work. Bear in mind that the word 'storytelling' carries a lot of baggage. We have found that some people see the activity as childish; may equate it with reading; or may even think of it as lying: 'I don't tell stories', said one lady whom we tried to interest in the group.

Top tips

- Include the familiar, such as pantomime tales, but bring in stories from other traditions as soon as possible.
- Trust the group to find the meanings that are right for them.
- Try to link the group in to your local story circle, which can be found through national networks like the Society for Storytelling (www.sfs.org.uk) – invaluable for opportunities to hear and tell the stories.

Where to go

Openstorytellers offer training: www.openstorytellers.org.uk.

Learning to Tell is a resource which includes everything you need to teach a 30-week course, with an example DVD, and is available from the British Institute of Learning Disabilities: www.bild.org.uk.

Sources for legends abound on the Internet. Visit https://www.sfs.org.uk for links and resources. In every country you will find a range of opportunities to develop your own storytelling skills, from residential to one-day events. Storytelling festivals are wonderful ways of learning new stories and skills and networking.

Acknowledgements

Thanks to all the company members Jane Harwood and Derryn Street, who worked with us to develop the course and Ruth Hill for her interview work. The original project was supported by the British Institute of Learning Disabilities and by Somerset Community Team for Adults with Learning Disabilities, funded through the Big Lottery Fund and the Esmée Fairbairn Foundation.

Notes

1 Films of performances and animations for both stories can be found at https://www.openstor ytellers.org.uk.
2 https://en.wikipedia.org/wiki/Children_of_Lir.

References

Branch, K., Fleet, C., Grove, N., Lumley-Smith, T. & Meader, R. (2018). What Peter means to us: Researching the past and present of Peter the Wild Boy. In C. Goodey, P. McDonagh & T. Stainton (Eds), *Intellectual disability: A conceptual history 1200–1900* (pp. 148–161). Manchester: Manchester University Press.

Grove, N. (2004). It's my story. *Community Living*, 17(3), 16–18.

Grove, N. (2009). *Learning to tell: A handbook for inclusive storytelling*. Kidderminster: BILD Publications. Available at: www.bild.org.uk.

Grove, N. (2015). Finding the sparkle: Storytelling in the lives of people with learning disabilities. *Tizard Learning Disability Review*, 20(1), 29–36.

Grove, N., Parsley, A., Lewis, C. & Meader, R. (2022). People with learning disabilities as community storytellers. In C. Holmwood, S. Jennings & S. Jacksties (Eds), *The international handbook of therapeutic stories and texts*.

Johnson, L. (2009) How I create creativity (2): Defining who I am. *Speech and Language Therapy in Practice*, November, 26–28.

Kondrat, D. & Teater, B. (2009). An anti-stigma approach to working with persons with severe mental disability: Seeking real change through narrative change. *Journal of Social Work Practice*, 23, 35–47.

Labov, W. & Waletzky, J. (1976). Narrative analysis: Oral versions of personal experience. In J. Helm (Ed.), *Essays on the verbal and visual arts* (pp. 12–44). Seattle, WA: University of Washington Press.

Peterson, C. & McCabe, A. (1983). *Developmental psycholinguistics: Three ways of looking at a child's narrative*. New York: Plenum Press.

Renfrew, C. (1997). *Bus Story Test*. Milton Keynes: Speechmark.

Schieffelin, E. (2014). Listening to stories with an anthropological ear. In A. Gersie, A. Nanson & E. Schieffelin (Eds), *Storytelling for a greener world: Environment, community and story based learning* (pp. 154–167). Stroud, Glos: Hawthorn Press.

Vygotsky, L. (1978). *Mind in society*. Cambridge, MA: Harvard University Press.

Walmsley, J. & Johnson, K. (2003). *Inclusive research with people with learning disabilities: Past, present and futures*. London: JKP Publishers.

Chapter 24

The autistic storyteller

Sharing the experience of otherness

Justine de Mierre

My passion has always been for reaching outsiders in society with story. I realise now this probably stems from experiencing that 'otherness' and wanting that connection myself, growing up as an undiagnosed autist.

That passion has taken my telling from schools to prisons, pubs to literary festivals, streets to libraries. Along the way I've worked with autistic children and adults – both diagnosed and undiagnosed, speaking and non-speaking – in countless story and drama projects over the last 30 years. It might seem odd that I only realised I was autistic in 2017 (diagnosed 2019), but when the stories in the public realm about what it is to be autistic are vague at best and inaccurate and damaging at worst, it's actually not that surprising. False perceptions even within the medical profession are common and many (particularly non-males) are left un- or mis-diagnosed. This leaves autistic individuals without that rich understanding of themselves and their community that can transform the quality of life.

In my online advocacy, I work hard to share information that changes society's dominant narrative of autists as tragedy or inspiration. As storytellers, I believe it's our responsibility to understand the power and prevalence of those narratives and fully grasp the negative impact it has on us as autistic people. When tellers fully embrace autistic communication forms (both verbal and non-verbal), understand our autistic culture and take care to notice and stop themselves when they are imposing neuro-normative ideas on us in story, then they can really change the lives of participants. A good tale for us raises up our difference, celebrates our culture and supports a generation of autists to be proud of who we are instead of ashamed of what we're not.

How I came to be a storyteller

I had been working as a performer and theatre maker since the late 90s, but it was on a short programme with the amazing theatre company Oily Cart,[1] working on a scratch show in a swimming pool for non-verbal audiences that I first met a professional storyteller. Only then did I realise that my passion for stories could be my work – I didn't have to wait until I was old and wise to call myself a storyteller! When I shared this with another artist on the project she invited me to tell stories to a group she ran for autistic children.

My journey with being autistic and my journey with being a storyteller have always been inescapably intertwined and echoed each other. I have always told stories: and so had always been a storyteller, I just hadn't claimed the identity. It was the same with being autistic – I had always stimmed, always struggled socially, always retreated to my safe fantasy world, always been hyperlexic – I just hadn't claimed my autistic identity either.

DOI: 10.4324/9781003159087-24

More than that though, storytelling was a more direct form of performance than theatre and so suited my autistic nature better. There wasn't the sensory overload of all the rigmarole that accompanies a theatre production to tell a story. There wasn't the drain of social interaction from dealing with other people, or the inevitable painful misunderstandings. Storytelling was an art form where my natural autistic tendency to talk at length on something I was passionate about was not vilified as rude or egocentric, but I actually got paid to do it! Storytelling was the place where my truest nature was acceptable in a non-autist society. Suited up in my storytelling garb at a festival or on the street I had permission to go up to complete strangers and engage them in something I cared about – in my civvies they'd probably run a mile! I suppose that's why it felt a bit like coming home.

The advantages of being an autistic storyteller

Being autistic and experiencing the world the way I do gives me some in-built advantages in my telling that non-autistic tellers might have to work a bit harder to achieve. Here are just some of them.

Instinctive inclusiveness

As an autist, I am continually adapting what I do and how I do it to manage my own needs in a world not designed for me, and meet the needs and expectations of others who communicate and understand things in ways that don't come naturally to me. So, when I tell, my style is instinctively inclusive and adaptive in-the-moment to every need and response that I notice. And noticing responses is something I'm highly sensitised to because I naturally notice detail and because I need this skill to get by in the world.

In telling I will therefore make any number of changes in the moment to respond to my audience. I might change my tone, introduce sensory rhythms or actions, move from sitting to walking – all without planning if I spot in the moment a need within the audience. This comes naturally because I'm so accustomed to adaptation, and my autistic hyper-focus is trained on getting that story across by whatever means necessary. (There is a great irony in the neurotypical myth of us being inflexible when every beat of our existence involves such adaptations, simply because few understand that we are not making a fuss but actually experience the world differently. I often wonder how non-autists would cope with unexpected change if they were already doing so much just to exist in the space.)

A teenager on one of my projects once said 'Other people say they listen to us and want to hear our ideas, but you actually do'. Autists mean what we express, in whatever communication form; to do otherwise is hard and painful. That clarity and directness allows us to engage people on the edges of society, who can spot from a long way off someone who is well meaning but lacking in understanding or sincerity. (It's also why I work better with those who take me at my word, and not those so involved in a world of unspoken inferences and social nuance that they assume additional meanings and refuse to hear otherwise.)

Making spontaneous connections in the moment – mid-story!

The autistic brain is an amazing thing. When someone says a word or shares an idea with me, every association I've ever had with that word or idea is instantly at the front of my mind. Autistic brains make more connections than non-autistic brains[2] and in my experience such connections are also different. Executive dysfunction means I can't remember where I put my glasses down two seconds ago, but autistic recall means I can remember in videographic detail everything I've ever heard about llamas! It's an incredibly useful attribute for things like Extreme Storytelling[3] where I take a word or idea thrown in by an audience member mid-story and instantly weave it into the narrative with virtually no thought required. It's worth knowing if you're working with autists that this is something we can't switch off, it's like breathing, which means that being presented with too many ideas at once (be that knowledge, sensory or emotional information) can be like having too many computer tabs open at once, and the brain can freeze and stop functioning. If you spot that, reduce the sensory, emotional and informational input (close the tabs!) and the autistic person should soon recover.

A different understanding of what listening looks like

The first time I truly owned my autistic identity in a professional space was in a workshop where I felt safe to say, 'I'm going to close my eyes when people are talking so I can hear them better'. The difference was transformational. I took in 50 per cent more information than I ever would have done otherwise. For many autists, asking them to open their eyes and look at you when you're telling orally means you're actually asking them to hear you less, because they're having to take in so much more than just your words resulting in overload. Bear this in mind with multi-sensory storytelling too – sometimes in a desire to reach those with sensory differences we can overwhelm with props, textures, sound and light, when keeping one channel of sensory input might make for a more coherent story to someone for whom 'sensory' is their first language.

Another way autists are able to focus with all that sensory noise is to stim. Stimming is a self-stimulating activity such as flapping hands, playing with a sensory toy, making vocal noises, jumping, spinning, hair twisting, pen chewing, etc, etc. Its purpose can be to calm, to comfort for enjoyment or to focus. Non-verbal advocate and blogger Nico Boskovic[4] described it to me recently as being in a constant stream of sensory input. Stimming keeps you at the top of your sensory stream so you can actually take things in. The traditional "sit still and don't fidget" instruction that goes along with so much storytelling means that those autists who need to stim to focus are excluded from full engagement in the story. (The danger of distracting others can usually be managed with careful positioning and building opportunities for participants' stims to be part of the story – there are often flapping birds in my tales!)

Thus, my wider understanding of the listening process means that I know when participants who might appear to others to be distracted/uninterested are actually engaging. With that knowledge, I can make sure they're allowed to carry on whilst I tailor my telling accordingly.

Ensuring stories and outcome measures aren't damaging to autists

In therapeutic and educational settings, well-meaning practitioners often use stories to 'help' autists to be more 'normal'. Despite good intentions, this is inherently damaging to our self-worth and, if used repeatedly, to our mental health. Educators may be aware that this is a problem, but unsure how to handle it (Hodge, Rice & Reidy, 2019). I understand that might be challenging for some to hear, so let me try separate out the issues.

There is nothing inherently wrong in a social story that tells neurodivergent people what to expect in a certain situation and how others might behave. That is useful information enabling us to understand and prepare for the world we live in and to manage expectations about unfamiliar cultures. However, stories used to change our behaviour and tell us how we 'should' behave, without any acknowledgement that these are purely arbitrary neurotypical norms convey the damaging message that our culture, what is comfortable for us, is wrong and should be removed from human experience. That's not the same as educating us about the dominant culture we live in so we can navigate it better.

Even worse damage can be done when project outcomes are measured by behavioural changes that more closely resemble neurotypical norms. These are often seen as success because parents, carers and teachers are happy that participants seem to fit in better and seem happier – because who wouldn't be happy to get a break from being constantly reprimanded for doing what comes naturally. However (see above) autists are highly adaptive. We will respond to this training, but the 'masking' that results is really mentally unhealthy, leading to burn out, usually later in life when decades of pressure takes their toll. And no one tends to measure outcomes decades on. Mental health issues are rife within the adult autistic community and we take our own lives at a rate up to eight times higher than that in the non-autistic population (Cassidy & Rodgers, 2017). We are far less likely to seek help from doctors because we're trained to ignore our natural responses, and far less likely to be taken seriously when we do, dying from treatable conditions at a higher rate than the non-autistic population.[5] This is unsurprising but it needs to stop – we deserve a higher average life expectancy than just 54 years (Hirvikoski et al., 2016).

As an autistic teller I have the advantage that these damaging narratives are very obvious to me, whilst neurotypical tellers may struggle to pick apart decades of ingrained social understanding to see how arbitrary such things are. Often people will describe neurotypical norms as "human nature" and that really does need challenging because when you do that, you inadvertently imply neurodivergent people are not human, which is deeply problematic. For example, did you know that small talk is broadly considered impolite in autistic culture? When every word an autist hears is naturally taken literally and all the information to do with that word or idea comes instantly to mind, saying 'Hi, how are you?' without meaning exactly that is distracting and irrelevant, hence impolite. Neurotypical brains are wired for socialisation not information, so they need small talk as a segue to the information. Autistic brains are the opposite, we connect socially through the sharing of information. Where autistic culture is unhampered, we will generally speak directly (neurotypicals often describe it as 'talking at' each other) about things that interest us. Efficiency is important to us so why would you take up someone's time in something trivial? When practitioners tell and make stories with an understanding of both cultures – as the wonderful Evaleen Whelton at Ausome Training[6] does – then real change happens and the two neurologies are able to connect in a way that is manageable for both.

Modelling being autistic and accepting autistic culture in public spaces

As an autistic storyteller I have the advantage that by simply doing my job in public, sharing my identity and modelling inclusive practice, I have the power to change perceptions, as happened when street telling for Flipside Festival in Lowestoft. Essentially I was approaching people in the street and asking if they fancied a story – obviously in cape and top hat because apparently that makes it okay! I spotted a couple of teenagers hanging out near their families and approached one of them to see if I could get them to make a story with me (there's an art to doing this in a way that works – I wouldn't advise it for the inexperienced!). The kids' mum shouted over 'Good luck love he's autistic!' which gave me the opportunity to say: 'Don't worry darling, so am I, let's go!' And we did! He would only make a story relating to his specific special interest in a video game, but we collaborated in real time as I followed his direction and added my input, as his mother watched on amazed. Before her eyes, an entirely unplanned, unexpected creative event had happened on their trip to the shops and her autistic teenager had not only coped but joined in and enjoyed it. The look on her face was everything. The pride in him that someone had taken a real interest in his special interest enough to make a story about it was everything. Before this, she thought her kid wouldn't engage in anything, she watched that engagement happen with a total stranger on the street, and now she can't think that anymore because she saw it with her own eyes. That knowledge changes lives.

When I go into a space as an autistic storyteller and people see me do what I do, those new to neurodiversity see that autism isn't what they think it is. When I accept stims and kids engaging with their backs to me, I show others that it's okay to do that too. When I switch into more sensory telling I show others that's normal. When I include shout-outs, celebrate interruptions and incorporate them within our story, I embody autistic culture and bring it into acceptance without ever having to preach. When non-autists experience this, their understanding is changed in some way, small or large, and so every future interaction with autistic people is subtly or dramatically altered. For autists, they are witnessing their natural ways of being treated as being just as acceptable as non-autistic ways. Non-autistic parents, teachers and carers see autistic culture being accepted, celebrated. They see autists engage in ways they never thought possible. That can change everything for those they care for and work with.

The challenges of being an autistic storyteller

Of course, there are many challenges in being an autistic teller. Here are just a few of them and how I try to overcome them. I hope they may provide some insight into how you might improve things when working with neurodivergent artists, audiences and participants.

The nature of getting storytelling work

Storytelling is a niche art form, and to work as a professional teller and make a decent enough living requires a lot of socialising, networking and building relationships. All of these are hard for an autist and take a huge amount of emotional and social energy which is physically as well as mentally draining. More than that though, in networking conversations there is an expected level of social nuance and understanding of unspoken suggestions that as an autist I literally cannot pick up on. I am a Cambridge graduate, a Fellow of the Royal Society of the Arts and a Clore Cultural Leadership fellow and with all of that you would think I had the most wonderful contacts book – and if I had any clue how to develop and maintain working relationships with the many powerful and influential people I've met locally and nationally over the years I'd probably be far better off and better known than I am! Where I've seen obviously autistic people do better in such situations is where from a young age they have been encouraged in their directness and their natural communication, so they dare to be direct rather than trying to mask to fit in, and where those differences are then accepted and supported by those around them. Sadly for all of us, that is the exception rather than the rule. The point is in most art forms, storytelling included, many work opportunities rely on who you know and how well you relate to them, and when your neurology is different to those with influence and money to impact your career, a lot of those opportunities pass you by. What this means is, if you want to involve neurodivergent professionals in your work – and I can't stress how important it is that you do that, particularly if your participants are neurodivergent – then you will have to seek them out and directly ask them, because without that we may never appear on your radar, or know you are looking for us.

Sensory overwhelm, recovery times and how online telling helps

Telling is a full-on sensory experience – there are people and smells and sights and sounds and my brain is involved in the story and adapting. In the moment of telling I am carried by being at the top of my sensory stream, but afterwards I will be exhausted and need recovery time. Having a 'spiky profile', i.e. we're at times capable of amazing things and at times incapable of getting off the sofa, is a common autistic experience and many of us are content with that – why limit yourself just because you need a lot of rest?

However it can be challenging to explain this to others who can't see why I can't do more sessions in a day or week as they see only the time involved and not the sensory impact. Foolishly I do often breach my limits to please clients and then I can't work for a month, so this is counter-productive in the long run. If you want to make your project autist friendly, building in that recovery time is extremely important for tellers, facilitators and participants, and can transform the quality of the work.

Interestingly, when storytelling had to move online because of the pandemic, it changed those parameters a lot and meant more work was possible. The sensory overwhelm and executive function requirements of travel, finding your way around a venue, dealing with people and the lack of a private space for retreat and recalibration were all gone in an instant. Zoom storytelling has led many to re-think what genuine inclusivity actually looks and feels like, and that is no bad thing.

Challenging the storytelling gatekeepers

The world of professional storytelling is full of debates centring around what good telling is, who is allowed to do it, where and how – followed by how wrong or disrespectful people are who don't do it that way. It's exhausting. For me, there is no 'right' way to tell. Stories don't care how they are told or by who, they just get out there – spouted over pints down the pub, whispered from grandmothers' lips, woven by playwrights into theatre or scribbled down by authors. When people try to gatekeep who tells by insisting on rules and methods, they discourage or exclude the very voices that need to be heard – those without the luxury of time or money for hours of contemplation and research but just a passion to tell and make it what they live for. Those voices are those of outsiders, often the neurodivergent, and often those that most need the support of a community – much more so than the comfortable middle class who seem to dominate it. Those that live off their wits and 'blag' it – telling a tale half heard from a mate and welding it with fragments of others – are the natural descendants of a storytelling tradition that goes back centuries before Victorian scholars started writing folk tales down. Recognising that venerates the contribution of those 'outsider' tellers – and their power to reach audiences those gatekeepers never would. For me, this is the important thing: it feels like right now the world needs to hear more, not less, from those that experience things differently, who can shed new light and insight on age old problems – and the direct visceral experience of one human painting a story in the mind of another is the one of the best ways I know of doing that.

Notes

1 https://oilycart.org.uk (Accessed 1.5.21).
2 E.g. https://www.cell.com/neuron/fulltext/S0896-6273(14)00651-5 – although almost all studies assume it is a fault rather than a natural variation (Accessed 1.5.21).
3 A form of spontaneous story creation that I originally developed as part of the hospital projects with Ladder to the Moon.
4 https://www.facebook.com/nikoboskovicPDX (Accessed 1.5.21).
5 https://www.spectrumnews.org/news/for-autistic-adults-a-hospital-stay-carries-high-risk-of-death (Accessed 1.5.21).
6 https://ausometraining.com (Accessed 1.5.21).

References

Bennett, M., Webster, A., Goodall, E. & Rowland, S. (2018). Negating the impact of the "Autism can be cured" myth: Creating inclusive societies for autistic individuals. In M. Bennett, A. Webster, E. Goodall & S. Rowland (Eds), *Life on the autism spectrum: Translating myths and misconceptions into positive futures* (pp. 81–102). Singapore: Springer. Available as free e-book to download at: https://link.springer.com/book/10.1007%2F978-981-13-3359-0 (Accessed 1.5.21).

Cassidy, S. & Rodgers, J. (2017). Understanding and prevention of suicide in autism. *The Lancet (Psychiatry) Correspondence*, 4(6), E11. doi:10.1016/S2215-0366(17)30162-1 (Accessed 1.5.21).

Hirvikoski, T., Mittendorfer-Rutz, E., Boman, M., Larsson, H., Lichtenstein, P. & Bölte, S. (2016). Premature mortality in autism spectrum disorder. *British Journal of Psychiatry*, 208(3), 232–238. doi:10.1192/bjp.bp.114.160192 (Accessed 1.5.21).

Hodge, N., Rice, E. & Reidy, L. (2019). 'They're told all the time they're different': How educators understand development of sense of self for autistic pupils. *Disability & Society*, 34(9–10), 1353–1378.

Chapter 25

Tales from the heart

Testimonies from storytellers with learning disabilities[1]

Sayaka Kobayashi, The Arts End of Somewhere and Openstorytellers

Japan: Sayaka Kobayashi

Sayaka Kobayashi is a performance storyteller whom the editor first met in 2011. She is skilled at recalling stories, even in English, which she does not speak as a natural language. She often accompanies herself on a traditional musical instrument. Her storytelling is powerful and joyous, and she is a highly valued member of the Japan Storytelling Network which organises festivals and events. Mrs Kobayashi is her daughter's effective business partner and support for her work. She and storyteller Mrs Yumiko Mitsudo helped Sayaka put together this account of her life and work.

My history

I would like to live keeping my pace, engaging in creating art, without being self-conscious, so I decided to be a storyteller.

First my teacher in the primary school for special needs told me that I could become a voice actor as I was good at reading books aloud. I took part in a storytelling competition for disabled people held by the Wataboshi project of Tanpopo-no-Ye and got a place when I was 13 years old.

After that, I was trained for three years how to tell stories before big audiences by Naoko Nakagawa, the Wataboshi instructor. Since then I have performed on stage several times a year, at some events with famous musicians. After graduating from a special high school, I took a job cleaning rooms and doing easy office work at Toyota Boshoku Create Staff (K.K) and also volunteered at a social welfare service corporation for several years.

I continued my storytelling though, and after five years quit the job to earn my living as a storyteller. But it is difficult to do this, and I rely on my pension for persons with disabilities.

When I became busy with storytelling, I started having panic attacks. So after consulting with a doctor, I try not to be on stage more than once a month. My mother and I realised I needed a support network of friends and a safe social space. So we founded Yumepalet (Dream-palette), for which I now act as an ambassador with my mother's help. We at Yumepalet love culture and art, work with some local people, including those with disabilities, to contribute to society through self-expression activities. I am now less anxious. My friends often come to watch me perform stories and cheer me on.

DOI: 10.4324/9781003159087-25

My thoughts on stories and storytelling

For me, a storyteller is one who conveys a story with related scenes of the story, and my role is to deliver the tales devised in my own way to the hearts of the audience. The stories I like to tell are those that give us courage, bright and gentle images, cherish our lives. I remember stories by linking the word images which I know or have seen in pictures, one after another. It takes a long time to memorise a story and retain it in the brain, especially for me. This is why I do not want to tell stories that are sad or harsh – they stay with me. Examples of my favourite stories are my personal story 'Life'; the poem: *The Sorrow of a Snail* and picture book: *Buying Mittens* by Nankichi Niim (1913–1943); *The Mountain of Flowers* by Ryusuke Saito (1917–1985).

The Mountain of Flowers. A young girl called Aya wanders a little too deep into the mountains while gathering wild herbs and gets lost. She meets the Yamanba, an old mountain witch, who shows her the secret of the magnificent flowers blooming around them. The Yamanba knows all about Aya and how she helps her family. Aya learns how she and the villagers are connected to the flowers and landscape: A good deed makes a flower bloom. In one version told to the editor (by another storyteller from Watashobi) Yamamba asks Aya to tell others that she is not an ogre, just an old woman who likes to live on her own in nature. It is a wonderful story for challenging prejudice.

Disabilities and storytelling

I think there is no wall between storytellers with and without disabilities. I have learned storytelling among people with disabilities at Wataboshi and I know many storytellers with no disability through the Japan Storytelling Network. The most important thing is that the storytellers feel the story with the skin and present their best images through storytelling to their audience.

My message to storytellers is:

> You with disabilities can realise your dream if there are people around you who understand and help you. I realise that we can develop ourselves, whether or not we have disabilities, through working as ambassadors, as I do for the Yumepalet Group. And also if people with different disabilities support each other, they can have happy lives.

Sayaka's performances are always well received. Here are comments after the concert in November 2019 where she told, her personal story 'Life', a well-known folktale 'The special pot' and recited the poetry of the much loved author Nankichi Niimi.

> I could have the clear images of the story.
> I was healed a lot by your storytelling.
> I was much moved and admired the way you changed your voice, tone and pitch.
> I could feel the depth of the story.
> I couldn't help shedding tears in your storytelling.

Sayaka gained the Toyota Culture New Face Award of Toyota City Cultural Promotion Foundation in 2019.

Find out more

Sayaka's blog: http://blog.livedoor.jp/sayakakobayashi.

Yumepalet group: https://yumepa-let.amebaownd.com (both of these are only in Japanese but can be translated via the internet).

Tanpopo-no-ye: https://tanpoponoye.org/english.

The Japan storytelling network aims to spread and develop the storytelling culture. Through storytelling, we tend to build peaceful and cultural societies. Mainly we hold a biennial storytelling festival in Japan and also some events including Kamishibai.[2] http://www.japankatarinet.jp/index.html.

Scotland: The Arts End of Somewhere – Storytelling company

Our history

We are an arts collective brought together through our passion for drama and storytelling. We chose this name because we want people to know that art can be created by anyone and is for everyone. We have been working on our multi-sensory storytelling project since May 2019 and we are all now good friends.

We became storytellers by doing a training course with Maureen (Maureen Phillip, PAMIS) for two days. We did some workshops during the summer whilst we were doing some acting. We thought that it was interesting learning new things, trying to do them in front of an audience of people with a disability, and we really enjoy it.

We have been on a journey learning about how to tell stories. We have researched and written them and learnt how to tell them in front of an audience. This has all been part of our training.

Our thoughts on stories and storytelling

We've created lots of multi-sensory stories: *Robert the Bruce and the Spider*, Harry and Ruby's story *The Devil's Porridge, Robert Burns at Ellisland Farm, The Kippford Mermaid*, and we did a story about lockdown.

SARAH: We did the mermaid tale. It was fun.

KATIE: My favourite story is the mermaid one.

ZOE: I like *Robert the Bruce and the Spider* one because we got to use lots of props and we got to use our senses and a bit of acting.

COURTNEY: *Robert Burns at Ellisland* because I enjoyed going to the farm.

FAYE: I liked the lockdown story best. It was about coronavirus and lockdown because we were all in lockdown. We did that to explain better to disabled people. We told the story to help them and had a dance to thank people too.

SKYE: My favourite has to be the lockdown one. We wrote what we had done in lockdown and it is my favourite because of the dance.

SARAH: I liked *The Devil's Porridge* story because we mixed the ingredients (Sarah used cotton wool and coloured water to represent cordite).

INDIA: I liked the lockdown one.

As a group we have worked at Ellisland Farm, the Devil's Porridge Museum, at home, at Wigtown Book Festival and we told a story at the Burns Supper in Dundee for PAMIS.

What we like about storytelling is being reminded that people know you because of the stories. You've got fans in the background. It's amazing to actually have that. Before, we were known by our disability but now we are known as storytellers. We've got a lot more confidence and meeting the rest of the group helped.

We like the fact that we work as a team and we are all together and we are friends as well.

People clap their hands and say 'Well done'. This makes us happy and they say 'Well done, you can go for it'.

We feel really proud of ourselves learning about storytelling and all the opportunities we have.

Acknowledgements

We thank all the parents and support workers who support the collective, PAMIS, and those who fund our activities: the Holywood Trust and Creative Scotland.

Find out more

https://pamis.org.uk/creative-arts/the-arts-end-of-somewhere.

England: Openstorytellers

Our history

We are Openstorytellers, a company of storytellers with learning disabilities. We are based in Frome in Somerset. The company has been going since 2004, and under its present name since 2009. We work with supporters who help us plan and deliver our story performances, and we meet every week to practise our skills and learn new stories. We won a storytelling community award for our company some years ago.

It helps you to tell a story. Some people find it hard to tell a story if they have no speech, they might have hearing impairments but they can use a Big Mack switch or show pictures to tell a story of themselves. We all came to the company in different ways. Some of us had done drama and enjoyed acting, and most of us have done the Learning to Tell course (see Chapter 23). Three of us (Katie, Clemma and Robin) worked as peer mentors on Storysharing courses in homes and day centres, about ten years ago, and that gave us skills to help people to share their own stories and use Big Macks (see Chapter 19).

Robin trained with Nick Hennessey, a well-known storyteller in the UK. Robin says:

> Because of my hyperactivity I can use my hands and like to stand to tell stories and use my body. People say I'm quite good, I've got a good way of showing my expression after working with Nick Hennessey and we learned about narrative, and using tai chi Chinese movement to tell stories with my hands.

Our thoughts on stories and storytelling

We tell at festivals and events, in libraries, at stately homes like Barrington Court.[3] We run training courses, like Halsway Manor residential folklore centre, or for social workers or teachers or health professionals. We also perform in special and mainstream schools. We have told abroad as well, like a conference in Holland. Lockdown has moved us online and it's been difficult, we want a big audience and real life people not just on TV screen, but we have managed to keep going. Recently we took part in a conference run by Learning Disability England. We tell many different kinds of stories – myths, legends and folktales, and stories about our own lives. We have been researching and telling some stories from history – about Peter the Wild Boy and Fanny Fust.[4] For that one we had to do a lot of historical research and we worked with Bristol University. Tim, Clemma and Katie helped to put together the application to the Heritage Lottery Foundation to get the money for this project, and it was because they used their own words that we were successful.

Everyone has different ideas about what they like to tell.

TIM: I like doing exciting and funny stories. I do my own stories – I write them myself (for example, he tells a version of *Goldilocks and the Three Bears* which ends up in a bloodbath, it's funny and horrifying all at the same time!). I like giving pleasure through the stories, this is special to me.

Tim enjoys working in a group and telling solo.
Charlotte's first story was *The Cracked Pot*, about a woman who has two pots, one perfect and one cracked. The perfect pot is rude about the cracked pot, but through the crack comes water which as it drips, allows flowers to grow along the path. Charlotte won our annual Bardic Chair competition telling this story which made her very happy. She likes to work in a group.

CHARLOTTE: I just really wanted to tell my story it really interested me, and I liked acting it out.
KATIE: I like to tell my own stories and work in a group. I told Anansie stories. I like to tell stories in the nursing home and help people with their memories and stories of their life. We can use storyboards and help them in a team.
CLEMMA: I like to tell all different stories, my favourite one is *Silly Jack* and I like being the mother character who keeps getting fed up each time he does something wrong. I like playing all the different characters.
ROBIN: I like to tell myths and legends and folk tales because I like the history and the local stories, places in the UK and all round the world.

The contribution of storytellers with learning disabilities

As people with learning disabilities, we are letting people know that just because you have a learning disability doesn't mean you can't be a storyteller. We are all role models and we can use different ways to tell stories. Katie says, 'It's ok to have a disability and people think we can't tell stories but we can and it makes us feel good. I practise in my bedroom. People say well done but it's ok to be nervous.'

We get a lot out of storytelling

ROBIN: I first started with Nicola in day services in 2003. I wanted to do storytelling instead of my day service so I stopped going there. I did training in storytelling with Jem and now I have a career and a job, as a storyteller and as an artist. I have an artist business where I do illustrations and capture important events like conferences. I've won awards for that too and I've been really pleased to be seen worldwide. Storytelling means I can get out and tell stories, don't have to sit in a box reading a book, go to places and get people to watch.

CLEMMA: It's special because it brings out the sparkle and joy and it's good to be with your friends. People say it's good and they enjoy listening to me. It means I'm in a group I enjoy, and part of a team and that means a lot to me.

KATIE: It gets me out of my nutshell, perform on stage and take part in competitions and performances. I look forward to the future of storytelling.

Acknowledgements

We would like to thank all the people who help us: Leah Harwood who did this interview; Jem Dick, Simon Blakeman, Ben Waller and Kay Williams who have facilitated the group meetings; volunteers Lesley Hughes and Angie Hyde-Mobbs; and our Director, Alex Mac-Neil. We are grateful to our funders, Arts Council England, and the Big Lottery.

Find out more

www.openstorytellers.org.uk.

Notes

1   There is some confusion about terminology. Internationally, academics use 'intellectual disabilities' to avoid confusion with the American designation of 'learning disabilities' as specific reading, writing and numeric difficulties. However, in the UK, the term 'learning disabilities' is generally used by self advocates. In Japan, it is still common to refer to 'mental handicap'. For the purposes of this chapter it is an editorial decision to use *learning* rather than *intellectual* disabilities, respecting the views and language of the storytellers themselves.

2   Traditional Japanese storytelling using a box frame with picture cards.

3   A National Trust venue in southwest England.

4   Real people who lived in eighteenth-century England, both with severe intellectual/learning disabilities, as we would now understand the term. https://www.openstorytellers.org.uk/story telling-company.

Appendix 1

Storytelling organisations

There are societies and centres for storytellers and storytelling all over the world. You will find storytellers, resources, links to story collections and research. This is a personal selection.

United Kingdom

Society for Storytelling: https://www.sfs.org.uk.
Scottish Storytelling Centre: https://www.scottishstorytellingcentre.com.
George Ewart Evans Centre for Storytelling: https://research2.southwales.ac.uk/george-ewart-evans-centre-storytelling.
The Story Museum, Oxford: https://www.storymuseum.org.uk.
Discover: Children's Storytelling Centre: https://discover.org.uk.
Verbal Arts Centre, Derry/Londonderry: https://www.theverbal.co.
Storytellers of Ireland: www.storytellersofireland.org.

International Project MYS – My and Your Stories

The MYS Toolbox for multimedia storytelling provides inclusive tools to empower learners to tell, re-tell and share each-others' stories in imaginative and compelling ways.
www.atempo.at/mys
rixwiki.org/mys
@MYSkeyaction3project
@MYS_project_eu #MeandYourStories

Europe

Europe/UK collaborative project MYS-My and Your Stories. The MYS toolbox for multimedia storytelling provides inclusive resources for developing personal storytelling in schools. Available at: rixwiki.org/mys.
Federation for European Storytelling: https://fest-network.eu.

AustralAsia

Federation of Asian Storytellers: https://www.feast-story.org.
Australia: https://australianstorytellers.org.au, https://www.roadtorefuge.com.
New Zealand: https://maoristorytelling.weebly.com.

National Storytelling Network

See https://storynet.org for the Healing Story Alliance which offers resources and training for therapeutic storytelling.

Americas

National Storytelling Network: See https://storynet.org for the Healing Story Alliance which offers resources and training for therapeutic storytelling.

Canada: https://www.storytellers-conteurs.ca.

First Nations storytelling teaching: https://firstnationspedagogy.com/stories.html.

Index

Printed in Great Britain
by Amazon

36200572R00132